101 Ways to Score Higher on Your NCLEX:

What You Need to Know About the National Council Licensure Examination Explained Simply

By J. Lucy Boyd, RN, BSN

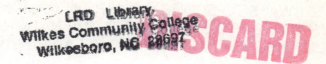

101 WAYS TO SCORE HIGHER ON YOUR NCLEX: WHAT YOU NEED TO KNOW ABOUT THE NATIONAL COUNCIL LICENSURE EXAMINATION EXPLAINED SIMPLY

Copyright © 2010 Atlantic Publishing Group, Inc.
1405 SW 6th Avenue • Ocala, Florida 34471 • Phone 800-814-1132 • Fax 352-622-1875
Web site: www.atlantic-pub.com • E-mail: sales@atlantic-pub.com
SAN Number: 268-1250

ISBN-13: 978-1-60138-250-4 • ISBN-10: 1-60138-250-2

Library of Congress Cataloging-in-Publication Data

Boyd, J. Lucy, 1966-
  101 ways to score higher on your NCLEX : what you need to know about the National Council Licensure Examination explained simply / by J. Lucy Boyd.
     p. ; cm.
  Includes bibliographical references and index.
  ISBN-13: 978-1-60138-250-4 (alk. paper)
  ISBN-10: 1-60138-250-2 (alk. paper)
  1. Nursing--Examinations, questions, etc. 2. Nurses--Licenses--United States--Examinations--Study guides. I. Title. II. Title: One hundred one ways to score higher on your NCLEX.
  [DNLM: 1. Nursing--Examination Questions. WY 18.2 B7888z 2009]
  RT55.B69 2009
  610.73076--dc22
                    2009037325

Printed in the United States

Printed on Recycled Paper

PROJECT MANAGER: Melissa Peterson • mpeterson@atlantic-pub.com
INTERIOR DESIGN: Samantha Martin • smartin@atlantic-pub.com
ASSISTANT EDITOR: Angela Pham • apham@atlantic-pub.com

We recently lost our beloved pet "Bear," who was not only our best and dearest friend but also the "Vice President of Sunshine" here at Atlantic Publishing. He did not receive a salary but worked tirelessly 24 hours a day to please his parents. Bear was a rescue dog that turned around and showered myself, my wife, Sherri, his grandparents Jean, Bob, and Nancy, and every person and animal he met (maybe not rabbits) with friendship and love. He made a lot of people smile every day.

We wanted you to know that a portion of the profits of this book will be donated to The Humane Society of the United States.   —*Douglas & Sherri Brown*

The human-animal bond is as old as human history. We cherish our animal companions for their unconditional affection and acceptance. We feel a thrill when we glimpse wild creatures in their natural habitat or in our own backyard.

Unfortunately, the human-animal bond has at times been weakened. Humans have exploited some animal species to the point of extinction.

The Humane Society of the United States makes a difference in the lives of animals here at home and worldwide. The HSUS is dedicated to creating a world where our relationship with animals is guided by compassion. We seek a truly humane society in which animals are respected for their intrinsic value, and where the human-animal bond is strong.

Want to help animals? We have plenty of suggestions. Adopt a pet from a local shelter, join The Humane Society and be a part of our work to help companion animals and wildlife. You will be funding our educational, legislative, investigative and outreach projects in the U.S. and across the globe.

Or perhaps you'd like to make a memorial donation in honor of a pet, friend or relative? You can through our Kindred Spirits program. And if you'd like to contribute in a more structured way, our Planned Giving Office has suggestions about estate planning, annuities, and even gifts of stock that avoid capital gains taxes.

Maybe you have land that you would like to preserve as a lasting habitat for wildlife. Our Wildlife Land Trust can help you. Perhaps the land you want to share is a backyard— that's enough. Our Urban Wildlife Sanctuary Program will show you how to create a habitat for your wild neighbors.

So you see, it's easy to help animals. And The HSUS is here to help.

THE HUMANE SOCIETY
OF THE UNITED STATES.

2100 L Street NW • Washington, DC 20037 • 202-452-1100
www.hsus.org

Trademark Statement

All trademarks, trade names, or logos mentioned or used are the property of their respective owners and are used only to directly describe the products being provided. Every effort has been made to properly capitalize, punctuate, identify and attribute trademarks and trade names to their respective owners, including the use of ® and ™ wherever possible and practical. Atlantic Publishing Group, Inc. is not a partner, affiliate, or licensee with the holders of said trademarks.

The "NCLEX" name and logo is a registered trademark and property of National Council of State Boards of Nursing, Inc.

The "NCLEX-PN" name and logo is a registered trademark and property of National Council of State Boards of Nursing, Inc.

The "NCLEX-RN" name and logo is a registered trademark and property of National Council of State Boards of Nursing, Inc.

The "Visa" name and logo is a registered trademark and property of Visa International Service Association CORPORATION.

The "MasterCard" name and logo is a registered trademark and property of MasterCard Worldwide.

The "American Express" name and logo is a registered trademark and property of American Express Company.

The "NCSBN" name and logo is a registered trademark and property of National Council of State Boards of Nursing, Inc.

The "Ensure" name and logo is a registered trademark and property of Abbott Laboratories Corporation.

The "Advil" name and logo is a registered trademark and property of American Home Products Corporation.

The "Bextra" name and logo is a registered trademark and property of Pharmacia & Up John Company Corporation.

The "Celebrex" name and logo is a trademark and property of G.D. Searle & Co. CORPORATION.

The "Darvocet" name and logo is a trademark and property of aaiPharma, LLC LIMITED LIABILITY CORPORATION.

The "Demerol" name and logo is a registered trademark of Alba Pharmaceutical Company, Inc.

The "Dilaudid" name and logo is a trademark of E. Bilhuber Inc.

The "Duragesic" name and logo is a registered trademark of Johnson & Johnson Corporation.

The "Indocin" name and logo is a registered trademark of Merck & Co.

The "Percocet" name and logo is a registered trademark of Endo Laboratories, INC.

The "Tylenol" name and logo is a trademark of The Tylenol Company.

The "Ultram" name and logo is a registered trademark of Johnson & Johnson Corporation.

The "Vicodin" name and logo is a registered trademark of Knoll Pharmaceutical Corporation.

The "Lortab" name and logo is a registered trademark of UCB Pharma Inc.

The "Vioxx" name and logo is a trademark of Merck & Co Inc.

The "Retrovir" name and logo is a registered trademark of Burroughs Wellcome Co.

The "Septra" name and logo is a registered trademark of Burroughs Wellcome Co.

The "Cipro" name and logo is a registered trademark of Bayer Aktiengesellschaft Joint Stock Company.

The "Diflucan" name and logo is a registered trademark of Pfizer Inc.

The "Flagyl" name and logo is a registered trademark of G.D. Searle & Co.

The "Keflex" name and logo is a registered trademark of Eli Lilly and Company Corporation.

The "Tamiflu" name and logo is a trademark of Hoffman La Roche INC.

The "Vancocin" name and logo is a trademark of Viropharma Incorporated Corporation.

The "Vibramycin" name and logo is a registered trademark of Chas. Pfizer & Co., Inc.

The "Zovirax" name and logo is a registered trademark of Burroughs Wellcome Co.

The "Zithromax" name and logo is a registered trademark of Pfizer Inc.

The "Coumadin" name and logo is a registered trademark of Endo Products Inc.

The "Cytoxan" name and logo is a registered trademark of Mead Johnson & Company.

The "Nolvadex" name and logo is a registered trademark of Imperial Chemical Industries Limited.

The "Taxol" name and logo is a registered trademark of Bristol Myers Squibb Company.

The "Accupril" name and logo is a registered trademark of Warner-Lambert Company Corporation.

The "Aldactone" name and logo is a trademark of Pharmacia & Up John Company Corporation.

The "Altace" name and logo is a registered trademark of Hoechst Aktiengesellschaft Company.

The "Bumex" name and logo is a registered trademark of Hoffman-La Roche Inc.

The "Capoten" name and logo is a registered trademark of E. R. Squibb & Sons, Inc.

The "Cardizem" name and logo is a registered trademark of Marion Laboratories Inc.

The "Catapres" name and logo is a registered trademark of Boehringer Ingelheim G.M.B.H. Corporation.

The "Cordarone" name and logo is a registered trademark of Omnium Financier Aquitaine Pour L'Hygiene et la Sante (Sanofi).

The "Pacerone" name and logo is a registered trademark of Upsher-Smith Laboratories, Inc.

The "Coreg" name and logo is a registered trademark of SmithKline Beecham P.L.C.

The "Cozaar" name and logo is a registered trademark of E. I. du Pont de Nemours and Company.

The "Crestor" name and logo is a trademark of IPR Pharmaceuticals Inc.

The "Diovan" name and logo is a registered trademark of Novartis Corporation.

The "Hytrin" name and logo is a registered trademark of Abbott Laboratories Corporation.

The "Hyzaar" name and logo is a registered trademark of E. I. du Pont de Nemours and Company.

The "Inderal" name and logo is a registered trademark of Imperial Chemical Industries Limited.

The "Isordil" name and logo is a registered trademark of American Home Products Corporation.

The "Lanoxin" name and logo is a registered trademark of Burroughs Wellcome & Co.

The "Digitek" name and logo is a trademark of Bertek Pharmaceuticals Inc.

The "Lasix" name and logo is a registered trademark of Hoechst Aktiengesellschaft Corporation.

The "Lipitor" name and logo is a registered trademark of Pfizer Ireland Pharmaceuticals Corporation.

The "Lopressor" name and logo is a registered trademark of Ciba-Geigy Corporation.

The "Lotensin" name and logo is a registered trademark of Ciba-Geigy Corporation.

The "Norvasc" name and logo is a registered trademark of Pfizer Inc.

The "Plavix" name and logo is a registered trademark of Elf Sanofi Corporation.

The "Pravachol" name and logo is a registered trademark of E. R. Squibb & Sons, INC.

The "Procardia" name and logo is a registered trademark of Pfizer Inc.

The "Rythmol" name and logo is a registered trademark of Helopharm W. Petrik GMBH & CO.

The "Levothroid" name and logo is a registered trademark of Rhone-Poulenc Rorer Pharmaceuticals Inc.

The "Flexeril" name and logo is a registered trademark of Merck & Co Inc.

The "Robaxin" name and logo is a registered trademark of A.H. Robins Company, INC.

The "Zyloprim" name and logo is a registered trademark of Burroughs Wellcome & Co. (U.S.A.) Inc.

The "Adderall" name and logo is a registered trademark of Richwood Pharmaceutical Company, Inc

The "Ambien" name and logo is a registered trademark of Synthelabo Corporation.

The "Ativan" name and logo is a registered trademark of American Home Products Corporation.

The "Celexa" name and logo is a trademark of Forest Laboratories, Inc.

The "Concerta" name and logo is a trademark of Alza Corporation.

The "Cymbalta" name and logo is a registered trademark of Eli Lilly and Company.

The "Depakote" name and logo is a registered trademark of Sanofi Corporation.

The "Desyrel" name and logo is a registered trademark of Mead Johnson & Company Corporation.

The "Effexor" name and logo is a registered trademark of American Home Products Corporation.

The "Elavil" name and logo is a registered trademark of Merck & Co., Inc.

The "Geodon" name and logo is a trademark of Pfizer Inc.

The "Haldol" name and logo is a registered trademark of McNeil Laboratories, Incorporated.

The "Klonopin" name and logo is a registered trademark of Hoffmann-La Roche Inc.

The "Lexapro" name and logo is a trademark of Forest Laboratories, Inc.

The "Librium" name and logo is a trademark of ICN Pharmaceuticals, Inc.

The "Paxil" name and logo is a registered trademark of SmithKline Beecham Corporation.

The "Prozac" name and logo is a registered trademark of Eli Lilli and Company Corporation.

The "Restoril" name and logo is a registered trademark of Sandoz, INC.

The "Risperdal" name and logo is a registered trademark of Johnson & Johnson Corporation.

The "Seroquel" name and logo is a registered trademark of Imperial Chemical Industries PLC.

The "Valium" name and logo is a registered trademark of Hoffmann-La Roche INC.

The "Vistaril" name and logo is a registered trademark of Chas. Pfizer & Co., INC.

The "Wellbutrin" name and logo is a registered trademark of Burroughs Wellcome Co.

The "Xanax" name and logo is a registered trademark of UPJOHN COMPANY.

The "Zoloft" name and logo is a registered trademark of Pfizer Inc.

The "Zyprexa" name and logo is a registered trademark of Eli Lilly and Company.

The "Allegra" name and logo is a registered trademark of Merrell Pharmaceuticals.

The "Atrovent" name and logo is a registered trademark of Boehringer Ingelheim International GmbH.

The "Combivent" name and logo is a registered trademark of Boehringer Ingelheim Pharmaceuticals, Inc.

The "Flonase" name and logo is a registered trademark of Glaxo Group Limited.

The "Nasonex" name and logo is a registered trademark of Schering Corporation.

The "Proventil" name and logo is a registered trademark of Schering Corporation.

The "Serevent" name and logo is a registered trademark of Glaxo Group Ltd.

The "Singulair" name and logo is a registered trademark of Merck & Co., Inc.

The "Theo-Dur" name and logo is a registered trademark of Key Pharmaceuticals, INC.

The "Zyrtec" name and logo is a registered trademark of UCB Pharma.

The "Cortisporin" name and logo is a registered trademark of Burroughs Wellcome & Co.

The "Antabuse" name and logo is a registered trademark of AYERST, MCKENNA & HARRISON LIMITED CORPORATION.

The "Narcan" name and logo is a registered trademark of Endo Laboratories.

The "PowerPoint" name and logo is a registered trademark of Microsoft Corporation.

The "Benadryl" name and logo is a registered trademark of McNeil Healthcare Limited.

The "GoLYTELY®" name and logo is a registered trademark and property of BRAINTREE LABORATORIES, INC.

The "Jell-o" name and logo is a registered trademark of Kraft Foods Holdings, Inc.

Dedication

"I wish to thank my husband and best friend, Sammy, for his endless support during this extended project. To our children and grandchildren, who bring the boundless hope of the future to me daily. I also wish to thank Melissa Peterson, the best editor of all time, for her guidance and expertise.

I dedicate this book to the many nursing graduates who shall hold it in their hands as they anxiously stand between two worlds — that of student and that of healer. And may I always remember to thank the thousands of patients who humbly placed their lives into my hands."

Table of Contents

Chapter 2: What to Expect on the NCLEX 47

Chapter 3: How to Prepare for the NCLEX 77

Chapter 4: Coordination and Management of Care 93

Chapter 5: Safety and Infection Control   117

Chapter 6: Health Promotion and Maintenance   133

Chapter 7: Psychosocial Integrity 157

Chapter 8: Basic Care and Comfort   181

Chapter 9: Pharmacological and Parenteral Therapies 199

Chapter 10: Reduction of Risk Potential 235

Chapter 11: Physiological Adaptation   261

Foreword

By Patricia Carroll
RN, BC, CEN, RRT, MS

Congratulations on making it through nursing school! While the NCLEX may seem daunting now, it is simply a long review of what you have already learned. You have made it through the hardest part; now, you have just one mile left on the journey.

This book is your guide for that last leg. Just as the Sherpas — the native experts — guide mountaineers in the Himalayas, Author J. Lucy Boyd is your NCLEX Sherpa, and *101 Ways to Score Higher on Your NCLEX* is your compass.

I wish a book like this was available when I took the NCLEX many years ago. Boyd avoids the trap many review books fall into and does not try to reteach nursing school. Instead, she walks you through how the test is designed, what to expect from the questions, and — just as important — what to expect from the actual mechanics of taking the computer-based test. You will discover that the NCLEX is not shrouded in mystery. By carefully reading this book, you will learn what the NCLEX is really testing for, how to approach the each type of question, and how to minimize mistakes while you are taking the exam.

Be sure to pay special attention to the "Smart Strategies" throughout the book. These tips and hints make this book particularly valuable. They will help you focus on the key aspects of the information and will keep you from being bogged down with details that are not as important — something that can really eat up your review time.

I have been an item writer for the National Council for State Boards of Nursing and for professional specialty certification exams. In fact, I took a course in test construction. NCLEX questions follow very specific rules and are extensively tested before they are used to assess your knowledge. In fact, you will test new questions when you take the exam. While you will not know which ones they are, new questions will be part of your exam. The test creators carefully review each sample question's results before it becomes part of the official exam. Answers that seem clear to item writers and reviewers may not be clear to new nurses taking the boards, so the questions are modified or thrown out. You can be assured that there are not any "gotcha" questions waiting for you. The sample tests in this book will allow you to practice questions that follow the NCLEX format.

The size of this book is ideal for carrying it with you to study on breaks or when you find yourself with time to kill. Get out your highlighter and a pen, mark it up, fold over the pages, and make it your personal study guide. Use the checklists and timelines to stay on track.

I will never forget how excited I was when I tore open the envelope that told me I passed the NCLEX so many years ago. Earning your nursing license is the first step on a new journey. For me, that journey has led through critical care, medical-surgical and emergency nursing, home care, consulting, teaching, being an award-winning medical writer and health columnist for the *New York Daily News*, and being a repeat guest on *The View*.

Your future is limited only by your imagination. Where will your journey take you?

Patricia Carroll RN, BC, CEN, RRT, MS
FREDDIE video award winner: Pass NCLEX!

Registered nurse Pat Carroll has been called "America's Nurse" and "Heloise on Health." Her warm, engaging style has been featured on television and radio, including *CNN Headline News, Fox News Channel, The View,* and dozens of local news programs nationwide. Her *PBS* special, *Hints for Health: A Nurse's Notebook,* made its national debut in August 2004 and she won a Golden Lamp Award from the Center for Nursing Advocacy in 2003 for providing one of the best media portrayals of nursing.

Pat began her career as a respiratory therapist, a graduate of Upstate Medical University in Syracuse, New York. She returned to school to become a registered nurse and is a proud alumna of Excelsior College School of Nursing in Albany, New York, the largest nursing school in the United States and one of ten Centers of Excellence in nursing education, designated by the National League for Nursing. Pat was a charter member of the Tau Kappa Chapter of the international honor society for nurses, Sigma Theta Tau, at Excelsior. The school named her one of 30 "exceptional graduates" of 100,000 to celebrate the school's 30th anniversary.

Pat is an award-winning author of *Community Health Nursing: A Practical Guide, Nursing Leadership and Management: A Practical Guide, The Surgical Nurse's Managed Care Manual,* which was named *American Journal of Nursing's* Book of the Year, and her book for consumers, *What Nurses Know and Doctors Don't Have Time to Tell You.* She has extensive experience in ER nursing, critical care, home care, community health, and traditional in-patient hospital care of adults and children. She is board certified as a registered respiratory therapist and in emergency nursing and nursing professional development.

Preface

Congratulations on your graduation from nursing school! Your excitement is likely tempered with mild anxiety about the upcoming NCLEX® (National Council Licensure Examination). This book will walk you through exactly what to expect and will prepare you for success. We have received advice from many experts on the best way to study for this exam. Unlike most of the other review guides you might find, this book is organized just as the creators of the exam organized the test. You will learn to think like the test question writers, optimizing your chances for success.

The test requires two main skills:

Memorization – You must know normal laboratory values, drug indications and side effects, symptoms of various diseases, typical treatments for many conditions, and how to prepare clients for surgical procedures. You will rely on your memory for many of the questions.

How this book prepares you for memorization questions:

You will find the majority of topics that may arise on the exam listed. Many of these topics are expounded on to help you understand the depth of knowledge you should have in each area. Short quizzes are provided for tough material to assist in memorization.

Critical Thinking – You must be able to figure out what you should do in various situations. Many of the questions will ask you: What should you do first? What is the priority? The nursing board needs to know that you will make appropriate decisions when facing both typical and atypical circumstances.

How this book prepares you for critical-thinking questions:

The skills related to critical thinking are discussed in the early chapters. You will learn how to answer questions based on Maslow's Hierarchy of Needs, the ABCs (airway, breathing, circulation), stable versus unstable, and more. Quizzes will reinforce your critical-thinking skills, and practice examinations will reinforce your confidence.

This book also devotes itself to explaining the basics of the NCLEX application process. All the needed resources are described in detail. You will learn exactly what you need to study and also how to study effectively. We will walk you through each moment from eight weeks pre-exam to the last minute of the test. All your questions — major and minor — will be answered as you read through the pages. As a nursing school graduate, you can pass the NCLEX, and being thoroughly prepared will greatly increase your chances of doing so on the first try.

Why This Book Is the Best Study Guide for You

1. It is based on the actual examination. Most of the review books you may find are set up exactly like nursing school was, but it is best to get in the habit of categorizing and thinking in the same way that the exam is organized.

2. It assists with both critical-thinking skills and memorization. Most review books only cover one or the other.

3. It has ample review material, quizzes, and two practice exams. Many of the review books you may find are practice examinations only. This does not aid in memorization or provide a review of topics on the examination.

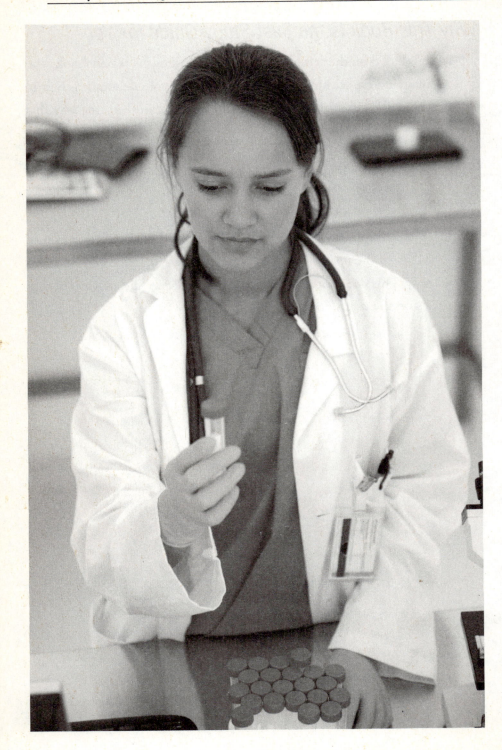

Introduction

101 Ways to Score Higher on Your NCLEX is intended to assist nursing school graduates with passing the NCLEX. This book should be used in conjunction with nursing textbooks and your classroom notes to prepare for test day. It was designed to be used as a reference for studying for the NCLEX while also giving helpful tips and advice for passing the exam. Use this book as an assistive tool for directing your study efforts. Because it is not possible to cover all topics taught while in nursing school, some sections throughout the book have been expanded, while others give a brief overview of what test takers need to know in order to succeed on the exam.

The Organization of the Book

Chapters 1-3 of the book will prepare nursing school graduates to take the NCLEX. Providing timelines to direct your study efforts and procedures for registering for the exam, these chapters offer test takers insider information they need to know to thoroughly study and prepare for the NCLEX. Chapter 1 reviews the question formats you will see on the NCLEX and offers advice for approaching each specific type of question. Chapter 2 breaks down the NCLEX-PN® (for practical nurses) and NCLEX-RN® (for registered

nurses) and lists the topics covered on each test according to the NCSBN®
(National Council of State Boards of Nursing). Chapter 3 provides a study
timeline starting eight weeks prior to the test up to the actual day of testing.
Tips on avoiding test anxiety are included in this chapter.

Chapters 4-11 offer an in-depth overview on the topics covered on both
nursing examinations. These chapters highlight each topic and offer some
expanded sections to help test takers review important information that
may appear on the exam. Each chapter includes a skills and terms-to-know
checklist for gauging your preparedness on each topic.

The book also provides several appendices to further prepare you for success on the exam. A helpful list of abbreviations used in nursing is included, as well as two practice tests with answers and extended explanations.
A complete listing of the contact information of individual state boards of
nursing provides test takers with an additional resource, should they have
questions on their specific state's examination.

Conventions Used in This Book

Pronouns

For ease of reading, nurses, physicians, and clients are referred to alter-
nately in the feminine and the masculine.

Licensed Practical Nurse/Licensed Vocational Nurse

References to both licensed practical nurses and licensed vocational nurses
(found in two states) are listed as licensed practical nurses or LPNs.

Skills Checklists

You will find skills checklists within many of the chapters, and you should
know how to perform each skill. If you are not comfortable with a particu-

lar topic, you can find further information later in the chapter or in your nursing textbooks and notes. Be aware that any lists in the book may be incomplete, and there could be additional skills that you will need to have. Refer to **www.ncsbn.org** for the latest information needed for the exam.

Use of the Term "Client"

The NCLEX refers to patients exclusively as clients; therefore, this book is written using the same terminology, so the term will be familiar to you while taking the exam.

Smart Strategies

Throughout this book, you will find 101 exciting strategies to help you ace the NCLEX. They will be labeled "Smart Strategies" and marked with special boxes for your convenience.

Case Studies

As part of bringing you the most practical advice for passing the NCLEX, we have obtained opinions from some of the best nursing educators in the country. These instructors and professors work daily with graduating students who continue to take their respective NCLEX examinations and have offered their best advice on passing the NCLEX. You will find these Case Studies inserted at the end of Chapters 4-10.

Quick Quiz

Short mini quizzes are scattered throughout Chapter 4-11 to test your knowledge on specific subjects. Answers to these quizzes can be found in Appendix D.

Chapter 1

Countdown to Test Day

The Structure of the Test

Test questions will appear one at a time on a computer screen. When you answer a question, the next question will appear. You cannot go back to any questions, nor can you leave any questions blank. There is no penalty for guessing, so make your best educated guess if you do not know the answer.

How to Sign Up for the NCLEX-PN or NCLEX-RN

Smart Strategies

- Do not miss your state's deadline for signing up to take the test.
- Make sure you give your name exactly as it is printed on your identification.
- Do not misplace your Authorization to Test.

1. Submit your application for a license to your state Board of Nursing. Some boards have deadlines; be sure you are aware of the rules for your state. If you do not have an application, you may obtain one by contacting the state Board of Nursing for the state in which you wish to practice.

2. Decide if you wish to be contacted by e-mail or U.S. mail. If you provide an e-mail address when you register for the NCLEX, all correspondence will arrive in that manner. If you do not give an e-mail address, you will receive correspondence by U.S. mail only. You must consider if you will be moving (which is often common after graduation), or if your e-mail is unreliable or could be changing.

3. Register for the exam. You have three options for registration.

    •   You may register online at **www.pearsonvue.com/nclex**. You will be asked for your name exactly as it will be listed on the identification you bring with you to the testing center. You must provide your e-mail address, mailing address, telephone number, and date of birth. While it is not required, you will also be asked your mother's maiden name, gender, Social Security number, ethnicity, maiden name, former name, and when the former name was last used. You will be asked how you wish to pay the $200.00 application fee; if you have taken the NCLEX before; the name, city, and state of your nursing school; the month and year of your graduation; and which state board you are taking the test for. If you are registering online, you may pay by credit or debit card — Visa®, MasterCard®, or American Express® — or money order, cashier's check, or certified check. Have your credit card or debit card available when you register. If you pay by credit card or debit card, the registration process is then complete. If you pay by money order, cashier's check, or certified check, you will need to print a confirmation document that you will mail along with the payment.

    •   You may register by mail. If you do not have a registration form, contact the NCSBN at **www.ncsbn.org** for information on how to obtain one. Carefully fill out the registration form, as a computer will read it, and mail it in along with a money order, cashier's check, or certified check to the NCSBN.

- You may register by telephone by calling 1-866-49NCLEX in the United States. It is suggested, but not required, that you have a completed registration form in front of you when you call. You will be asked information as it appears on the form. You can pay by credit card or debit card — Visa, MasterCard, or American Express.

4. Receive your Authorization to Test (ATT). The Authorization to Test will expire in 60 to 365 days, depending on your state Board of Nursing. Receiving the ATT means that you have been authorized to take the NCLEX by your state Board of Nursing. You must take the ATT with you when you take the exam.

5. Schedule to take the examination at a Pearson Professional Center. You can find a list of locations at **www.pearsonvue.com/nclex**. You may take the exam at any center you wish; it does not have to be in the state that you wish to become licensed in. You may schedule the examination online or by telephone. Refer to the information on the ATT for where to call and write down the date and time you are given. Ask for directions if you need them.

6. You must take one acceptable form of identification to the test center. Acceptable forms of identification include:

- U. S. driver's license, issued by your state's department of motor vehicles
- U. S. state identification, issued by your state's department of motor vehicles
- Passport
- U. S. military identification

The identification must be current (not expired) and contain your photograph and signature. Exception: If your driver's license has expired, you may bring in the renewal slip along with the expired license. The writing and signature must be in English. Learner's and driver's permits are not acceptable identification.

What to Expect When You Arrive at Pearson Professional Center

Smart Strategies
- Plan to be early to the testing center.
- Take the exam tutorial online so that you will know what to expect.

The NCSBN says that you should plan to arrive at least 30 minutes early; in this book, we recommend arriving an hour early. This gives you extra time for any problems that may arise. Bear in mind that they will accept you if you are up to 30 minutes late, should you have a transportation emergency. If you are running late, go to the facility and see if they will still accept you.

Friends, relatives, or children who accompany you may not wait in the testing center, nor may they speak with you during the exam time. If you need someone to give you a ride to the testing center, prepare accordingly.

You will present your ATT and your approved form of identification with identical name. Your fingerprint, photograph, and signature will be taken. Be aware that you will be observed during the entire examination. A video and audio recording will be taken of your examination process. You will be re-fingerprinted each time you enter and leave the testing room. You may not leave the building during your breaks. You may not contact anyone via telephone, e-mail, or in-person after you begin testing. You will be given a note board and marker for use during the test. You may request a new board at any time. A secure storage space will be provided to you to store your personal items during the test.

The following items are not allowed in the testing center and should be left at home or in your vehicle:

- Textbooks
- Notebooks
- Any other study aids
- Cameras
- Tobacco
- Photographic equipment or devices
- Weapons (i.e. guns, knives, swords, daggers, etc.)

The following items are *not* allowed in the testing room:

- Papers, including scratch paper
- Books
- Pens/pencils (testing is done via computer — no writing utensils are necessary)
- Purses
- Wallets
- Watches
- Beepers
- Cell phones
- Any other electronic devices
- Hats
- Scarves
- Coats

Exceptions may be made for religious apparel. The NCSBN rules state that you may not eat, drink, or use tobacco in the testing center, but you should confirm this if you feel you may need a snack during the testing period.

You will be given an erasable note board and marker for solving questions. Some test takers write down information on the board as soon as the testing time begins. For example, they may write lab work values they are afraid they will forget. It is recommended that you ask for the earplugs that the testing center supplies to test takers.

When you complete the test, a survey will appear on the screen inquiring about your testing experience. When you complete the survey, you will raise your hand. Your note board will be taken, and you will soon be dismissed.

You can view the tutorial that you will be given on exam day at **www. pearsonvue.com/nclex**. Ensure that you are comfortable with the calculator, the exhibits/charts, and the way you must scroll down to view all the possible answers to some of the questions. Notice the timer, called a clock, in the top right corner that tells you exactly how much time you have left to complete the exam. Practice navigating the tutorial until you feel completely comfortable with all the tools.

You must raise your hand and await permission to take breaks during the test.

Special Considerations for International Candidates

If you take the NCLEX outside of the United States, you must pay an international scheduling fee of $150. You may also be subject to a "Value Added Tax." You can find detailed information regarding the scheduling of your test at **www.ncsbn.org**.

Test Question Types

Smart Strategies
- Concern yourself much more with standard format questions than alternate format questions.
- Answer math questions to the decimal requested.
- Take your time and be precise when answering a hot spot question.
- Make sure that you have scrolled down to read all the answer choices for each question.

Test questions will either be in standard format or alternate format. These types are explained in the following sections.

Standard Format Questions

The vast majority of the questions you will encounter on the test will be standard format questions, which are multiple-choice questions with four answers to choose from. The four possible answers are labeled 1, 2, 3, and 4. You will mark the appropriate answer and click "Next."

Alternate Format Questions

Some of the questions on the test will be in an alternative format. These alternative formats include multiple-response questions, fill-in-the-blank questions, hot spot questions, exhibit questions, and drag and drop/ordered response questions.

The bulk of the questions will be in the standard format, and you should not expend too much energy focusing on the alternative format questions. The NCSBN indicates that, if your exam includes only the minimum number of questions, you may only have one or two alternative format questions on your entire test.

Multiple-Response Questions

These questions state, "Select all that apply" or similar wording. Between one and all five of the answers will be correct. You will mark your choices and click "Next."

Tips for Answering Multiple-Response Questions

If you are prepared for standard format questions, you should be ready for multiple-response questions. Take each answer and ask yourself if it is a correct answer. Do not worry about whether you find one or all five answers to be correct. There could be one, two, three, four, or five correct answers.

Fill-in-the-Blank Calculation Questions

These math questions require an exact answer. Carefully record your answer and click "Next."

💡 Tips for Answering Fill-in-the-Blank Questions

You should take advantage of the calculator feature on these questions, even if you feel you know the answer. You may also use the note board you are given to work out the answer. Do not hesitate to ask for a fresh board if you need one. Be careful to follow the directions exactly. An example of specific directions might be, "Record your answer using two decimal places."

Do not stress yourself if math is not your strong suit. There will be very few math questions on the exam, and you will not fail solely because of the math questions. If you wish to study to improve your math skills for these questions, do not make it more than 5 to 10 percent of your study effort.

Hot Spot Questions

These questions require you to put the cursor where the correct answer is and click enter. An example of this type of question is: Where do you put the stethoscope to listen to an apical pulse? A picture of a chest would be available and you should place the cursor exactly where you would listen. Then, click "Next."

💡 Tips for Answering Hot Spot Questions

Take your time and picture the human body. Recall any references.you have learned, such as rib counts or other body landmarks. Do not confuse the left and right sides of the body. Your cursor must be in precisely the correct spot.

Exhibit Questions

On these questions, you will see the question, four possible answers labeled 1, 2, 3, and 4, and a button to view an exhibit. The exhibit will show you information that you must use to answer the question. Pick the correct answer and hit "Next."

 Answering Exhibit Questions

Make sure that you look at each tile of the exhibit. Tiles provide additional information needed to answer the question, and there may be several of them. Use your board as necessary to record the contents of one tile so that you can access that information while you view the other tiles. Be especially careful to read the question carefully. Try to ascertain the correct answer before looking at the possible answers. Come up with your own answer and see if one of the possible answers matches yours. It is wise to spend an extra few minutes on these questions. An example of an exhibit question can be found on the NCLEX tutorial on the NCSBN Web site.

Drag and Drop/Ordered Response Item Questions

For these questions, you will read a question and drag the responses into the correct order. An example of this type of questions is: Put the following steps in order for preparing to clean a stage III decubitis wound.

 Answering Drop/Ordered Response Questions

These questions will rely largely on common sense. If you are uncertain of the answer, think through the possibilities and imagine each step. Some steps must logically come before other steps. Take a few extra minutes to make sure you have placed each step in its proper sequence.

The Computer Adaptive Testing (CAT) Process

Smart Strategies

- Do not convince yourself you are not doing well during the test. Remember, the test is created to give you questions at the border of your knowledge, and you will only answer about half of the questions correctly.

- Ignore the counter tracking the number of questions you have completed as you take the test. As described below, you can pass the exam having completed anywhere between the minimum number of questions (85) to the maximum number (265).

- If you do not know an answer after several minutes of consideration, make your best guess. Eliminate the obviously wrong answers and pick the most likely choice.

The NCLEX is a test that attempts to accurately rate your level of knowledge on the subject, called computer adaptive tests. Many myths exist about the Computer Adaptive Testing Process. Here are the facts:

The NCLEX-PN contains from 85 to 205 questions. Of these, 25 are called pre-test questions and do not count. The maximum time limit for the NCLEX-PN is five hours. The NCLEX-RN contains from 75 to 265 questions. Of these, 15 are pre-test questions that do not count. The maximum time limit for the NCLEX-RN is six hours.

The test can end at any point between the minimum and maximum number of questions. It will end when it can be determined with 95 percent accuracy whether you will pass or fail. If the test ends at the minimum number of questions, it could either mean you passed or failed; the test continuing to the maximum number of questions could also mean you passed or failed.

The test will continue until you pass with 95 percent certainty; you fail with 95 percent certainty, you reach the maximum number of questions, or time runs out. If you do not know an answer, make your best guess. You should not, however, engage in rapid guessing when time is almost out. To pass the exam, the test taker's performance must be above the passing standard (typically 95 percent). When the computer determines with 95 percent accuracy that the test taker will either pass or fail the exam, the exam will end. As stated above, the test can also end when the maximum number of questions has been reached or if the time limit runs out.

If you answer a question correctly, the next question will be slightly harder. If you answer incorrectly, the next question will be slightly easier. But do not try to figure out if the questions are getting easier or harder. Just focus on responding.

The test is created so that you will answer about half of the questions correctly. This leads many to feel as if they have failed the test. Do not be discouraged if it seems like you are missing many of the questions; just continue.

Passing the Exam

Pass rates are sobering for repeat candidates, making it imperative for repeat test takers to establish the reasons for their failure. Common reasons include:

- A language barrier
- Test anxiety
- Illness or lack of sleep
- Poor preparation
- Difficulty "thinking" in terms of what the questions are asking

What to Do If You Have a Language Barrier

Smart Strategies

- If your English is not perfect, strongly consider taking a class in both English and medical English.

- Ask a practicing U.S. nurse from your country of origin to explain to you any cultural differences in care and communication between the two countries.

If a candidate has difficulty understanding English, he needs to take necessary courses to improve his language skills. While studying medical terminology is important, it is equally important to understand all the words in a question. One misunderstood word can easily cause someone who actually knows the correct answer to miss the question.

What to Do If You Have Test Anxiety

Smart Strategies

- If you have previously failed the NCLEX due to anxiety, consider discussing the test anxiety with your primary care provider. She may have some helpful treatment options.

While anxiety is also discussed elsewhere in this book, here we will discuss the importance of not "psyching yourself out" during the test. Many who fail the NCLEX report that they started staring at the clock or worrying about the number of questions they had answered. You can pass at the minimum number of questions, the maximum number of questions, and anywhere in between. The only concern you need to have with the clock is to remember to pace yourself. Spend at least one minute on each question, and realize that you can spend several minutes on many of the questions if you need to. While it is possible to run out of time before the questioning ends, it does not happen very often.

What to Do If You Are Ill or Did Not Sleep Well

Of course, prevention is best, but if you wake up sick or feeling the effects of a poor night's sleep, try the following:

- Eat a light breakfast if at all possible. If you cannot eat, try to have a smoothie or nutritional supplement. Do not go into the test with low blood sugar.
- Drink a caffeinated beverage if you normally do.
- Take any supplies that you could potentially need: medication, inhalers, cough drops, tissues, and so on.
- Visualize yourself resting at home after the test.

What to Do If You Are Poorly Prepared

Poor preparation will mainly affect your ability to do well on questions that require memorization. Your critical-thinking skills should still be intact, and you should use them to your advantage. For many of the questions, the correct answer can be reasoned, even if you do not recall many of the specifics discussed in the question. For example:

- You know that infections cause fever, especially before they are successfully treated. Thus, you may be able to answer a question on infections or fevers only by using your critical-thinking skills.

- You know that elderly clients are more prone to falls, fractures, side effects from medication, and development of most diseases. Thus, you may be able to answer questions on any of these topics using only critical-thinking skills.

Your critical-thinking skills can assist you in excluding some of the possible answers and increase your chances of answering the question correctly.

What to Do if You Have Difficulty with the Format

Some graduates have trouble with the format of the test, in that it comprises scenarios instead of direct questions. Follow these guidelines if this is an issue for you:

- Try to imagine how your instructor would answer the question.
- Visualize the scenario being described.
- Have an "effective nursing care" mentality. Remember the various roles of the nurse and do not answer the question as the physician would.

Pass Rates

The pass rates for the first quarter of 2009 include the following:

NCLEX-PN

- First time test-takers passed 83.19 percent of the time.
- Repeat test-takers passed 37.41 percent of the time.
- U.S.-educated test-takers passed 75.66 percent of the time
- Internationally educated test-takers passed 31.79 percent of the time.

NCLEX-RN

- First time test-takers passed 80.86 percent of the time.
- Repeat test-takers passed 38.82 percent of the time.
- U.S.-educated test-takers passed 82.45 percent of the time.
- Internationally educated test-takers passed 34.57 percent of the time.

From these statistics, it is difficult to determine whether the low success rate of repeat test-takers is indicative of the fact that they simply do not know the material, or whether experiencing an initial failure damages their confidence

Chapter 2

What to Expect on the NCLEX

This chapter provides an overview of subjects covered on the NCLEX according to the National Council of State Boards of Nursing (NCSBN). Each individual subject will be covered in greater depth in Chapters 4-11.

Clients Defined

When taking the NCLEX-RN, be aware that clients are defined as individuals, families, and groups.

When taking the NCLEX-PN, note that clients are defined as individuals, families, and significant others.

The following information specific to the NCLEX-PN and NCLEX-RN is copyrighted by the National Council of State Boards of Nursing and is used with their written permission.

The NCLEX-PN

Smart Strategies

- Carefully read the categories and subcategories for the topics on the test. Understanding the structure of the NCLEX will help you immensely when studying.

The content of the NCLEX-PN Test Plan is organized into four major Client Needs categories. Two of the four categories are further divided into a total of six subcategories:

A. Safe and Effective Care Environment

   1. Coordinated Care

   2. Safety and Infection Control

B. Health Promotion and Maintenance

C. Psychosocial Integrity

D. Physiological Integrity

   1. Basic Care and Comfort

   2. Pharmacological Therapies

   3. Reduction of Risk Potential

   4. Physiological Adaptation

Integrated Processes

The following processes fundamental to the practice of practical/vocational nursing are integrated throughout the Client Needs categories and subcategories:

- **Clinical Problem-Solving Process (Nursing Process)** – A scientific approach to client care that includes data collection, planning, implementation, and evaluation.

- **Caring** – Interaction of the practical/vocational nurse and clients, families, and significant others in an atmosphere of mutual respect and trust. In this collaborative environment, the practical/vocational nurse provides support and compassion to help achieve desired therapeutic outcomes.

- **Communication and Documentation** – Verbal and nonverbal interactions between the practical/vocational nurse and clients, families, significant others, and members of the health-care team. Events and activities associated with client care are validated in written and/or electronic records that reflect standards of practice and accountability in the provision of care.

- **Teaching and Learning** – facilitation of the acquisition of knowledge, skills, and attitudes to assist in promoting positive changes in behavior

Distribution of Content

Smart Strategies

- Learning the percentages of each type of question on the test is one key to scoring well. Try to focus your study time in a similar ratio to the test question ratios. In other words, do not spend 33 percent of your time studying psychosocial integrity when it only comprises 8–14 percent of the test questions.

- Safety and infection control may not have been highly emphasized during your nursing education. Make sure you spend about 11 percent of your study time on these topics.

Client Needs	Percentage of Questions from Each Category or Subcategory
A. Safe and Effective Care Environment	
1. Coordinated Care	12-18%
2. Safety and Infection Control	8-14%
B. Health Promotion and Maintenance	7-13%
C. Psychosocial Integrity	8-14%
D. Physiological Integrity	
1. Basic Care and Comfort	11-17%
2. Pharmacological Therapies	9-15%
3. Reduction of Risk Potential	10-16%
4. Physiological Adaptation	11-17%

Overview of Content for the NCLEX-PN

All content categories and subcategories reflect client needs across the life span in a variety of settings.

A. Safe and Effective Care Environment

The practical/vocational nurse provides nursing care that contributes to the enhancement of the health-care delivery setting and protects clients and health-care personnel.

1. Coordinated Care – The practical/vocational nurse collaborates with health-care team members to facilitate effective client care.

Related content includes but is not limited to:

- Advance Directives
- Advocacy
- Client Care Assignments
- Client Rights
- Confidentiality/Information Security

- Collaboration with Interdisciplinary Team
- Concepts of Management and Supervision
- Continuity of Care

- Establishing Priorities
- Ethical Practice
- Informed Consent
- Information Technology
- Legal Responsibilities

- Performance Improvement (Quality Improvement)
- Referral Process
- Resource Management
- Staff Education

2. Safety and Infection Control –The practical/vocational nurse contributes to the protection of clients and health-care personnel from health and environmental hazards.

Related content includes but is not limited to:

- Accident/Error/Injury Prevention
- Ergonomic Principles
- Handling Hazardous and Infectious Materials
- Home Safety
- Internal and External Disaster Plans

- Medical and Surgical Asepsis
- Reporting of Incident/Event/ Irregular Occurrence/Variance
- Restraints and Safety Devices
- Safe Use of Equipment
- Security Plan
- Standard/Transmission-Based /Other Precaution

B. Health Promotion and Maintenance

The practical/vocational nurse provides nursing care for clients that incorporates knowledge of expected stages of growth and development, and prevention and/or early detection of health problems.

Related content includes but is not limited to:

- Aging Process
- Ante/Intra/Postpartum and Newborn Care
- Data Collection Techniques

- Health Promotion/ Screening Programs
- High-Risk Behaviors
- Human Sexuality

- Developmental Stages and Transitions
- Disease Prevention
- Expected Body Image Changes
- Family Planning
- Immunization
- Lifestyle Choices
- Self-Care

C. Psychosocial Integrity

The practical/vocational nurse provides care that assists with promotion and support of the emotional, mental, and social well-being of clients.

Related content includes but is not limited to:

- Abuse or Neglect
- Behavioral Management
- Coping Mechanisms
- Crisis Intervention
- Cultural Awareness
- End-of-Life Concepts
- Grief and Loss
- Mental Health/Illness Concepts
- Religious or Spiritual Influences on Health
- Sensory/Perceptual Alternation
- Situational Role Changes
- Stress Management
- Substance-Related Disorders
- Suicide/Violence Precautions
- Support Systems
- Therapeutic Communication
- Therapeutic Environment
- Unexpected Body Image Changes

D. Physiological Integrity

The practical/vocational nurse assists in the promotion of physical health and well-being by providing care and comfort, reducing risk potential for clients, and assisting them with the management of health alterations.

1. Basic Care and Comfort – The practical/vocational nurse provides comfort to clients and assistance in the performance of their activities of daily living.

Related content includes but is not limited to:

- Assistive Devices
- Elimination
- Mobility/Immobility
- Non-Pharmacological Comfort
- Interventions
- Nutrition and Oral Hydration
- Palliative/Comfort Care
- Personal Hygiene
- Rest and Sleep

2. Pharmacological Therapies – The practical/vocational nurse provides care related to the administration of medications and monitors clients who are receiving parenteral therapies.

Related content includes but is not limited to:

- Adverse Effects
- Contraindications and Compatibilities
- Dosage Calculations
- Expected Effects
- Medication Administration
- Pharmacological Actions
- Pharmacological Agents
- Side Effects
- Agents
- Side Effects

3. Reduction of Risk Potential – The practical/vocational nurse reduces the potential for clients to develop complications or health problems related to treatments, procedures, or existing conditions.

Related content includes but is not limited to:

- Diagnostic Tests
- Laboratory Values
- Potential for Complications of Diagnostic Tests/Treatments/ Procedures/Surgery or Health Alterations
- Therapeutic Procedures
- Vital Signs
- Potential for Alternations in Body Systems

4. Physiological Adaptation – The practical/vocational nurse participates in providing care for clients with acute, chronic, or life-threatening physical health conditions.

Related content includes but is not limited to:

- Alterations in Body Systems
- Basic Pathophysiology
- Fluid and Electrolyte Imbalances
- Medical Emergencies
- Radiation Therapy
- Unexpected Response to Therapies

The NCLEX-RN

The content of the NCLEX-RN Test Plan is organized into four major Client Needs categories. Two of the four categories are further divided as follows:

A. Safe and Effective Care Environment
1. *Management of Care*
2. *Safety and Infection Control*

B. Health Promotion and Maintenance

C. Psychosocial Integrity

D. Physiological Integrity
1. *Basic Care and Comfort*
2. *Pharmacological and Parenteral Therapies*
3. *Reduction of Risk Potential*
4. *Physiological Adaptation*

Integrated Processes

The following processes are fundamental to the practice of nursing and are integrated throughout the Client Needs categories and subcategories:

- **Nursing Process** – A scientific problem-solving approach to client care that includes assessment, analysis, planning, implementation, and evaluation.

- **Caring** – Interaction of the nurse and client in an atmosphere of mutual respect and trust. In this collaborative environment, the nurse provides encouragement, hope, support, and compassion to help achieve desired outcomes.

- **Communication and Documentation** – Verbal and nonverbal interactions between the nurse and the client, the client's significant others, and the other members of the health-care team. Events and activities associated with client care are validated in written and/or electronic records that reflect standards of practice and accountability in the provision of care.

- **Teaching/Learning** – Facilitation of the acquisition of knowledge, skills, and attitudes promoting a change in behavior.

Distribution of Content

Client Needs	Percentage of Questions from Each Category or Subcategory
A. Safe and Effective Care Environment	
1. Management of Care	13-19%
2. Safety and Infection Control	8-14%
B. Health Promotion and Maintenance	6-12%
C. Psychosocial Integrity	6-12%
D. Physiological Integrity	
1. Basic Care and Comfort	6-12%
2. Pharmacological and Parenteral Therapies	13-19%
3. Reduction of Risk Potential	13-19%
4. Physiological Adaptation	11-17%

Overview of Content for the NCLEX-RN

All content categories and subcategories reflect client needs across the life span in a variety of settings.

A. Safe and Effective Care Environment

The nurse promotes achievement of client outcomes by providing and directing nursing care that enhances the care delivery setting in order to protect clients, family/significant others, and other health-care personnel.

1. Management of Care – Providing and directing nursing care that enhances the care delivery setting to protect clients, family/significant others, and health-care personnel.

Related content includes but is not limited to:

- Advance Directives
- Establishing Priorities
- Advocacy
- Ethical Practice
- Case Management
- Informed Consent
- Client Rights
- Information Technology
- Collaboration with Interdisciplinary Team
- Continuity of Care
- Staff Education
- Legal Rights and Responsibilities
- Concepts of Management
- Performance Improvement (Quality Improvement)
- Confidentiality/ Information Security
- Referrals
- Consultation
- Resource Management
- Delegation
- Supervision

2. Safety and Infection Control – Protecting clients, family/significant others, and health-care personnel from health and environmental hazards.

Related content includes but is not limited to:

- Accident Prevention
- Medical and Surgical Asepsis
- Disaster Planning
- Emergency Response Plan
- Reporting of Incident/Event/ Irregular Occurrence/Variance
- Ergonomic Principles
- Safe Use of Equipment
- Error Prevention

- Security Plan
- Handling Hazardous and Infectious Materials
- Standard/Transmission-Based/ Other Precautions
- Home Safety
- Use of Restraints/ Safety Devices
- Injury Prevention

B. Health Promotion and Maintenance

The nurse provides and directs nursing care of the client and family/significant others that incorporates the knowledge of expected growth and development principles; prevention and/or early detection of health problems; and strategies to achieve optimal health.

Related content includes, but is not limited to:

- Aging Process
- Health Promotion Programs
- Ante/Intra/Postpartum and Newborn Care
- Health Screening
- Developmental Stages and Transitions
- Lifestyle Choices
- Family Systems
- Principles of Teaching/Learning
- Growth and Development

- High Risk Behaviors
- Disease Prevention
- Human Sexuality
- Expected Body Image Changes
- Immunizations
- Family Planning
- Self-Care
- Health and Wellness
- Techniques of Physical Assessment

C. Psychosocial Integrity

The nurse provides and directs nursing care that promotes and supports the emotional, mental, and social well-being of the client and family/significant others experiencing stressful events, as well as clients with acute or chronic mental illness.

Related content includes but is not limited to:

- Abuse/Neglect
- Psychopathology
- Behavioral Interventions
- Religious and Spiritual Influences on Health
- Chemical and Other Dependencies
- Sensory/Perceptual Alterations
- Coping Mechanisms
- Situational Role Changes
- Crisis Intervention
- Stress Management
- Cultural Diversity
- Support Systems
- End-of-Life Care
- Therapeutic Communications
- Family Dynamics
- Therapeutic Environment
- Grief and Loss
- Unexpected Body Image Changes
- Mental Health Concepts

D. Physiological Integrity

The nurse promotes achievement of client outcomes by providing and directing nursing care that enhances the care delivery setting in order to protect clients, family/significant others, and other health-care personnel.

1. Basic Care and Comfort – Providing comfort and assistance in the performance of activities of daily living.

Related content includes but is not limited to:

- Assistive Devices
- Nutrition and Oral Hydration
- Personal Hygiene
- Mobility/Immobility

- Complementary and
  Alternative Therapies
- Palliative/Comfort Care
- Elimination

- Rest and Sleep
- Non-Pharmacological
  Comfort Interventions

2. Pharmacological and Parenteral Therapies – Providing care related to the administration of medications and parenteral therapies.

Related content includes but is not limited to:

- Adverse Effects/
  Contraindications
- Parenteral/Intravenous
  Therapies
- Blood and Blood Products
- Pharmacological
  Agents/Actions
- Central Venous Access Devices

- Pharmacological Interactions
- Dosage Calculation
- Pharmacological Pain
  Management
- Expected Effects/Outcomes
- Total Parenteral Nutrition
- Medication Administration

3. Reduction of Risk Potential – Reducing the likelihood that clients will develop complications or health problems related to existing conditions, treatments, or procedures.

Related content includes but is not limited to:

- Diagnostic Tests
- Laboratory Values
- Potential for Complications
  from Surgical Procedures and
  Health Alterations
- Monitoring Conscious
  Sedation
- Therapeutic Procedures

- System Specific Assessments
- Vital Signs
- Potential for Alterations in
  Body Systems
- Potential for Complications
  of Diagnostic Tests/
  Treatments/Procedures

4. Physiological Adaptation – managing and providing care for clients with acute, chronic, or life-threatening physical health conditions.

Related content includes but is not limited to:

- Alterations in Body Systems
- Medical Emergencies
- Fluid and Electrolyte Imbalances
- Pathophysiology
- Hemodynamics
- Radiation Therapy
- Illness Management
- Unexpected Response to Therapies
- Infectious Diseases

The Nursing Process as It Relates to the Exam

Assessment

Smart Strategies

- If you feel you are not prepared for assessment questions and are not currently working in health care, practice assessing family and friends. Use imagined ailments, but think of the actual assessment you would do for the diabetic client, the hearing-impaired client, or the underweight teen.

Nursing assessment includes assessment of the client and assessment of any ongoing process, such as bleeding or pain. An assessment is always the first response of the nurse. Assessment should not be delegated to subordinates. Questions on the NCLEX will test whether you know what factors to assess for a given condition and if you understand normal assessment findings.

Example assessment questions include:

- What is a normal heart rate for a 3-year-old child?
- What are the normal complaints of a client in labor at 2 centimeters?

- Describe the normal shape of the chest of a client who has had progressive COPD for ten years.
- Describe the stool of an adolescent with cystic fibrosis.
- What is the normal weight range for a 25-year-old man who is 70 inches tall?

Assessment questions utilize both your memorizing and critical-thinking skills. It may help you to visualize the scenario in the question. If you do not automatically know the answer to the question, think about everything you do know about the condition being discussed. Some of the answers will be detractors; that is, they can send your thinking process in the wrong direction and cause you to miss the correct answer.

Analysis

Smart Strategies

- If you feel you are not prepared for analysis questions, ask your study friends to quiz you on these types of questions. Examples include:

  - The client is complaining of double vision. What could be wrong?
  - The client has an inflamed toe. What could be wrong?
  - Your client's heart rate has doubled in four hours. What do you anticipate your orders to be?

Nursing analysis involves taking your assessment findings and any other data available to you — such as lab results — and analyzing the client's needs. These needs can be anticipated by considering the process and sequelea of the health challenges facing the client.

Example analysis questions include:

- The client has just learned that she has Stage II lymphoma. She is convinced that she will not live very long. The nurse must consider the facts about lymphoma as well as her knowledge of the stages of grief. Combining these with her assessment findings and the client's biopsy results, she can properly analyze the needs of the client.

Analysis questions will test your critical-thinking skills.

Planning

Smart Strategies

- If you feel you are not prepared for planning questions, create imaginary clients and write care plans for them. Update them according to imaginary changes.

- Ask yourself, for an imaginary client, what five things the nurse can do to improve his or her health.

- As you take the exam, view the nurse's job as two-fold. You create a plan for the client's care from the nursing standpoint. You also carry out physician orders, which you must be able to anticipate. Think of both of these responsibilities as you consider the planning questions.

One of the primary functions of a nurse is to create and follow a plan of care for the client. These are created from both the analysis of the client's condition and the anticipation of the client's needs. For the purposes of NCLEX questions, it is generally assumed that a RN will develop the client's care plan in most health-care settings.

Example planning questions include:

- The nurse must anticipate that a client with severe COPD may need extra pillows. He or she may also require extra time to eat and possibly limitations on casual visitors. The nurse will plan for his varied needs in the nursing care plan.

- A client headed to surgery can be anticipated to have anxiety, questions, and possibly insomnia. The nurse will have these considerations in mind when creating the nursing care plan.

- Planning can also involve preparing for a procedure. This may be a procedure that the nurse performs, one in which she assists, or one that she prepares for the physician. NCLEX questions may test your knowledge of the steps involved in planning for a procedure, such as treating a wound or administering an enema.

Planning questions require both your memorization and critical-thinking skills.

Implementation

Smart Strategies

- If you feel you are not prepared for implementation questions, spend time reading skills and procedures manuals. Think through various procedures and talk them through with or practice them on your study friends.

Nurses implement treatments, client and family education, medication administration, specialized feedings, and many other tasks. The nurse must recall how to perform these tasks and will be tested on the implementation of these tasks on the NCLEX. Some of the questions can be expected to refer to what step should be done first and which step is incorrect.

Implementation questions will test your memory of various skills, such as administering the proper insulin dose, teaching a client how to walk on crutches or with a walker, and how to feed a client with a gastric feeding tube.

Implementation questions will utilize your memorizations skills.

Evaluation

Smart Strategies

- If you feel you are not prepared for evaluation questions, you may have a lack of confidence in your nursing abilities in general. Remember your victories while in clinicals — the times you provided excellent care or successfully performed a task.

- Consider the desired outcomes for an imaginary client who is admitted to the hospital. For the client with severe hypertension, it will be a reduction in his pressure to near-normal levels. It may also be the addressing of any primary problems that led to the hypertension. It may include his understanding of and adherence to a low-sodium diet; it may be his participation in stress management classes.

- Once again, view the nurse's job as two-fold. While your main focus will be on whether nursing objectives have been met for a particular client, you should also look at whether the medical treatment objectives were met.

- If, upon evaluation, you determine that nursing objectives have not been met, or need to be altered, you must update the plan of care. Expect to see these types of scenarios on the NCLEX.

Nursing evaluation is a critical component of the nursing process. It is the means by which you determine if treatment is meeting the expected outcome.

Example evaluation scenarios include:

A client arrives with a stage III decubitus wound. The care plan objective is to reduce the wound to a stage II by the end of 14 days. The wound is measured and assessed daily during treatment. After 14 days, the nurse will evaluate whether the desired outcome has been met.

The NCLEX will consist of many evaluation questions. These questions will test your memorization. The nurse must know how to evaluate outcomes and what to do if the desired outcome has not been achieved.

Additional evaluation scenarios include:

A care plan for a morbidly obese client includes assisting her to lose ten pounds in 30 days. A diet and exercise program has been planned and implemented. At the end of the 30 days, the client has lost 11 pounds. The objective has been met.

A care plan for an outpatient client with type II diabetes includes stabilizing his blood sugar and not allowing it to climb over 200 mg/dl. When tested, his blood sugar is 235. The objective has not been met. The nurse must determine if the care plan needs correcting; for example, whether a more stringent diet and exercise plan is needed, or if the client has been noncompliant with his diet, his exercise plan, or his medication regimen.

Some of the questions will relate directly to the nursing process. For example, you must assess a problem before you plan what to do.

Evaluation questions test your critical-thinking skills. For questions in which you do not know the answer, it can be helpful to think about which step of the nursing process the question describes. Is it asking you to assess the client? Evaluate the outcome of therapy? Plan the steps to a procedure? Understanding the question in this way will help to eliminate possible incorrect answers and lead you to the correct one.

Caring

Caring in nursing relates to the services you provide as well as the empathy you show your clients and their families. Care must be given in a non-hurried, non-judgmental fashion. It must be remembered that clients are at their worst in the hospital setting. With that said, caring may also be given in the form of setting limits for client-patient relationship. The nurse must have sound judgment to be able to handle each situation. The client depends on her to maintain calmness and order, regardless of the circumstances.

A Word about Empathy

Smart Strategies

- For any test question on the NCLEX, think empathy, not sympathy.
- Remember that calling the client pet names, or anything besides Mr. Jones (or sometimes by their first name in a psychiatric setting), is inappropriate. Answer the test questions in that context.

Empathy involves considering how you might feel if in the same situation that the client or family finds themselves in. This does not mean that you should anticipate their behavior to mirror what yours would be.

Questions on empathy may appear in the following manner on the NCLEX:

A 6-year-old girl has just been diagnosed with Stage IV cancer. Treatment begins immediately. The father arrives at the hospital, obviously intoxicated. What should the nurse do first?

1. Call the physician and report the situation.
2. Find out if someone can escort the father home.
3. Ask the mother if the father is an alcoholic.
4. Tell the father that he is being inappropriate and harming his child.

Answer: 2. The nurse should find out if someone can escort the father home. This is a non-judgmental response based upon the nurse realizing that the father may be using alcohol to cope with his new grief and fear.

Empathy must not be confused with sympathy. Displays of sympathy disempower the client and give her a victim status. Questions regarding empathy should be expected on the NCLEX.

Communication

Smart Strategies
- Expect communication questions to be on the NCLEX, and be aware that they can seem "tricky" upon first reading them. Think through the basic principles of healthy communication when you answer them.

Communication with the Client and Family

There are many forms of therapeutic communication. Below, you will find some of the general principles you are expected to know for the purposes of the test.

Talking

The nurse should speak in a calm, authoritative tone. Speaking with authority allows the client to feel safe, and speaking calmly facilitates open communication.

Body Language

The nurse must attempt to keep herself open to the client's needs. Body language such as crossed arms and poor eye contact can cause the client to feel as if his needs are not a priority. A smile or therapeutic touch can be healing to a client and can alleviate his anxiety.

Therapeutic communication skills are first learned, then developed over years of nursing practice. You will be expected to understand the basic skills on the NCLEX.

Ask Open-Ended Questions

Examples of open-ended questions include:
- How do you feel about the treatment plan?
- How are you dealing with your wife's cancer diagnosis?

Questions to be Avoided

- **Closed-Ended Questions**: These questions only allow for a short answer, such as "yes" or "no," and do not give clients the option to discuss their feelings. They effectively end the therapeutic communication process. Examples of closed-ended questions include:

  - Do you accept the treatment plan?
  - Do you realize you are being discharged tomorrow?

Improvements upon these examples include:

  - How do you feel about the new treatment plan?
  - How do you feel about being discharged tomorrow?

- **Leading Questions**: These questions can cause the client to feel as if you want a simple answer and do not want to be bothered with any specific issues. A passive client may feel pressured to answer in the manner he feels you want to hear. Examples of leading questions include:

- You are all right with your new diet, aren't you?
- Isn't it wonderful that you are going to live with your son?

Improvements upon these examples include:

- Tell me how you feel your new diet is going to work out.
- How do you feel about going to live with your son?

- **"Why" Questions in the Mental Health Field**: Clients often do not know "why" they have committed a particular behavior. This type of question can put the client on the defensive and end the therapeutic communication process. Examples of "why" questions include:

  - Why did you strike your wife?
  - Why did your throw your food?
  - Why won't you come out for dinner?
  - Why are you making that noise?

Harmless negative behaviors are sometimes best ignored rather than making an issue of them. Rewarding positive behaviors may be the best therapeutic approach. Improvements upon these examples include:

- Let's talk about your aggression toward your wife.
- You came out of your room for dinner and ate most of your meal. I am proud of you. Would you like to listen to your favorite music now?

Other Communication Principles to Remember

Silence can be therapeutic; sitting quietly with a client can be helpful. Elderly clients are frequently inclined to enjoy sitting quietly with others, thus asking a question and giving the client time to talk can also be conducive.

Avoid Authoritarian Responses: The nurse must not sound as if she is directing the client's life. Likewise, she must not trivialize the client's concerns. Sounding authoritarian closes communication with many clients, as their experience with parents was often to listen and not speak. It diminishes the client's confidence in his decision-making.

Examples of authoritarian responses include:

- If your husband has an issue with your breast removal, you should leave him, anyway.
- You do not need to worry about the surgery; thousands of men have had this surgery and you will be fine.

When you encounter a communication question on the NCLEX, think back to all you have learned about therapeutic communication. Find the answer that is most appropriate for the multiple-choice questions. Often, all or most of the answers will sound correct, and it will be your task to determine which is the most correct.

Ask yourself the following questions about communication questions:

- Does this answer facilitate open communication?
- Which answers will cause the client to stop speaking about how he feels? These answers should be avoided.
- Which answers convey judgment? These answers should also be avoided.

Communication with other Medical Professionals

Your communication with physicians and staff must be to-the-point, polite, and professional. It should involve facts and observations. Instead of calling a physician and saying, "Mrs. B is having a myocardial infarction," you should explain her symptoms and what has been done for her thus far. For example, "Mrs. B. has been complaining of chest pain for 15 minutes. She has been given three nitroglycerin with no relief. She states that the pain is in the left side of her chest, steady and unrelenting. She is pale and diaphoretic."

Communication regarding clients must be kept confidential. You should not discuss clients in an elevator or any public area where you could be overheard. Nurses should also not be heard describing their personal problems to other staff around clients or families. This is unprofessional and causes the client to be uncertain if you can focus on her needs.

Documentation

Smart Strategies

- Be prepared for documentation questions, which are one of the last things you do in a crisis. They must be objective, not subjective. It is a good idea to quote the client if it helps to clarify circumstances, such as "My right arm is killing me. I am ready to end it all."

- Keep in mind what is documented — what you witnessed (your assessment) and what you did (the care you gave). You will frequently document passing information regarding the client to another care provider, whether the physician or the nurse to whom you are transferring the client's care.

The number one rule of documentation is: Stick to the facts. The nurse does not diagnose in her notes; she simply describes what she sees, hears, feels, and smells. She discusses the client's orientation, assessment, reaction to treatment, or refusal to eat. She quotes the client when necessary, such as "I won't eat because I'm going to die anyway." She documents the care she has given, including checks on the client, medication given, treatment administered, and client teaching provided along with outcome.

Documentation questions on the NCLEX will be straightforward. Care is documented; assessments are documented. In a crisis situation, the client must be assessed and procedures must be implemented. In such a question, documentation is usually not the first step the nurse would take.

The client's interaction with his family members may be documented. Questions that relate to his understanding or lack of understanding of his diagnosis should be documented. Sound nursing judgment, combined with facility policy, will dictate what you document in the client's notes.

Keep in mind that documentation serves two important purposes:

1. Ensures a legal record of the client's care is available.
2. Documentation serves as communication between health-care workers to ensure continuity of care.

Teaching / Learning

Smart Strategies

- Be prepared for a number of questions related to teaching on the NCLEX. You must know the best way to teach a particular client a particular task or topic, and how to evaluate whether your teaching was effective.

The nurse is constantly teaching her clients. She must explain what to expect with certain disease processes, how to properly use an inhaler, and how to perform umbilical cord care.

Ideal client or family teaching includes a demonstration and a return demonstration.

Examples of teaching scenarios include:

- A new diabetic must be taught how to compute, draw up, and self-administer insulin.
- A client who has just had a myocardial infarction must know which foods to eat and how much.
- A new mother may need to know how to breast-feed her baby.

Teaching involves:

- A rationale for why the teaching is needed. For example, why the client needs to get her blood glucose under control.
- An explanation of what the client needs to know, such as how to care for his surgical wound.

The most effective way to explain is by demonstration when possible. It is good to give the client written materials to keep for future reference as little may be retained at first. The client also needs to know who to contact if she has questions.

Allow for a return demonstration. The client or family member should perform the task in front of you or verbalize to you what you have just said. This ensures that you were understood properly.

Many NCLEX questions focus on client teaching. You will be given a variety of answers and be asked, "Which response by the client indicates the need for further education?" These questions require your memorization of disease processes and appropriate therapeutic interventions.

As you study any given topic in preparation for the NCLEX, ask yourself how you would teach the topic to the client or family. For example, not only must you know how to perform ileostomy care, you must be able to teach the client how to perform the self-care. You must be able to teach the diabetic client how to monitor blood glucose, administer insulin, count calories, and watch for complications.

NCLEX questions can be divided into several categories, such as according to client need or according to which part of the nursing process they require. You may encounter a question that involves your knowledge of peptic ulcers, therapeutic communication, and the nursing process. Do you need to spend time deciding which category a question falls into? Not if you know the answer. If you do not, it is helpful to think about everything you do know about peptic ulcers. Then, ask yourself, Which answer is the most therapeutic? Which part of the nursing process does this question involve? You may find these questions helpful, or they may only raise your anxiety; you will learn what is helpful to you as you review the practice tests. If thoroughly analyzing the question only confuses you, you may be better off to visualize the situation as if it were actually your client. Another tip that may help is to imagine what a nursing textbook would say about the situation in the question.

Anatomy and Physiology

Smart Strategies
- Know your anatomy and physiology. In the abdominal and chest area, know the location of the organs and important landmarks. Know the veins used for IVs.

While direct anatomy and physiology questions are not found on the exam, you will need to have a good grasp on the workings of the human body.

You should know about pregnancy, the birthing process, and the changes that a human encounters from infancy to adulthood.

Entry-Level Practice

Smart Strategies

- Think as a new nurse when answering the test questions. You are not expected to know information that a seasoned nurse would know from experience.

Keep in mind that you are being tested on what you should know as a nursing school graduate. Therefore, the NCLEX will contain questions about the things you learned in nursing school and clinicals. An occasional mistake candidates make is to answer the questions as a physician would. Instead of thinking of a medical treatment first, think of what a new nurse would do in the situation described in the question.

Considering the level of the questions should help you to answer them correctly and to avoid being anxious about the questions. You are not expected to know what a labor and delivery nurse of ten years' experience would know. Feel confident in knowing you have been taught everything you need to know to pass the exam. Utilizing your memory and your critical-thinking skills is all that is required.

Chapter 3

How to Prepare for the NCLEX

When You Should Take the NCLEX

Three factors should be taken into consideration when deciding when to schedule your exam.

- Pick a low-stress time. It is best not try to study for and take the exam during a move, while planning a wedding, or when a loved one is critically ill. Make certain your life is not in crisis or upheaval when you prepare for the test — it needs to have your complete concentration.

- Consider the amount of study time you need. If it has taken you many years to complete nursing school, or you do not remember the information you learned early on in your nursing education, you should plan a good deal of study time prior to taking the exam.

After considering the first two factors, realize that it is best to take the test as soon as possible after graduation. Your memory will fade with each day that passes; do not put off the test because you are dreading it. That feeling will worsen, not improve, the longer that you put it off.

Understanding the Basics of Maslow's Hierarchy of Needs

Smart Strategies

- Use the Maslow test for questions concerning what to do first or what is priority in specific situations. Meet the most basic needs of your clients, then move to higher level needs.

The humanistic psychologist Abraham Maslow theorized the hierarchy of human needs. He believed that only after basic needs are met can humans work toward meeting higher needs. The pyramid outlines the various human needs, beginning at the bottom.

Maslow's theory is standard nursing practice. An understanding of this hierarchy is fundamental to correctly answering many of the questions on the NCLEX.

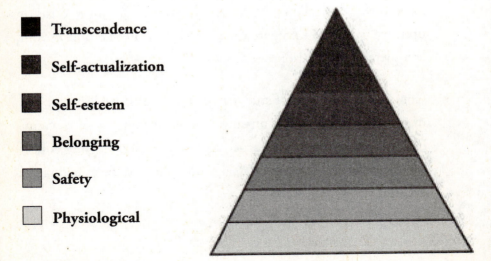

Transcendence

Self-actualization

Self-esteem

Belonging

Safety

Physiological

Physiological Needs: Physiological needs include breathing, eating, drinking, excreting, sleeping, sex, and homeostasis.

Safety Needs: Safety needs include housing, proper temperature, and physical safety.

Love and Belonging Needs: Love and belonging needs include needs for family, friends, and intimacy.

Self-Esteem Needs: Self-esteem needs include belonging, self-worth, confidence, respect of others, and achievement.

Self-Actualization Needs: Self-actualization needs include achieving one's individual potential.

Questions regarding the meeting of needs will ask you what you should do first for a client, or which client you should assess first.

The following is an example of a question regarding assessing a client's needs:

The nurse is assigned the following four clients. Which should she assess first?

1. A client with kidney stones who is sad her family has not visited
2. A two day post-op client complaining of pain
3. A client in traction who is asking for assistance with bathing
4. A client with asthma who was having difficulty breathing an hour ago

The correct answer is four. Breathing difficulties involve "physiological needs," the greatest need in Maslow's hierarchy. Secondly, you would care for the client in answer two. Relief from pain is a "safety need." Third, you would speak with the client in answer three, who is requesting help bathing, which is also a safety need (but of lower rank than pain). Client number three should be told when to expect assistance. Finally, you would check on the client in answer one, who has a "love and belonging need."

Strategies for Answering Questions

Smart Strategies

- Realize that the exam questions depict scenarios. Practice visualizing scenarios and what you would do in each case.

With a difficult question, consider what a textbook would say. Many review guides will tell you that there is a "real world" and an "NCLEX world." Actually, the correct answers are based on the ideal circumstances all nurses should strive for. Answer questions in that context. When reading a question, do not consider that the scenario may include a short-staffed unit or a physician who does not want to be bothered after-hours. If you have previously worked in a facility where these types of problems occurred, do not envision that atmosphere. Envision an ideal environment and base your answers on that instead.

Do not study more than three hours at a time. Your brain becomes fatigued after that point, and your retention begins to decline. If you can only study on weekends, study three hours, rest or get some physical activity, and study three more hours. Try to squeeze in at least an hour of study time most days of the week, if at all possible. Consider studying during commuting time (as long as you are not actually driving), television time, time spent waiting for appointments, or time waiting for others. Carry this book with you at all times for impromptu study sessions.

Highlight the places in the book you need to study further. Repeat things aloud. Be your own instructor and quiz yourself constantly.

Remember to reward yourself for progress. Pamper yourself with a movie, a long bath, a good book, or whatever you like. Acknowledging your accomplishments will help to build the confidence you will need on exam day.

Preparing for the NCLEX — Week by Week

Eight Weeks Before the Exam

Smart Strategies
*   Pinpoint your weaknesses.
*   Avoid studying the history of nursing. You will not find questions related to history on the NCLEX.
*   Focus your time on nursing topics. Nursing questions and perhaps a few mathematics questions will be all you see on the exam.

Review all the materials you have from nursing school. Look at the test questions you missed if your old tests are available to you. Look over all your notes and your nursing books.

Study Resources

Old Tests, Reviews, and Notes

Highlight areas you had trouble with. Make yourself a small stack of the information you need to study. It can include all your old tests with wrong answers highlighted, or your notes from class with pages turned down and areas highlighted.

Look over your old tests and notes. Write down the areas you do not feel competent in. You may have missed some questions early in your nursing education on topics you fully understand now. Skip those. You need to determine exactly where your deficits lie today. You can skip any material on the history of nursing.

By now, you should have a firm grasp on where you need to focus the majority of your study time. Review the materials from school and, as you move forward, take notes on items you still have difficulty remembering. As you record this information, you are creating a miniature review book personalized for you.

Textbooks

Only concentrate on the books directly related to nursing. You do not need to study your psychology or chemistry books, for example. Put bookmarks or turn down pages at the places you know you need to study further.

Below, write down the top three areas you need to concentrate on the most. Utilize this to help shape your study plan.

I feel least confident in the following areas:

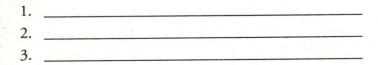

1. _____
2. _____
3. _____

Eight Week Checklist

	I have reviewed my nursing textbooks.
	I have reviewed my old notes.
	I have made note of the areas in which I feel unconfident.
	I have put together a good study resource from these materials.
	I have studied at least 15 hours this week.

Seven Weeks Before the Exam

Smart Strategies

- When testing yourself, concentrate on questions that involve scenarios. These are the questions that duplicate the NCLEX. The practice tests in this book contain 100-percent scenario-type questions to help you best prepare for the NCLEX.

- Discover if you are apt to misread questions. If so, learn to slow down and relax as you read. You do not want to miss even one question on the NCLEX because you misread it.

- If you miss practice questions that require memorization, focus your study on that. Create your own lists and flash cards and read aloud to yourself. Close your eyes and repeat what you just said.

- If you miss practice questions that require critical thinking, take the questions apart. Think them through step by step.

Take Practice Test One if you have not yet taken it. Were the questions you missed memorization or critical-thinking questions?

If you missed more questions due to not having information memorized, focus the majority of your efforts there. And if you missed more questions due to critical thinking, practice taking the questions apart and analyzing what the question is truly asking.

Did you miss more than one question because you misread it? You need to work more slowly and read each question and set of answers twice. The questions in this book are similar to the questions that will be on the NCLEX, so it will be helpful to familiarize yourself with their format.

Seven Week Checklist

	I have taken Practice Test One.
	I have taken steps to improve my memorization skills.
	I have taken steps to improve my critical-thinking skills.
	I have studied at least 15 hours this week.

Six Weeks Before the Exam

Read Chapters 4 through 7. Identify any areas you do not feel comfortable with. Spend the majority of your time focusing on becoming proficient in those areas. Read the review material in each of the chapters, as well as your notes and books from nursing school.

Six Week Checklist

	I have read Chapter 4.
	I have read Chapter 5.
	I have read Chapter 6.
	I have read Chapter 7.
	I have pinpointed my weaknesses from the chapters and studied the material thoroughly, both in the book and in my nursing materials.
	I have studied at least 15 hours this week.

Five Weeks Before the Exam

Read Chapters 8 through 11. Identify any areas you do not feel comfortable with. Review your textbooks and old notes from nursing school on the topics you have found you are most deficient in.

Five Week Checklist

	I have read Chapter 8.
	I have read Chapter 9.
	I have read Chapter 10.

	I have read Chapter 11.
	I have pinpointed my weaknesses from the chapters and studied the material thoroughly, both in the book and in my nursing materials.
	I have studied at least 15 hours this week.

Four Weeks Before the Exam

As you read your study materials (this book and your notes and books from school), take time to envision the various scenarios. Imagine the questions that could be asked about each topic. Review all areas of your nursing notes and textbooks.

Four Week Checklist

	I have reviewed all the material from nursing school.
	I am working on both memorization and critical thinking as I study.
	I consult with peers when needed regarding any unfamiliar material.
	I have studied at least 15 hours this week.

Three Weeks Before the Exam

Smart Strategies

- Know your drugs. Become familiar with the most common drugs, both prescription and over the counter. Know their uses, contraindications, and side effects.

- Know your lab values. Follow the list in this book and quiz yourself often until you have reliably memorized each value.

- Know your abbreviations. It is not as important to memorize them as much as it is to recognize what they mean. For example, a question may reference administering TPN or giving a drug PRN.

Continue to review all topics. Update your list of topics that you still do not feel proficient in. Quiz yourself on drugs and lab values, and mark the ones you missed — as well as the ones you guessed on.

Three Week Checklist

	I have spent time studying all topics that I expect to see on the exam.
	I have updated my list of topics that I still feel uncomfortable with.
	I have reviewed common lab values.
	I have reviewed the common drugs.
	I have reviewed the medical abbreviations.
	I have studied at least 15 hours this week.

Two Weeks Before the Exam

Smart Strategies

- Get lots of exercise. It helps your brain to process the information you are memorizing and relieves stress, as well.
- If you use a study buddy, make sure the bulk of your time is spent on topics you need to study.

Focus your study on the areas in which you remain weak. If you are working with a study buddy, make sure you are spending the bulk of your time on the areas you need to work on. Work together only on areas you both need to focus on.

Get plenty of aerobic exercise. It reduces stress and helps your brain to function better.

Two Week Checklist

	I have studied my weak areas.
	I have exercised adequately to keep down my stress levels and help my brain to function optimally.
	I have studied at least 15 hours this week.

One Week Before the Exam

Smart Strategies
- Make a trial run to the testing center.
- Keep working on memorizing any facts you have difficulty with.

If you have never been to the testing center, make a trial run on the same day and time — one week earlier — of your appointment.

Take the second practice test. Fully review any questions you missed and also any areas in which you still feel weak.

Stay away from people with influenza, a cold, a stomach virus, or anything else you could possibly catch. Wash your hands frequently. Eat well to keep your immune system healthy. If you are dealing with anxiety, you may wish to take a multivitamin or a B-complex vitamin daily. Do not attempt a new diet, and continue to exercise. Taking these steps will reduce the likelihood that you will wake up sick on test day and allow you to feel better during the actual exam.

One Week Checklist

I have taken practice test two.
I am continuing to work on areas in which I feel uncomfortable.
I have made a trial run to the testing center.
I am making a concerted effort to stay healthy.
I have studied at least 15 hours this week.

The Day Before the Exam

Smart Strategies
- Retake the NCLEX tutorial. You want to feel 100-percent comfortable with the format when you enter the testing room. Practice the calculator and all available buttons.

- Go to the Web site **www.pearsonvue.com/nclex** and take the tutorial. Practice using the calculator, exhibit, and scrolling feature. Do this even if you have done it before. You want the workings of the test computer to be fresh on your mind. It will reduce anxiety as well as speed things up until test day.

- Review your notes for one to three hours. Do not attempt to answer practice questions. Simply review any areas you are not confident about, and read out loud to yourself.

- Make sure you have plenty of gasoline in your car, or secure another means of reliable transportation.

- Have a snack and beverage ready to take for the exam breaks, if allowed.

- Avoid eating any unfamiliar foods or foods that can cause food poisoning or gastrointestinal upset.

- Have a healthy breakfast planned, and make sure it contains plenty of protein. Aim to eat around 500 calories. This is not the time for calorie-cutting, as your brain will need energy and you will not want to feel hungry while you are trying to concentrate. If you do not cook, or you feel you will be too nervous to cook, plan to get a good breakfast somewhere on the road and figure this into your commute time.

- Plan your clothing for test day. Have an extremely comfortable outfit that you feel confident in. Plan comfortable shoes and non-restrictive undergarments.

- Go to bed in time to have eight to nine hours of sleep.

Exam Day: What to Take, What to Wear, What to Avoid

Smart Strategies

- Be prepared physically for test day. Follow the listed advice to arrive calm and ready to pass.

- Spend a few minutes remembering your graduation day and the summation of your accomplishments. Allow this to give you confidence.

Bring these items on test day:

- Picture identification
- Authorization to Test document
- Directions to testing center
- Purse or wallet with money for lunch and/or emergency car repair
- Snack
- Beverage
- Prescription medications
- Over-the-counter medication for headache or stomachache (optional)
- Cell phone in case your car breaks down

Things to remember:

- Get up with plenty of time to accomplish everything you need to.
- Wear the comfortable clothing you planned.
- Eat a healthy, substantial breakfast.
- Leave with at least an hour to spare, based on your dry run the previous week.
- Do not try to cram this morning. Save your energy for answering the critical-thinking questions.

What to Avoid on Exam Day

Delays: Check and double-check any childcare arrangements. Set two alarm clocks. Make sure you have no other obligations for the day that you have forgotten to reschedule.

Family Conflicts: When you are tense, it is a vulnerable time for a fight to break out. Carefully think about anything you say, and do not allow yourself to become angry or distracted if others do not seem to care that you are anxious. Any issues can be cleared up after the testing is complete.

Health Problems: Consider toothaches, headaches, stomachaches, gas, diarrhea, hypoglycemia, and so on. You must take care of yourself prior to and during the exam. Avoid a spicy or high-fiber breakfast, or anything you have never eaten before.

Dealing with Exam Anxiety

Your anxiety level on this exam will likely mirror your experiences with other critical exams. If you know that you commonly suffer from test anxiety, take steps to be prepared. Everyone is different, and no perfect plan exists. Read the following tips to see which might be of benefit to you.

Meditation and Deep Breathing: Many people utilize concentration or breathing techniques to alleviate or prevent anxiety. Taking slow, deep breaths in through the nose, holding for several seconds, and breathing out through the mouth can be calming. Visualizing yourself with your nursing license can be of benefit.

Feeling Prepared: Spending time studying and answering practice questions can leave you calm at test time. Realizing that you graduated nursing school and understanding that the test focuses on entry-level nursing practice should also relieve anxiety.

Taking Breaks: Taking a minute to look away from the exam, stretch, and visualize a beautiful outdoor scene can be beneficial. Walk around for a couple of minutes, if you feel you have time. Remember, you can take both the scheduled and unscheduled breaks. Truly relax during your break times, even if just for a few minutes.

Utilizing the Earplugs: If hearing the noises of others raises your anxiety level, use the earplugs that are provided to you. If you do not get them when first offered, but decide you want them later, do not hesitate to ask.

Closing Your Eyes: Simply closing your eyes can greatly reduce your anxiety level. This turns off the stimulation from the amygdala and leads to calmness. Perhaps you have seen a crocodile calm down when a large dark cloth is thrown over its eyes — this is the same principle. Reduce your emotional stimulation. Ignore any sounds in the room and say to yourself, "I feel very peaceful."

If Anxiety Takes Hold

Smart Strategies

- If you get anxious during the test, take a break.

Unless you have less than an hour left to complete the exam, get up and take a break. Walk around in the area where you can, have a snack or drink, and think of calming aspects of your life, whether these are the faces of your children, a beach vacation you took, or your future plans. Massage your shoulders and stretch. Sit quietly with your eyes closed if you need to. If there is no privacy, go into a bathroom stall if necessary. Return to the exam only when you feel ready. Breaks are acceptable during the test. Keep in mind, however, that they do take away from your available time.

When you return to the test, carefully read the questions to yourself. It can be hard to concentrate when you are anxious. Visualize the scenario depicted in the question and in each of the possible answers.

Keeping Your Perspective

The NCLEX exam is important — but it may not be as important as you are imagining it to be. Many candidates inflate the importance of passing the exam in their mind; in reality, you will survive whether you pass or not. Remember that, while inconvenient, the test can be taken again. Putting extreme importance on the exam will only increase your anxiety level and decrease your effectiveness.

Chapter 4

Coordination and Management of Care

At the beginning of Chapters 4 – 11, you will find a skills checklist and terms-to-understand list. The chapters review topics that test-takers should be familiar with in order to excel on the NCLEX exam. Ensure you know how to perform the listed functions and mark accordingly any that are unfamiliar or you feel you need extra review on.

Skills Checklist

I am unfamiliar	I am somewhat familiar	I am completely familiar	Skill
			Create and update a care plan
			Maintain client privacy
			Function as client advocate
			Refer clients to community resources
			Know how to care for a client with Advance Directives

			Understand when and how to report client conditions to authorities
			Know how to obtain informed consent and how to ensure informed consent is obtained
			Review management outcomes
			Understand cost efficiency methods and utilize them when planning client care
			Supervise care by licensed and unlicensed personnel
			Receive and transcribe physician orders
			Educate other staff members via in-services
			Assign care based on staff members' education and experience
			Triage clients

Terms to Understand

I am unfamiliar	I am somewhat familiar	I am completely familiar	Term
			Advance directive
			Client advocacy
			Client rights
			Quality improvement
			The five "rights" of delegation

Advance Directives

The Patient Self-Determination Act of 1990 states that facilities must provide clients with information about advance directives. Advance directives can include a living will and a durable power of attorney for health care (DPAHC). A living will spells out a client's wishes should he become incompetent or unable to express himself. A DPAHC specifies who may make health-care decisions for a client who is incompetent or can no longer express himself.

Living Wills may address:

- Withholding or discontinuing lifesaving procedures
- Cardiopulmonary resuscitation
- Mechanical ventilation
- Intravenous medications, hydration, or nourishment
- Enteral nourishment
- Syringe feedings

These issues may be addressed as permanent decisions, or they may change under certain circumstances such as terminal illness.

Each state has different laws about documentation and witness requirements for living wills. The nurse must check for an advance directive before initiating treatments, such as the insertion of a feeding tube.

Client Advocacy

The first responsibility of the nurse is to the client. This supersedes any responsibility to her employer, union, or any physician. If the nurse notes that the client does not understand the physician's instructions or diagnosis, she must bring the situation to light and see that it its resolved. She must follow protocol for medication and treatment orders that are out of the range of safety. She must act in the client's best interest. If the client cannot speak English, the nurse should follow facility policy for finding an interpreter. The role of client advocate is one of the most important roles of the nurse.

Case Management

Case management in nursing has several definitions.

In acute care primary nursing, it can refer to a system whereby a registered nurse is in charge of a client's total care. He collaborates with other disciplines to provide the best care for the client. The nurse is responsible for initiating, revising, and evaluating the care plan. He informs the client or family about resources available to assist the client after hospital discharge.

Case management in the acute care setting also refers to the functions of a non-clinical nurse who monitors the care of a client with an eye for minimizing expenses while providing the care needed by the client.

Outside the acute care setting, case management refers to the coordinated care of clients with complex medical or mental health issues. The case manager may see that the client has regular physician appointments, home health care, and/or counseling. He may oversee medication administration, treatment, or even financial affairs. His goal is to monitor the overall care of the client by collaborating with physicians, nurses, therapists, and family care providers. He may work with an insurance company to ensure that cost-effective care is being provided to the client.

Nurse care managers may be hired by hospitals, home health-care agencies, assisted living facilities, insurance companies, governments, families, or individuals.

Client Rights

Smart Strategies

- On the NCLEX, always take into consideration a client's rights when answering a question.

It is critically important for the nurse to know the scope of the client's rights at the facility where she practices. Violating a client's rights can lead to dismissal, loss of one's nursing license, a civil lawsuit, or criminal charges. Client's rights are frequently an issue in psychiatric facilities.

Client's rights, often called the Patient's Bill of Rights, may include:

- The right to privacy
- The right to receive visitors, phone calls, and private correspondence
- The right to leave against medical advice
- The right to refuse any medications, treatments, or surgery
- The right to be aware of the treatment plan

Many other rights may be included.

Local, state, and federal government laws may also give a client specific rights. Certain groups may have specific rights, such as:

- Elderly clients
- Disabled clients
- Children
- Research subjects
- Prisoners

Common nursing issues that may affect a client's rights include:

- A demented nursing-home client who refuses to take his medications
- A psychiatric hospital client who wishes to leave against medical advice

Client's rights may also include fiduciary issues, such as the right to receive necessary medical care regardless of ability to pay.

Clients should be made aware of their rights, and nurses must evaluate their subordinate's level of understanding of client's rights.

Collaboration

It is generally the function of the nurse to manage the interdisciplinary team treating a client. This team may include:

- Physicians
- Nurses
- Advance practice nurses
- Occupational therapists
- Respiratory therapists
- Physical therapists
- Psychologists
- Dieticians
- Social workers
- Pharmacists

The nurse keeps each member abreast of the client's overall condition, the treatment plan, and information specific to each professional's discipline. Interdisciplinary team member meetings may be held on a weekly basis, or sometimes less frequently. The subject of the meetings is the client's care and prognosis. At some facilities, the client or his family may participate in the meetings.

Management and Supervision

Smart Strategies

- When answering questions that involve management or supervision, assume the scenario is based in a hospital unless otherwise specified.

- Remember that LPNs are assigned routine care of stable clients, while RNs may be assigned complex care on unstable clients.

- When answering questions involving unlicensed, assistive personnel, assume their responsibilities involve assisting with activities of daily living or providing noninvasive care. Unlicensed personnel will never be assigned to do the work of a nurse.

Each member of the health-care team has a specified set of responsibilities.

Registered Nurses: Registered nurses manage the care of both simple and complex clients. They supervise unlicensed, assistive personnel, licensed practical nurses, and other registered nurses.

Licensed Practical Nurses: Licensed practical nurses provide care for clients with noncomplex needs. They supervise unlicensed, assistive personnel and, occasionally, other licensed practical nurses.

Unlicensed, Assistive Personnel:

- Assist with activities of daily living
- Assist with feeding clients
- May weigh clients
- May take vital signs on stable patients
- May record simple inputs and outputs

These responsibilities can vary depending on the staff member's level of experience. A licensed practical nurse of 20 years may be entrusted to tasks that a newly licensed practical nurse may not. A registered nurse who has spent ten years in critical care will be prepared to assume different responsibilities than the registered nurse who has worked in long-term care for the past five years.

Each area of an acute care hospital will have a management system. At the top may be a nurse manager or clinical nurse specialist. Each shift may then have charge nurses or team leaders. These may be the same or the registered nurses may rotate these positions. Other registered nurses will follow next, then licensed practical nurses and unlicensed, assistive personnel.

Here are examples of various management types. We will assume there are 30 clients in the medical/surgical wing of a small, rural hospital.

- Three registered nurses, three licensed practical nurses, and three unlicensed, assistive personnel are assigned to day shift. They are divided into three teams, with ten clients for each team. The registered nurse makes assessments and keeps up with physician orders. The licensed practical nurse administers the medications. The unlicensed assistant takes the vital signs on the stable clients; weighs clients; and assists with bathing, toileting, eating, and walking.

- Three registered nurses, three licensed practical nurses, and three unlicensed, assistive personnel are assigned to day shift. The registered nurses are each assigned to four of the less stable clients. The licensed practical nurses are each assigned to six stable clients. The unlicensed, assistive personnel take the vital signs of the licensed practical nurses clients and assist with bathing, toileting, eating, and walking for all clients.

- One registered nurse is the team leader. She makes the assignments for everyone. She assigns the other three registered nurses to four clients each and the four licensed practical nurses to four to five clients each. The one unlicensed assistant gives three baths and assists clients with feeding, toileting, and walking. The nurses perform the remainder of the care for the clients. The team leader handles admissions and assists with complex clients.

Many other management styles exist for acute care settings. Various styles exist for long-term care settings or home health care. It is important for the nurse to understand the exact level of his responsibilities and who his resources are for assistance. It is also important to remember that the licensed nurse is generally responsible for the actions of those acting at a level under her, whether licensed or unlicensed. Management personnel must constantly monitor whether the outcomes of each assignment create optimal strategies for the best client care.

The nurse must never accept an assignment she does not feel prepared for. If she is given a client who has a piece of equipment she has not been trained on, she must speak up and let her superior know.

Confidentiality

Client confidentiality must be maintained at all times. Nurses must safeguard all information about a client, including the fact that he or she is client at the facility. Follow the specific facility's policy regarding dissemination of information. A typical medical-surgical policy will be as follows:

- The client will sign a form acknowledging who may receive information regarding their condition. Anyone else will be directed to speak with the client or family.

A typical psychiatric floor policy will be as follows:

- No one may have information about the client unless they have a "code" given to them by the client. Calls for the client will be answered with "I cannot confirm nor deny that Mr. Smith is a client here."

Client information must not be discussed where visitors or other clients may hear. Charts must be protected from view. At some facilities, charts no longer have a visible name on the outside. Access to electronic records is carefully guarded, and views of a client's information are recorded. Clients cannot be forced to wear an armband, which can lead to medication and treatment errors.

Clients with a higher level of information security may include:
- High-profile clients
- Prisoners
- Psychiatric clients
- Obstetric clients and newborns

The Health Insurance Portability and Accountability Act (HIPAA) governs client confidentiality. For purposes of the NCLEX, questions should be answered in a manner that ensures confidentiality is protected to the fullest extent possible. Questions will not be too technical due to the wide variance among facilities.

Nursing Priorities

The nurse must triage all her clients to prioritize the order of assessments and care delivery. As discussed in Chapter 3, Maslow's Hierarchy of Needs should be remembered. Critical thinking will help the nurse establish which needs are urgent and which are non-urgent.

Pointers for Establishing Priorities

A client headed to surgery within hours will have priority over stable clients. The nurse must ensure the client's state has not changed precluding the surgery. She must also physically prepare the client for surgery. The nurse must note that the physician has obtained an informed consent for the procedure. Most facilities will have a preparation checklist for the nurse to follow, such as:

- A client with breathing problems must have priority over stable clients.

- A client in danger of serious bleeding, such as a post-op client, must have priority over stable clients.

- A client who is a fall risk must be monitored more closely than other clients.

- All clients must be checked on at least every 30 minutes or more frequently, according to facility policy. Call bells must be in reach with extra monitoring for clients who cannot use the call light, or do not understand it.

On the NCLEX, priority questions can seem tricky. As you read each possibility, ask yourself what can happen if care to that client is delayed. You may also need to look at the probability that any given client may deteriorate.

Priority questions can also refer to just one client and ask you which of his needs you should meet first, or which of his body systems you should assess first.

While these questions involve a bit of memorization, they predominantly utilize critical-thinking skills that cannot be studied for. Trust that you are prepared to answer these.

Ethical Practice

Nurses frequently deal with ethical issues. Common ethical issues in the health-care setting include:

- The level of care to be supplied to clients who cannot afford to pay

- End-of-life care, such as withdrawal of life-saving treatments
- The giving of large doses of pain medications to fragile clients
- The administration of placebo medications
- Rationing of health care, such as deciding which clients may receive organ transplants
- The level of care to be given to newborns with serious complications

Points to Remember about Ethical Practice

- Opinions can vary as to what constitutes good, ethical practice.
- Many facilities have an ethics committee or an ethicist who can help with ethical dilemmas.
- Laws come before ethics in treatment decision-making.

Gray Areas

The nurse will encounter many episodes of gray areas relative to ethics. Good nursing judgment must be used in nursing practice and in answering ethics questions on the NCLEX. The following are some examples of gray areas:

- A woman seems verbally abusive to her child. The nurse also realizes the family is under incredible stress, as another sibling has cancer. Does the nurse report the woman?

- A staff member seems to be under the influence of alcohol or drugs, but the nurse cannot be sure. Does the nurse report them?

- An order is given for a large dose of narcotic analgesic to a comatose client who does not appear to be in pain. Does the nurse trust the physician knows what she is doing, or does she suspect the physician is trying to euthanize the client and refuse to administer the medication?

Encountering a Gray Area

When you encounter a gray area:
- Look at your facility's policies and procedures manual.
- Ask your supervisor.
- Ask the ethicist or ethics committee.

As the nurse gains experience, he will begin to draw on those experiences for answers to ethical dilemmas. For the purposes of the test, answers should err on the side of caution. If you are asked what you should do in a certain situation, think first of client safety. Secondly, think of good nursing or medical practice. One answer should strike you as being "textbook" correct.

Informed Consent

Principles of Informed Consent

- Informed consent is required for hospital or other facility admission; surgery and other invasive procedures; some non-invasive procedures; and the initiation of new medications.

- Identify the appropriate person to give informed consent. This could be the client, the client's durable power of attorney for health care, the spouse, the child, the parent, or a legal guardian. The person giving consent must be capable of comprehending the possible outcomes of the procedure. Consent for surgery must be obtained prior to the administration of a mind-altering medication or sedation.

- The appropriate person to obtain informed consent is the person performing the procedure. For hospital admissions, it may be the nurse or someone in the admissions office. For medication admin-istration, it will be the nurse. For a surgical procedure, it will be the physician performing the surgery. It is the responsibility of the nurse to ensure that an informed consent has been obtained prior to the surgery. The nurse must inform the physician if the client asks questions after signing the consent indicating that they do not truly understand the procedure.

- Informed consent for a procedure or medication includes explain-ing the rationale, risks, side effects, possible complications, antici-pated effect, and alternatives.

- Ideally, written literature will be given for the client to reference later.

- If the client does not speak English, it becomes even more important to ascertain that the client understands the procedure and the paper he is signing. Follow facility policy for the use of interpreters.

- The client or other party must sign that they understand the proce-dure and consent to it. The consent must go in the client's chart.

- Each facility will have a policy regarding emergency surgery and lack of consent.

Information Technology

The nurse must have basic knowledge of information technology in order to access information for her clients and their families. She may also use this technology to learn the best way to provide her nursing care.

The nurse must be capable of receiving and transcribing physician orders via sophisticated technology. She must be able to access online client re-cords and documents in the records as needed.

Legal Rights and Responsibilities

The nurse must be aware of her legal responsibilities to her clients at all times. Some common issues of legal rights and responsibilities follow:

Client Abandonment

Not showing up for one's shift, particularly without notice, can constitute client abandonment. Falling asleep can also be considered client abandonment. The nurse cannot leave her designated area without leaving her clients with someone who accepts them during her absence.

Client abandonment can become an important issue in private-duty nursing. If the next scheduled nurse does not come to replace the nurse on duty, she may have to stay with her client until her employer finds a replacement. This can also happen in other health-care settings, due to inclement weather or other circumstances.

A chronically late nurse can wreak havoc in her health-care setting, as other nurses must adapt to her schedule to ensure appropriate, legal client care.

Physician Orders

The nurse must follow the written or verbal orders of the physician. He must understand the policy regarding verbal orders, such as when the physician must sign them, for his state and facility. He must understand the state and facility policy on faxed orders or orders via the Internet.

Nurses who work in a physician's office must understand state law regarding prescriptions, such as which medications can be called into a pharmacy and by whom.

Lack of Training

The nurse must not accept an assignment he knows he has not been trained or educated to complete.

Reporting Requirements

The nurse must understand under which circumstances he must report certain incidents or conditions. These reporting requirements will vary according to state and county law. Incidents that typically require reporting include:

- Gunshot wounds or stabbings
- Domestic violence
- Child abuse
- Certain sexually transmitted diseases
- Tuberculosis
- Certain other communicable diseases
- Elder neglect or abuse
- Animal bites
- Neglect or abuse of a disabled person

Documentation

Nurses are legally required to document client care, including findings of client status, medications and treatments administered, and outcomes. They must document client refusals of treatment.

Errors and Incidents

Nurses are required to report medication errors and other incidents such as client falls. Many of these reports remain internal to the facility, but an account of the incident must also be recorded in the client's care documentation (nurse's notes). At some facilities, near-miss incidents should also be reported via incident report.

Medical Research

In the medical research arena, adverse events and serious adverse events must be reported to the pharmaceutical company, facility's institutional review board, and federal government.

Responsibility for Actions of Others

The nurse must report improper actions on the part of other personnel caring for clients. This can include working while impaired, client neglect or abuse, or any malpractice noted. They may be required to intervene if unsafe client circumstances exist.

Performance Improvement (Quality Improvement)

The nurse must know how to perform the following duties:

- Define performance improvement or assurance activities

- Report identified client-care issues or problems to appropriate personnel (such as nurse manager or risk manager)

- Participate in performance improvement or quality assurance process (such as formally collecting data or serving on quality improvement committee)

- Document performance improvement or quality improvement activities according to facility policy

- Utilize research and other references for performance improvement actions

- Evaluate the impact of performance improvement measures on client care outcome and resource utilization

The nurse must follow facility protocol on informing the necessary party of quality improvement issues related to client care. She must participate in conferences and data collection as required for quality improvement staff.

Nurses may be employed to work in the quality improvement setting. These nurses may have the following responsibilities, among others:

- Monitoring adverse events in the facility
- Communicating with administration or corporate figures about data collected
- Disseminating data to nurse managers and staff nurses to improve client care
- Keeping up with the latest trends in health care by utilizing research
- Evaluating quality improvement efforts for quantifiable results

Quality Improvement

The nurse must follow facility protocol to inform quality improvement of client care issues that should be addressed. She must participate in conferences and data collection as required for quality improvement staff.

Nurses may be employed to work in the quality improvement setting. These nurses may have the following responsibilities, among others:

- Monitoring adverse events in the facility
- Communicating with administration or corporate figures about data collected
- Dissemination of data to nurse managers and staff nurses to improve client care
- Keeping up with the latest trends in health care by utilizing research
- Evaluating quality improvement efforts for quantifiable results

Referrals

Nurses frequently make referrals or follow physician orders to facilitate referrals. Common referral needs include:

- Respiratory therapy
- Physical therapy

- Dietician services
- Occupational therapy
- Services of a medical specialist
- Speech pathology services

Resource Management

The nurse is responsible for ensuring that client supplies are available as needed. Oxygen, intravenous pumps, and suction machines are among the many possible supplies she must monitor. Supplies and equipment must be used in a cost-effective manner. The nurse may be responsible for charging clients or their insurance companies for supplies, either by checking them out of a supply area or, in some other way, recording their use.

She must see that the client does not run out of necessary supplies. On the hospital floor, this means ensuring that enough of the supplies are available for her shift and possibly the next. In the home-health and private-duty situation, she must ensure that enough supplies are on hand until a new order arrives.

The nurse must be proactive at anticipating the needs of her client. For example, if a home-care pediatric client frequently pulls out his feeding tube, she must have supplies on hand to reinsert the tube or the supplies she needs to keep the stoma open until the tube is reinserted by someone else.

The nurse must ensure that her subordinates do not waste supplies. This creates unnecessary expense for the client, her employer, the insurance company, and/or taxpayers.

Staff Education

It may be the responsibility of the nurse to participate in staff education.

Who Will be Educated

Nurses may be asked to educate their peers, subordinate nurses, unlicensed, assistive personnel, agency or pool nurses, new hires, or staff from other departments.

Education Topics

The nurse may be required to educate peers on the following topics:

New Techniques
- New restraint techniques in the psychiatric setting
- New communication techniques on the pediatric floor

New Equipment
- A new monitor in the Intensive Care Unit
- A new insulin pump on the medical / surgical floor

New Forms
- A new input/output record
- A new incident report form

Yearly In-services
- Updates on life-saving measures
- Other mandated topics

Orientation for New Employees
- Introduction to facility procedures
- Introduction to areas of the hospital and other employees

Mentoring of Less-Experienced Employees
- Answering questions
- Demonstrating procedures

Points to Remember about Staff Education

When the nurse has been asked to develop a staff education program:

- First, ascertain the purpose of the education.
- Plan the means of delivery. Will you use literature, an active discussion, a PowerPoint® presentation, or something else?
- Decide if there will be a pre-test and post-test to quantify that learning occurred.
- Evaluate whether the outcome is successful.

In many facilities, one or more nurses will be dedicated to staff education. Federal law, state law, or facility policy frequently mandate topics for staff education. Facilities may provide needed yearly requirements for staff, such as cardiopulmonary resuscitation or advanced life support. They may also assist licensed personnel in obtaining state-mandated continuing education credits. Each department will have its own staff education needs. Some topics must be taught to all clinical staff at a facility, including safety procedures and client confidentiality.

Quick Quiz #1

- Name three topics you may be asked to educate staff about in the nursing-home setting.

- Name three topics you may be asked to educate staff about in the home health-care setting.

- Consider what information you would include in your discussion.

Supervision

Supervision involves ensuring that other staff members are performing their tasks correctly and that quality, safe client care is achieved.

Supervision Hierarchy

- The nurse must know for whom she is responsible.

- The charge nurse in a department may be responsible for other registered nurses, licensed practical nurses, and unlicensed, assistive personnel.

- A registered nurse may be responsible for other registered nurses, licensed practical nurses, and unlicensed, assistive personnel.

- A licensed practical nurse may be responsible for other licensed practical nurses and unlicensed, assistive personnel.

Personnel working in an inferior position to the nurse may, in effect, be working under her nursing license. For this and many other reasons, it is an excellent idea to closely monitor any subordinates. Their actions could result in legal action against the nurse or disciplining of her license.

Principles of Supervision

Questions regarding supervision and delegation are commonly found on the NCLEX exam. The candidate should spend time studying these topics and considering different scenarios. The following are examples of different scenarios in which test takers may be tested on the NCLEX:

- Report must be given to each licensed nurse who is in charge of a client's care.
- Ensure that each staff member understands and accepts their assignment.
- Make sure that someone is responsible for clients during break and lunch times.

- Make sure that the staff members are trained and educated to perform their assignments.
- If a staff member seems to be impaired or falls asleep, take immediate action per facility policy. Client safety must be your first priority.
- Staff members who violate policy must be disciplined or reported per facility policy.
- Staff members who abuse or neglect clients must be removed from the client area immediately and disciplined or reported.
- The nurse must be available for questions or concerns from subordinate staff.

CASE STUDY: BRENDA BECKER

Assistant Professor of Nursing
Metropolitan State University
Saint Paul, Minnesota.

The students who pass the NCLEX on the first attempt generally have moved beyond rote memorization and can easily bridge theoretical concepts to case studies and clinical performance.

They have also prepared by reviewing test-taking strategies and content that may not be fresh in their minds. But on the other hand, students who fail the NCLEX on their first attempt generally are on the low end of the grade curve in class. They have found it difficult to apply theoretical concepts on course exams and clinical exercises. They may also doubt their test-taking abilities and second-guess exam answers.

Four weeks before the test, you should develop a plan for taking care of yourself during this time. If you are stressed, worried, and not sleeping well, the review time will not be helpful. Give yourself permission to take time for activities that will care for your mind and body. Read a book that has nothing to do with nursing, go to the gym or for a run, or go out with your friends or family. Reflect on how you react to stress and practice activities that will help you reduce the impact of stress during the NCLEX. Self awareness and preparation are critical tools for NCLEX success. Build a plan for study time and stick to it. Block time out on your calendar and make sure others know you need support and quiet time to study and prepare. Procrastination is your worst enemy, and that test date will arrive before you realize it!

CASE STUDY: BRENDA BECKER

On the day of the test, take a deep breath, believe in yourself, and do not panic.

It is beneficial for new graduates to review all areas of content as there is no guarantee of how the topics will progress for them during the exam.

The length of the study session needs to be suited to the strengths and preferences of the learner. Students can gain insight by taking a learning-style questionnaire and then tailoring that review process to their needs. Some candidates do well with short and intense sessions, while others need an hour or two to review and reflect on the content area.

Pharmacology is one of the weaker areas for new graduates. Generally, pharmacology is covered early in the nursing program to give the students a strong base for clinical. Depending on the clinical sites, there may be drug classes that a student never encounters and are only mentioned in the medical/surgical or specialty courses.

For those pesky math questions, practice, practice, practice. Find a routine and a method that works for you and stick with it. One safety check that students usually fail to do to ask themselves is: "Does this answer make sense in this situation?"

The student may have executed the math correctly, but failed to recognize a flaw in their initial formula, which results in a totally wrong answer. A logical double check is one more safety step beyond the math.

Math needs to be as natural as breathing in clinical practice. It is an essential part of safe, competent care. If students practice, adhere to a routine, and consider if the answer is safe and logical, clinical math will become easier and less stressful.

I think students must possess a certain degree of critical thinking to be successful in nursing school and on the NCLEX. Clinical and theory courses develop this innate skill through new content, application, and additional skills. Because health care and the human response are so complex, critical thinking in nursing is very different than other professions. Students, new graduates, and expert nurses must remain current in clinical practice and the application of critical thinking to patient care to be safe, competent practitioners.

Prior experience will benefit new graduates when they transition into an RN role. The experience with education, communication, and time management are invaluable in real world practice. Working in health care while preparing to take the NCLEX may provide depth of knowledge in one area, but will lack the breadth and theory base necessary to pass the NCLEX.

Chapter 5

Safety and Infection Control

Skills Checklist

I am unfamiliar	I am somewhat familiar	I am completely familiar	Skill
			Ensure that treatment and medication orders are appropriate
			Discover and correct dangers in home care environment, including risk of falls, fire, and poisoning
			Know how to properly care for cognitively impaired clients to ensure safety
			Set up a sterile field in the operating room, the client's room, and any other setting

			Participate in security plans relative to any health care unit
			Know how to use various types of walkers
			Be able to use all health care equipment and teach client and family how to use it correctly
			Safely use client restraints
			Be able to put on, use, and remove barriers such as gloves, mask, booties, eyewear, and gowns
			Report clients with reportable communicable diseases
			Know how to properly lift and transfer clients
			Educate client and family regarding use of sharps box and disposal of other waste
			Know how to perform clean technique
			Know how to perform sterile technique
			Know how to use infant and child car seats
			Complete a variance report
			Be able to triage clients in a disaster
			Be able to provide client care in disaster conditions

			Be able to implement each type of infection precaution and know when each is needed
			Keep client and self safe from infection and be able to educate others on infection control
			Utilize ergonomic principles in client care
			Implement fire and other emergency response plans
			Understand use of crutches
			Know how to handle biohazardous materials
			Be able to position clients in ways that do not compromise their skeletal and muscular health
			Implement seizure precautions
			Apply appropriate precautions for immunocompromised clients

Terms to Understand

I am unfamiliar	I am somewhat familiar	I am completely familiar	Term
			Allergies (food, drug, latex, etc.)
			Communicable diseases (methods of transmission, proper precautions)

Ergonomics

The nurse must utilize ergonomic principles when performing client care. The following are some general principles:

- Ask for help in lifting.
- Continually position pads under clients who need lifting or repositioning.
- Squat to pick up items. Do not bend over and lift.
- Use a Hoyer lift or other equipment to lift heavy clients.
- Sit appropriately in chairs.
- Raise the level of the bed to perform client care, such as bathing. Remember to lower the bed when the task is completed.

The nurse is expected to educate her client and family regarding safe ergonomic principles, such as teaching a spouse how to assist a client with transfer from a bed to a chair. A second example would include teaching a client with a herniated disc how to dress without worsening their condition.

Error and Injury Prevention

The nurse must ensure that she is working with the correct client. Most facilities utilize name bracelets. If the facility does not, use the method employed by the facility to identify the client.

Make sure that the order is legible and sounds appropriate given the client's condition.

The nurse must know the indications, side effects, and possible adverse effects for every medication she administers.

The nurse must know the client's allergies and avoid any medication or other substances that would trigger a reaction in the client.

Home Safety

Educating clients about home safety is very important in the home health and private duty setting. The hospital discharge nurse may also educate clients about safety issues prior to their return home.

Common issues to address during home safety education include:

- Throw rugs cause many falls each year.
- Clients walking on any type of floor other than carpet should wear non-skid house shoes.
- Confused clients should not have access to vehicle keys or access to dangerous equipment.
- Care must be taken when confused clients could turn on stoves, etc.
- Water temperature should be kept in a safe range.
- Refrigerated and pantry-stored food should be checked for freshness.
- A safety plan must be in place for bathtub or shower use.
- Fragile clients must have access to a telephone or other call system.
- If clients must traverse steps within the home, a safety plan should be in place.
- If clients use a walker or a wheelchair, the home must be prepared for the use of the adaptive equipment, i.e. barriers to movement must be removed.

If young children are in the home, the following topics should be discussed with the client:

- Poisons and all medications must be kept in locked cabinets.
- Guns and other dangerous items must be in locked cabinets.
- They must be protected from falls down steps.
- Furniture with sharp edges or glass furniture should be avoided.

- Adults must be educated on keeping items on the stove out of reach, such as turning pot handles inward.
- Small items that a child could swallow must be kept out of reach.
- Young children must never be left alone around water, such as a bathtub or pail of water.
- Unused electrical outlets must be childproofed.

The hospital discharge nurse must consider the discharge needs of the following types of clients:

- Clients with a sudden onset of visual impairment
- Clients who are weaker than upon admission
- Clients with new equipment for walking
- Clients with a history of falls or who are a high fall risk
- Clients leaving the hospital with ambulatory issues
- Clients with confusion, dementia, or delirium (family education needed)

Basics of Seizure Precautions

The following precautions should be taken by the nurse in instances where risk of seizure is prevalent:

- Pad the client's side rails.
- Keep the bed in the lowest position.
- Have oxygen available.
- Have suction equipment available.

Client care during a seizure includes:

1. Call for help; one staff member may need to call the physician while another assists the client. Do not leave the client alone.
2. If the client is standing or sitting, help him or her to the floor and provide padding under the head.

3. Maintain privacy as much as possible.
4. Remove restrictive clothing.
5. Place client on his side.
6. Administer oxygen if needed.

The priorities during a client seizure are maintaining an open airway and keeping the client from self-injury.

Client care after a seizure includes:
1. Notify primary care provider.
2. Suction mouth if necessary.
3. Keep client covered and warm.
4. Take vital signs, including pulse oximetry.
5. Perform neuro checks
6. Provide calm emotional support.
7. Document the following:
   – Time and duration of seizure
   – Aura or absence of aura
   – Whether client was incontinent
   – The parts of the body that were involved
   – Level of consciousness during and after seizure
   – Neuro check results after seizure
   – Head and eye deviation during seizure
   – Respiratory changes during or after seizure
   – Assessment of client after seizure, including paralysis, speech difficulties, weakness, physical complaints, behavior, and recollection of events.

Asepsis

Smart Strategies

• Be prepared for asepsis questions. If you did not have adequate instruction on preparing a sterile field during clinicals, study this book, your nursing books, and notes until you feel comfortable.

Quick Facts about Asepsis:

- Asepsis is the absence of infection-causing microorganisms.
- Sterile is the complete absence of any living organisms.
- Equipment can be sterile.
- Hands can be aseptic, but not sterile. Living organisms will always be present on humans.

Medical Asepsis

Medical asepsis includes hand washing, universal precautions, and the cleaning or disinfection of equipment.

The proper hand-washing procedures for medical asepsis are:

1. Remove any rings. Move watch to high on wrist.
2. Wet hands from wrist to fingertips with warm water.
3. Place bacteriostatic soap on hands and use friction for 30 seconds, thoroughly cleaning all surfaces from fingertips to wrists.
4. Rinse hands, fingertips first.
5. Repeat until hands are clean.
6. Dry hands, fingers first. Dry all the way to the forearms. Use a paper towel.
7. Turn off faucet with the paper towel.

This procedure should take two to four minutes.

The nurse must wash her hands before and after caring for each client. Fingernails must be kept short, clean, and filed. The only ring that should be worn is a wedding band. Nail polish should not be worn. Gloves must be worn when in contact with bodily fluids or when infection may be possible. Hands must be washed after removing gloves. All equipment must be cleaned thoroughly after each use. Stethoscopes should be cleaned between clients. Alcohol prep pads can be used to accomplish this.

A gown should be worn if contact with body secretions is likely. It should also be worn in reverse isolation.

A mask should be worn if there is danger of contact with an airborne organism. It should also be used if there is a danger of projectile bodily fluids.

Soiled dressings and other items contaminated with body wastes must be disposed of properly and promptly. The nurse will place these in a bag before leaving the client's bedside and place them in the soiled utility room or dispose of them according to facility policy.

Care must be taken with used linens. They should be kept away from the nursing uniform and never shaken. They must be folded with the soiled part inside and placed in a linen bag. They should then be taken to the hamper or linen chute. Linens must never be thrown on the floor.

Items that are used for multiple clients should be cleaned with a bacteriostatic cleaner — either a wash or a spray — between uses by different clients. These items include, but are not limited to, permanent thermometers (these use a disposable sheath), EKG leads, pulse oximetry, sphygmomanometers, and scales.

Do not wear gowns, gloves, or masks outside of a client's room. Remove them, place in the appropriate receptacle, and wash hands.

Needles, syringes, disposable blood collection equipment, IV insertion equipment, finger stick devices, and all other sharp disposable equipment must be placed in appropriate "sharps" containers. "Sharps" containers must not be allowed to become over-filled. Follow your facility's policy for reporting almost full containers. Never replace the cap on a needle or syringe.

Aseptic technique is also called clean technique. It is used for all general nursing care.

Surgical asepsis is also called sterile technique.

Quick Quiz #2

- Name the physical barriers utilized in sterile technique:

———   ———   ———   ———   ———   ———   ———

Sterile Field

The nurse must remember the basic rules for a sterile field.

- The sterile field must remain sterile.
- An open sterile container is no longer sterile.
- Gloved hands must stay above the waist at all times.

A sterile field includes a surgical gown, sterile gloves, a surgical cap, a surgical mask, protective eyewear, and shoe covers. A surgical scrub must be performed.

The procedures for performing a surgical scrub are:

1. Remove rings and watch.
2. Push pedal or otherwise turn warm water on and wet arms and hands from elbows to fingertips.
3. Apply antimicrobial soap and rub into arms and hands.
4. Using scrub brush, scrub all skin surfaces with a circular motion. Be sure to clean well into creases and all around fingernails. Continue for five to ten minutes.

5. Rinse hands thoroughly under warm water from fingertips to elbows.
6. Pat hands dry from fingertips to elbows with a sterile towel.
7. Turn off water.

Incident Reporting

Nurses must be aware of the policy at their facility for handling incident or variance reports. Some facilities also track near-miss incidents. When an incident occurs, the nurse may need to notify the client's admitting physician, family member, and the client themselves. You will also need to document within the nurse's notes any incident that affected the client.

Most facilities have a policy whereby incident tracking is non-punitive but used for quality improvement and educational purposes.

Equipment Safety

The most important thing to know about medical equipment is how to use it properly. Many facilities require all electrical equipment to be checked out by a safety department prior to use. The equipment is then marked as being checked for safety issues. When using medical equipment in any setting, the nurse must perform the following:

- Ensure that she knows how to use the equipment before beginning the procedure.
- Check for frayed electrical cords.
- Check for any obvious safety hazards, such as loose or missing parts.
- Perform a diagnostic test if it is available.
- For any equipment relating to a client, turn it on and observe it briefly to ensure that it is working properly before leaving the room.

Teaching Clients and Families How to Safely Use Equipment

The following procedures should be in place to teach clients to use necessary equipment:

- Ensure that the client feels well enough to learn how to use the equipment.
- Explain the purpose of the equipment and under what circumstances it should be used.
- Explain exactly how to use the equipment, including safety precautions the client should take.
- Ask for a return demonstration.
- Leave written instructions if possible.

In the hospital or nursing-home setting, ensure that the call light remains in reach.

In the home setting, leave a phone number to call for questions regarding the equipment.

Malfunctioning Equipment

If the nurse notes equipment to not be working properly, it is her responsibility to remove it from the client area and replace it. She should notify the safety department or other appropriate personnel for its repair or replacement.

Security

Security plans vary widely by facility and department. All facilities should have a plan for suspected fire and bomb threats. It is the nurse's responsibility to participate in all drills and to understand her role in an emergency. She must understand proper evacuation procedures.

Pointers for Security Plans:

- Client safety is paramount. Remove clients from immediate danger first.
- Call for help, both in terms of other staff and the fire department or other emergency department.
- Confine the threat if possible.
- Use equipment, such as fire extinguishers, if necessary.
- Evacuate if necessary. Ambulatory clients should be evacuated first.
- Work professionally to keep clients calm.
- Close client room doors when required.
- Communicate with fire department personnel when they arrive.
- Notify appropriate supervisors.

Special Security Plans for Newborn Nursery and Psychiatric Departments

The newborn nursery will have a specific security plan for dealing with missing newborns or suspicious persons. The nurse must be aware of the plan and her role in it.

Psychiatric departments will have lock-down procedures when needed. It is important for the nurse to participate in preparedness drills.

Restraint Use

Smart Strategies

- Fully understand restraint use, from a legal standpoint and whether they assist a client or impede him.

- When answering restraint questions on the NCLEX, remember to keep a client's dignity and privacy in mind.

The following principles should be followed when restraint use is necessary.

- The goal of restraint use must be client safety, not the convenience of staff.
- Any restraint used must be the least restrictive device necessary.
- Improvised restraints may not be used.
- Restraint use is subject to federal law, state law, and facility policy.
- Clients in restraints must be monitored carefully.
- Regular circulation checks must be performed if applicable.
- Restraint use must be by physician order, subject to facility policy.
- The purpose of the restraint must be explained to the client.
- Restraints must be removed every two hours for client movement, repositioning, and exercise.

Types of Restraints

Mechanical or Physical Restraints

These restraints include wrist restraints, vest restraints, ankle restraints, and belts. They are commonly made of cloth or leather. They are designed to restrict or prevent movement. Bedside rails and chairs with attached table devices can also be considered physical restraints.

Chemical Restraints

Chemical restraints are almost always illegal. They involve giving the client medications designed to cause them to sleep or restrict their ability to move freely.

Alternatives to Restraints

There are many alternatives to using restraints. Nurses should consider the following when using restraints:

- Toilet every two hours
- Utilize exercise programs

- Remove of IVs, catheters, and other invasive equipment as soon as possible
- Utilize wandering programs

Basics of Precautions

Smart Strategies

- Know your precautions. They are an important part of infection control.

The nurse must know the reasons for each type of precaution and how to implement each type.

Complete the following quiz to test your knowledge of infection precaution.

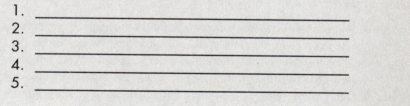

Quick Quiz #3

Name five types of infection precautions.

1. _____
2. _____
3. _____
4. _____
5. _____

CASE STUDY: JEFFREY BEZRUCIK, R.N., M.S.N.

Jeffrey Bezrucik graduated from Saint Francis Hospital School of Nursing. He received a Bachelor of Arts degree from Central Connecticut State University and a master of science degree from University of Connecticut. He has served as an instructor for more than 20 years in the Connecticut Vocational Education System. Bezrucik's areas of teaching include geriatric nursing, pediatric nursing, physical assessment, and medical nursing. His clinical areas include acute care, long-term care, and community settings.

CASE STUDY: JEFFREY BEZRUCIK, R.N., M.S.N.

Nursing school graduate who pass the NCLEX typically achieve an average of "B" or higher throughout the program; "catch on quickly with procedures and test taking," are well-organized, studious, and always well-prepared in class and clinical; and "mature acting." In comparison, those who typically fail on the first attempt are students who consistently "just pass" course work during the program, and are slow to "catch on"  with directions, both academically and clinically. They are never prepared, have an unstable personal life or finance problems, child care issues, or relationship issues. They are typically never on time for class and clinical.

Four weeks prior to you taking the NCLEX you should:

1. Read through your notes from the program.
2. Concentrate on reviewing notes in areas you did poorly with during the program.
3. If you had a history of poor test-taking skills, consider enrolling in a test-taking strategy course.

On the morning of the NCLEX, do not rush. Give yourself enough time to relax a little at home and get to the test site early. Have a good breakfast. Try to use some type of stress relief strategy.

I would suggest reviewing those courses taught at the beginning of the program and then any course (or content area) you had difficulty with. For adults, study no more than two-hour blocks. More than that causes an adult to not pay attention. Review basic algebra prior to taking NCLEX. When math questions arise, take a deep breath, relax, and do not panic. Think about the question before trying to do the calculation.

Yes, working in health care prior to taking the NCLEX can help. Many students have stated that they did not understand concepts while in school, but that it "came to them" while working in the clinical area. For any new grad, I feel that working in the clinical area helps to reinforce theory and practice, especially with multi-step procedures and critical-thinking skills.

Chapter 6

Health Promotion and Maintenance

Skills Checklist

I am unfamiliar	I am somewhat familiar	I am completely familiar	Skill
			Conduct a physical examination (RNs only)
			Explain birth control methods to sexually active clients, including contraindications to various methods
			Explain and assist with breastfeeding
			Provide care during and after circumcision
			Provide specialized care to clients undergoing life transitions
			Monitor a client in labor
			Explain the benefits of breastfeeding and bottle feeding an infant

			Explain the appropriate frequency of physician examinations for clients of various ages
			Anticipate and treat post-partum infection
			Conduct a psychosocial examination
			Teach a client to perform a breast self-examination
			Teach a client to perform a testicular self-examination
			Educate client about healthy weight loss and exercise
			Provide care to a new-born, both healthy and with health problems
			Anticipate and treat post-partum hemorrhage
			Provide umbilical care and educate family on follow-up care
			Explain immunization schedules for well clients and clients with chronic disease
			Take a comprehensive health history
			Compute expected delivery date (RNs only)
			Teach appropriate parenting skills
			Teach client about expected changes during puberty

			Teach a smoking cessation class
			Give a sitz bath to a postpartum client
			Know how to care for adult clients of every age
			Provide substance abuse education
			Provide care to the prenatal client
			Provide care to the postnatal client
			Provide care to the intranatal client during vaginal and caesarean birth
			Assess parental ability to care for newborn
			Check fetal heart rate
			Understand psychosocial responses to pregnancy
			Assess client for malnutrition and over-nutrition based on weight and other factors
			Be able to perform a vision assessment
			Be able to perform a hearing assessment
			Be able to educate clients regarding high-risk behaviors such as needle sharing
			Be able to discuss impotence with clients
			Explain procedures to children of various ages
			Understand role of ethnicity in hypertension

			Understand role of eth-nicity in diabetes
			Perform a scoliosis examination
			Be able to explain moral stages of development
			Be able to discuss meno-pause with clients
			Assess client's self-care abilities and deficits
			Facilitate process of client bonding with infant
			Teach parents about normal child growth and development

Terms to Understand

I am unfamiliar	I am somewhat familiar	I am completely familiar	Term
			Activities of daily living
			Alternative, complemen-tary, and homeopathic therapies
			Cultural differences in childbearing process
			Human growth and development
			Immunizations (includ-ing contraindications and adverse reactions)
			Risk factors for disease
			Screening examinations
			Sexually transmitted diseases

Ante / Intra/ Post Partum and Newborn Care

Smart Strategies

- Make sure that you feel comfortable with pregnancy and labor questions. If your clinicals in obstetrics and the newborn nursery were brief or early in your education, study and discuss scenarios with your peers until you feel comfortable.

- Know both the basics of a routine pregnancy and labor and the things that can go wrong.

- Understand the nurse's role in childbirth during problematic or emergency circumstances.

High Risk Pregnancy

Indicators of a high-risk pregnancy include:

- Maternal age over 35
- History of spontaneous abortion, stillbirth, or problems during birth
- Multiple fetuses
- Maternal hypertension
- Maternal diabetes
- Maternal kidney disease
- Maternal heart disease

Common complaints during the first trimester:

- **Complaint**: Nausea and vomiting
  Cause: Increasing levels of hCG and changes in carbohydrate metabolism
  Remedy: Avoid odors, especially food odors. Eat small, frequent

meals. Eat a cracker or toast first thing in the morning. Drink fluids only between meals. Avoid greasy or spicy foods.

- **Complaint**: Breast tenderness
  Cause: Increasing levels of estrogen and progesterone
  Remedy: Wear a supportive bra during all waking hours.

- **Complaint**: Urinary frequency
  Cause: The uterus pressing on the bladder
  Remedy: Void as soon as the urge is noticed. Consume fewer fluids at bedtime.

Common Complaints During the Second and Third Trimesters

- **Complaint**: Backache
  Cause: Change of the curve of the spine as the uterus enlarges
  Remedy: Perform pelvic tilt exercises. Avoid picking up heavy objects. Wear low-heeled shoes. Have rest periods.

- **Complaint**: Pyrosis
  Cause: Increased level of progesterone, displacement of the stomach by the enlarging uterus
  Remedy: Avoid greasy foods. Eat small meals.

- **Complaint**: Ankle edema
  Cause: Circulatory congestion of legs, increased capillary permeability, increased sodium levels
  Remedy: Have frequent rest periods with the legs elevated.

- **Complaint**: Varicose veins
  Cause: Venous congestion, weight gain
  Remedy: Elevate legs as much as possible. Wear support hose.

- **Complaint**: Constipation
  Cause: Increased level of progesterone, pressure against intestine by the enlarging uterus, iron supplements
  Remedy: Stay physically active. Increase fiber and fluid intake.

- **Complaint**: Hemorrhoids
  Cause: Pressure on the hemorrhoidal veins, constipation
  Remedy: Treat constipation. Avoid sitting for long periods. Take a warm sitz bath. (Do not take hot baths during pregnancy.) Try an ice pack.

- **Complaint**: Leg cramps
  Cause: Pressure of uterus on nerves, poor circulation to legs, calcium/phosphorus imbalance
  Remedy: Apply heat to area. Stretch affected muscles frequently.

Calculating Expected Delivery Dates (RNs only)

Calculate the due date according to Nagele's Rule. Add seven days to the first day of the last menstrual period and subtract three months from that date.

Quick Quiz #4

- First day of last menstrual period is January 1. Calculate the expected delivery date.

_____

- First day of last menstrual period is August 31. Calculate the expected delivery date.

_____

Maternity Care

Familiarize yourself with each step of childbirth. You must know the process of conception and zygotic, embryonic, and fetal development from conception to birth. Understand the basics of both normal and high-risk pregnancies. Be able to discuss the common problems encountered during pregnancy and labor. Be prepared for questions related to post-partum care.

Newborn Care

You must know how to care for both the normal and ill newborns, including premature newborns. You must know how to facilitate bonding between the newborn and family. Be prepared for questions related to infant nursing and bottle-feeding.

Human Developmental Stages

Erik Erikson, a Danish-German-American developmental psychologist and psychoanalyst known for his theory on social development of human beings, provided us with an effective way to assess developmental stages in infants, children, and adults. The chart below contains a brief review of his findings. You will note that the ages applicable to the stages overlap somewhat, and it is the clinician's responsibility to determine the client's true developmental age.

Name of Stage	Approximate Age	Developmental Task	Basic Strengths
Infancy	Birth to 18 Months	Trust vs. Mistrust	Drive and Hope
Early Childhood	18 Months to 3 Years	Autonomy vs. Shame	Self-Control, Courage, and Will
Play Age	3 to 6 Years	Initiative vs. Guilt	Purpose
School Age	5 to 12 Years	Industry vs. Inferiority	Method and Competence
Adolescence	10 to 18 Years	Identity vs. Role Confusion	Devotion and Fidelity
Young Adulthood	18 to 35 Years	Intimacy vs. Isolation	Affiliation and Love
Middle Adulthood	30 to 65 Years	Generativity vs. Self-Absorption or Stagnation	Production and Care
Late Adulthood	50 Years to Death	Integrity vs. Despair	Wisdom

Disease Prevention

Nurses educate clients about disease prevention. This is frequently done in the community at health fairs or other gatherings. The following are common topics:

- Heart disease prevention: Including a proper diet, exercise, stress management, and cholesterol management

- Diabetes prevention: By educating the public about metabolic syndrome and the advantages of a healthy diet, proper weight, and an exercise program.

- Cancer prevention: By promoting smoking cessation, a proper diet, and exercise

- Obesity prevention: By promoting a healthy diet and exercise program

- Asthma prevention for children: By encouraging parents not to smoke in the home

- Addiction prevention: By teaching young people the many dangers of illegal or misused prescription drugs and alcohol

Risk Factors Related to Disease

Non-modifiable risk factors include:

- Age
- Genetics
- Gender
- Race and ethnicity

Modifiable risk factors include:

- Obesity and overweight
- Smoking
- Drug use
- Poor sleep hygiene
- Poor oral hygiene
- Stress
- Environmental conditions
- Improper nutrition
- Lack of exercise

The nurse must teach clients about their modifiable risk factors to prevent disease and maintain their health.

Some common topics include:

- Talking to clients about smoking cessation. Provide literature about smoking cessation classes. Encourage the client to talk to their physician about pharmacological management of smoking cessation.

- Teaching clients about proper nutrition based on their disease risk factors. For example, those at risk for diabetes will need education on a healthy, low-glycemic diet. Someone at risk for heart disease will need education regarding a low-fat, low-cholesterol diet.

- Talking to clients about losing excess weight. Provide literature about support groups. Explain the details of a proper weight-loss diet and an exercise program specific to their abilities. Explain that a healthy weight loss is 1 to 2 pounds per week and never more than 3 pounds a week. Instruct them to avoid fad diets. Encourage them to speak to their physician before taking over-the-counter medications or supplements for weight loss. Tell the client what their healthy weight range is and that losing even ten percent of their body weight will lower their risk of disease. The nurse can be an excellent source of information and support to the overweight or obese client.

Expected Body Image Changes

The body image of a client will change over the course of her life. The nurse should facilitate the client's coping with these changes and help her understand what to anticipate. Common changes that frequently challenge clients include:

- **Entering pre-puberty and puberty**: Pubic hair, chest hair, and facial hair begin to grow. Genitalia changes, and female breasts grow in size. The male voice matures, and both sexes grow in height.

- **Pregnancy**: As well as weight gain, the pregnant client will experience excess fluid in her extremities. The changes of pregnancy devastate many women and interfere with the relationship they share with their significant other.

- **Aging**: Many physical changes occur in the aging body. Muscle atrophy and wrinkling are among the changes disconcerting to many clients. Hair may turn gray, white, or fall out. Aged individuals frequently cannot move as quickly as they could in younger years and can face incontinence and other unwelcome changes.

Family Planning

Nurses in certain settings will be responsible for educating clients about contraception and family planning. An entry-level nurse is expected to possess basic information about contraception.

Types of Contraception

- *Birth control pills*
  Common contraindications: Smoking, age over 35, risk of stroke, history of blood clots or stroke

- *Birth control patches*
  Common contraindications: Smoking, age over 35, risk of stroke, history of blood clots or stroke

- *Birth control injections*
  Common contraindications: Smoking, age over 35, risk of stroke, history of blood clots or stroke

- *Diaphragms*
  Common contraindications: Allergy to rubber or latex, physical abnormalities, repeated urinary tract infections, poor compliance

- *Intrauterine Devices (IUDs)*
  Common contraindications: Gynecological cancers, sexually transmitted disease, pelvic inflammatory disease

- *Condoms – male and female*
  Common contraindications: Poor compliance, allergy to ingredients

- *Rhythm method*
  Common contraindications: Poor compliance, age under 20 or over 40, irregular cycles

- *Spermicidal foams and jellies*
  Common contraindications: Poor compliance, allergy to ingredients

Birth control methods are frequently used in tandem. The need for protection from sexually transmitted diseases must be factored into birth control decisions. A condom should be worn during sexual intercourse — heterosexual or homosexual — for all but long-term, monogamous, disease-free partners who have another method of birth control.

In preparation for the NCLEX, test takers should be aware of the indications for each birth control method.

Clients who wish to plan families may need genetic counseling to determine the chances of their offspring having genetic defects. Clients who may wish to receive genetic counseling include:

- Clients whose partners are related to them
- Clients over age 30
- Clients with a personal history of physical or mental disorders
- Clients with a history of chemotherapy or radiation
- Clients with a family history of physical or mental disorders
- Clients who have had miscarriages or children born with birth defects
- Clients who do not know their family history

Family Systems

The nurse must realize the critical role of the family in client health or illness. A well-functioning family is a great asset in times of illness, injury, or disease. A poorly functioning family can lead to a weakened immune system, poor recuperation, and a poor prognosis.

Changes due to health issues have an impact on the family. A bread-winning father's myocardial infarction can upset the balance of the family. Children suddenly taking care of their parents are confused and in need of support. A cancer diagnosis in a child will shift family dynamics and resources significantly. Be cognizant of the impact of these changes and allow the client and family time for venting feelings, both individually and together. Be prepared to refer clients to appropriate resources when needed. These may include social workers, marriage and family counselors, support groups, and psychologists.

Religious and Cultural Influences on Family Systems

Nurses must have an understanding of the effect of religion and culture on families. If a woman who is seriously injured comes from a culture where the female prepares the meals and meets the basic needs of the family, the entire family system will be disrupted.

Other examples of religious or cultural influences include the man who does not want his children to assist with bathing him or a family who seems focused on the fact that their critically injured son will not be able to help with the family harvesting.

The nurse must remain nonjudgmental when caring for clients such as these. A nurse with cultural sensitivity will analyze how to best help the entire family in times of stress.

Family Roles and Structures

The nurse must ascertain the structure of the family she is caring for. She must learn whether it is a nuclear, blended, or adoptive family and what the family's specific needs are. In some families, the elders of the family (grandparents) will play a major role in the family. For others, they may be more distant. The nurse must take the time to understand the support system for the client and family.

It is the role of the nurse to assist the client and family with life transitions, whether the client is experiencing the birth of a baby or a terminal diagnosis.

Growth and Development

The nurse must apply the fundamentals of growth and development when caring for clients.

Explaining Procedures and Treatments

It is the responsibility of the nurse to explain any procedures or treatments she is to perform. She may also be responsible for follow-up questions regarding any treatment or surgery to be performed by a physician.

Children

For young children, a brief explanation shortly before the procedure is best. Explain that this is to help the child "feel better" or provide another explanation of why the procedure is to take place. Explain who will be present and whether a parent will be in attendance. Be kind but firm so that the child understands that the procedure must be done. If it is a quick procedure, let the child know. It may be helpful to mimic the procedure on a doll or an adult.

For older children, a brief explanation in words they understand should suffice. This can be given a day before a scheduled procedure if applicable. The main questions are likely to be, "Will it hurt?" and "Will I be OK?"

Adults

For adults, procedures should be explained as soon as they are ordered. The client has a right to know what to expect in his medical care. A basic rule is to speak at a 10th-grade level unless the nurse can see that the client does not understand. Refrain from using medical terms, and consider that the client is under stress at this time. Ask if the client has any questions when done. It is important to not seem rushed.

Health and Wellness

To assess the client's perception of her health status, simply ask. Questions can include:

- How would you rate your overall health — excellent, good, fair, or poor?
- Do you feel you are as healthy as others your age?

You may want to ask about mental as well as physical health. Research indicates that people who feel good about their health will generally have healthier lives than those who do not. It is important to encourage healthy habits and compliance with physician orders. Seniors, in particular, are affected by their self-perception of their health status.

Health Promotion Programs

Health promotion programs are excellent opportunities for nurses to disseminate health information to communities. This information can include:

- Safe sex practices
- Influenza and pneumonia immunization education
- Nutrition classes
- Exercise classes
- Stress management classes
- Skin cancer screenings
- Cholesterol screenings
- Hypertension screenings
- Natural childbirth
- Breastfeeding

Health promotion programs are frequently free of charge and aimed at specific demographics, such as the elderly, young adults, or those in poverty.

Breast Self-Exams

Teach adult female clients the following steps for breast self-examination. Let them know that most lumps and changes are benign, but must be checked by a professional. For further information, contact the American Cancer Society®.

1. Lie down with your right arm behind your head.

2. Use the pads of your three middle fingers on your left hand to feel for lumps in your right breast. Make overlapping small circular motions to feel the breast tissue. Begin with light pressure, then apply medium pressure, and finally apply firm pressure. Make sure to apply all levels of pressure to all areas of the breast. You may find a firm ridge in the lower curve of each breast. This is normal.

3. Move around the breast up and down from the side to the middle of the breast until you have completely covered the entire breast.

4. Place your left arm behind your head and examine your left breast in the same manner, using your right hand.

5. Stand in front of a mirror and press firmly downward on your hips. Look at your breasts for any changes in shape, size, contour, dimpling, scaliness, or redness.

6. Stand and examine your right underarm with your left hand while your right arm is slightly raised.

7. Examine your left underarm in the same manner.

8. Contact your health-care professional right away if you notice any changes in your breast or underarm.

High-Risk Behaviors

Nurses have a unique opportunity to discuss the ramifications of high-risk behavior with risk takers. Some of these behaviors include:

- Taking illegal drugs or misusing prescription drugs
- Alcohol intoxication
- Driving under the influence of mind-altering substances
- Driving while unsafely using technology (talking, accessing the Internet, or texting on a phone)
- Being in a motor vehicle without a seat belt
- Not getting proper sleep
- Illegal activities, especially with weapons

Immunizations

The following is a chart of recommended immunizations by the Centers for Disease Control (CDC) in the United States. Recommendations vary each year, and this chart should be used as a general guideline only.

	Birth	1 Month	2 Months	4 Months	6 Months	12 Months	15 Months
Hepatitis B	X				X	X (8 Months)	
Rotavirus			X	X			
Diphtheria, Pertussis, Tetanus			X	X	X		
Haemophilus Influenzae Type B			X	X		X	
Pneumococcal			X	X	X	X	
Inactivated Poliovirus			X	X	X		
Influenza					X		
Measles, Mumps, Rubella						X	
Varicella						X	
Hepatitis A						X	

	18 Months	19-23 Months	2-3 Years	4-6 Years	7-10 Years	11-12 Years	13-18 Years
Diphtheria, Pertussis, Tetanus				X			
Tetanus, Diphtheria, Pertussis						X	
Human Papillomavirus						X (3 Doses)	
Meningococcal						X	

Influenza	X		X (Yearly)	X (Yearly)	X (Yearly)	X (Yearly)	X (Yearly)
Hepatitis A	X						
Inactivated Poliovirus				X			
Measles, Mumps, Rubella				X			
Varicella				X			

	19-26 Years	27-49 Years	50-59 Years	60-64 Years	> 64 Years
Tetanus, Diphtheria	X (Every 10 Years)	X (Every 10 Years)	X (Every 10 Years)	X (Every 10 Years)	X (Every 10 Years)
Zoster				X	X
Influenza	X (Yearly)	X (Yearly)	X (Yearly)	X (Yearly)	X (Yearly)

Client Teaching

Numerous other vaccines may be indicated if the client did not receive earlier vaccines or if she has certain conditions or lives in certain conditions. The charts provide a basic immunization schedule for healthy children and adults in the United States.

Different clients learn best through different methods. Some prefer to read, while others prefer a live demonstration or discussion. Still others prefer a video. The nurse must take into account the client's grasp of the English language, his eyesight, hearing, and ability to read when deciding the best method for teaching. The client's general education level must be considered, as well.

Quick Quiz #5

Which of the following actions by the nurse is incorrect?

1. The nurse shows preschoolers a cartoon about properly brushing their teeth.
2. The nurse gives preschool children a demonstration on proper hand washing.
3. The nurse asks a group of preschoolers, "Who can tell me what happens at a hospital?"
4. The nurse gives a group of preschoolers a pamphlet about safe playground play.

Physical Examination (RNs only)

The nurse must know how to conduct a basic physical examination.

CASE STUDY: PATRICIA HINDIN, PHD, CNM

University of Medicine & Dentistry of New Jersey -
School of Nursing (UMDNJ-SN)
Suite SSB -1041
65 Bergen St. Newark, NJ 07101
Office: 973-972-4211
Fax: 973-972-8775
E-mail: hindinpk@umdnj.edu

Dr. Hindin is an assistant professor of nursing at the University of Medicine & Dentistry of New Jersey – School of Nursing.

Students who are active learners, motivated, organized, and make the most of all learning experiences generally pass the NCLEX on the first attempt. They usually have a study plan for the NCLEX and either take a review course or plan consistent and organized daily reviews of NCLEX questions, either online or from a review book. They usually have solid grades throughout the program.

Students who typically do not pass on the first attempt are students who have struggled during the entire nursing program. They are usually the students who have passed major courses such as medical/surgical nurse and senior capstone with a 75 percent (just passing), or have failed and repeated courses. They are usually weak in the basic sciences and have been borderline students throughout their academic careers.

Four weeks prior to the NCLEX, develop a study plan earlier than the last four weeks prior to the exam. Have the exam study plan in place and ready to "go" after graduation.

Pick a consistent time and place to study. If you are going to take your exam in the morning, study during this time in a quiet place or library. If you are an afternoon test-taker, study in the afternoon.

Practice one form of stress reduction everyday — whatever works for you — but decide on this along with your study plan. Running, yoga, or meditation are some ideas.

At UMDNJ-School of Nursing, students take an ATI comprehensive exam, which helps them identify their areas of strength and weakness. They then are provided with a three-day ATI review with an instructor from the company. The review course focuses on the weak areas of the class. Students preparing for the NCLEX should strengthen their weak areas, but still review all content for the exam.

CASE STUDY: PATRICIA HINDIN, PHD, CNM

I am not convinced we are really testing critical-thinking skills, but rather we are testing the student's ability to take NCLEX questions and skills involved in this exam. It becomes almost a game of how to answer the questions for the NCLEX rather than an intellectual test of critical thinking and how a nurse would really perform in those circumstances. However, that did not answer your question. I  think some people have more innate critical-thinking abilities than others, but also that the skills can be learned.

Length of study time is an individual choice that should be made by the student. At this point in their academic careers, they should have self-awareness and know when they study best and how often they need to take breaks.

On the morning of the test, have breakfast and spend about 10-15 minutes prior to the exam in quiet reflection and positive self-affirmation. Visualize yourself passing the exam. Focus on each question and give the best possible answer. Do not make up a story about the question, just answer what is asked.

Whether a graduate should work in health care while studying for the NCLEX depends on individual students and their abilities. I see strong academic students in full-time nursing internships who study while in the internships and pass NCLEX on the first attempt. I think the weaker students need to focus on studying and not deal with the stress of a new job while trying to pass a major exam.

Chapter 7

Psychosocial Integrity

Skills Checklist

I am unfamiliar	I am somewhat familiar	I am completely familiar	Skill
			Recognize client substance abuse or dependence, withdrawal, or toxicity
			Provide end-of-life care
			Lead and participate in group therapy (RNs lead and participate; LPNs participate)
			Recognize the abused or neglected client and be able to counsel her
			Know how to plan interventions the abused client
			Place client under suicide precautions

			Be able to inform client and family about various mental illnesses
			Care for clients who are hallucinating
			Develop trusting relationships with clients
			Provide appropriate care for clients with dependencies such as gambling, pornography, and sexual addiction
			Be able to contract with client who requires behavioral intervention
			Understand the basic workings of Alcoholics Anonymous and similar groups
			Care for client undergoing chemical withdrawal
			Care for client who has chemical toxicity
			Teach client appropriate stress management techniques
			Be able to explore client non-adherence to treatment plan
			Recognize client relapse
			Recognize signs and symptoms of specific mental illnesses
			Recognize symptoms that indicate clients are suffering from impaired cognition

Terms to Understand

I am unfamiliar	I am somewhat familiar	I am completely familiar	Term
			Behavioral management techniques (limit setting, positive reinforcement)
			Boundaries
			Coping mechanisms and defense mechanisms
			Crisis intervention
			Grieving and anticipatory grieving
			Reality orientation
			Spiritual distress
			Support system
			Therapeutic communication techniques (verbal and nonverbal)
			Therapeutic milieu

Abuse and Neglect

Abuse and neglect can take many forms. Physical abuse involves the striking of another person or inflicting pain on their body by another means. It can involve shoving or rough handling. Verbal abuse involves speaking to someone in a disrespectful manner. It may or may not involve the raising of the voice or intimidation. Emotional abuse involves disregarding the emotional needs of another party. Sexual abuse involves inappropriate words or behavior of a sexual nature toward someone who does not consent or is unable to consent, such as a minor or a mentally-incapacitated adult. Neglect involves not meeting the physical or emotional needs of another to whom we are responsible. It may or may not involve placing one's safety at risk.

The nurse must never abuse or neglect a client, nor allow any subordinate to do so. Knowledge or suspiciousness of anyone abusing a client must be reported and dealt with immediately.

Child abuse and neglect must be reported to the proper authorities in all states. Abuse and neglect of the elderly and disabled must be reported in some states and domestic violence must be reported in some states. It is the nurse's responsibility to know the laws of her state and to report accordingly.

The victim of abuse must never be blamed for her situation. Questioning must be straightforward and non-judgmental.

Signs of abuse include:

- Obvious bruising or other marks that have no logical explanation
- Bruises in various stages of healing
- The client moans or acts as if they have painful areas of their body
- Long sleeves or heavy garments during hot weather
- Lack of eye contact
- Puffy, swollen eyes from extensive crying
- Broken bones
- Poor self-esteem

Behavioral Interventions and Behavioral Management

You must understand the basics of behavioral interventions in both the psychiatric and non-psychiatric setting. You must understand the general principles of behavioral management relative to different client populations.

Reality Orientation for the Delusional, Delirious, or Demented Client

To provide delusional, delirious, or demented clients with the care they require:

- Provide a learning environment. Large calendars should be visible at all times with signs giving the date and day of the week. Windows are helpful to help distinguish time. Clocks should be visible.

- Give many verbal cues, such as "Here is breakfast," "Here is dinner," or "This is a good time to get ready for bed."

- Use the client's name frequently.

- Explain what will be happening next.

- Give correct but thoughtful answers to questions.

- Make suggestions of activities that the client can do, such as "Would like to watch television?" "Would you like to play a game?" "Would you like to exercise a bit?"

- For a client who is suddenly confused, provide emotional support and monitor the client closely.

Chemical and Other Dependencies

Smart Strategies

- Familiarize yourself with the issues that face nurses who care for addicted clients.

- Understand the basics of both detoxification and the long healing process from addiction.

- Be aware that clients can become addicted to many different types of things.

Alcohol Dependency

You must understand how to care for the client who is experiencing detoxification as well as later in their recovery. Know the medications typically given during detoxification and the types of therapy utilized to facilitate recovery from dependence. Be familiar with the destructive effects of alcohol on the body.

Tobacco Dependency

You should know the ramifications of tobacco dependency and the medications available to aid abstinence. Understand that counseling greatly enhances the success rate of smoking cessation.

Other Dependencies

Clients may become dependent on many types of pharmacological agents, both legal and illegal. They may also abuse and become dependent on other items, such as glue, paint, gasoline, and other solvents. NCLEX questions can also involve non-substance addictions, such as Internet addiction, gaming addiction, or pornography addiction.

For all dependencies, the client must develop new ways of coping with stress. Rehabilitation consists of withdrawing from the substance, which is often done as an inpatient. Most substances can be physically withdrawn from in three to five days. The client must be monitored closely during this period with his vital signs taken frequently.

The following are nursing interventions to be executed during withdrawal or detoxification:

- Vital signs are monitored every two or four hours per policy.

- Anti-anxiety and other medications are given as ordered.

- The client is kept from stressful situations and generally from the environment in which he became ill. Visitors are usually strongly restricted.

- Encourage good nutrition. Give vitamins and other supplements as ordered.

- Monitor closely for seizures.

- Provide a stable, secure environment. Ensure that the client understands the rules of the facility.

- Maintain suicide or elopement precautions if ordered.

When the client has successfully physically withdrawn, the emotional recovery process begins. Clients in the United States are frequently introduced to a 12-step recovery program. Inpatient clients are kept busy from the time they awaken until they go to bed. They will have individual and group therapy, attend educational classes, take part in family meetings, and be adapted to a healthy lifestyle of regular meals, exercise, and productivity.

Coping Mechanisms

Smart Strategies
- Instead of memorizing the names of the various coping mechanisms, consider which ones are healthy and which are unhealthy. Be prepared to answer questions accordingly as to whether client and family behaviors are adaptive or maladaptive.

Clients and families will develop coping mechanisms to deal with the stress of illness or injury. Coping mechanisms are crucial to the client's mental health. Some of the more common ones include:

- **Altruism**: Clients focus on helping others and not thinking about their own stressors. This is frequently seen on transplant floors and among pediatric clients.

- **Avoidance**: Clients avoid talking or listening to discussion about their diagnosis and prognosis. This is frequent among families as well.

- **Bargaining**: The client tries to bargain with fate, or his supreme figure, to change his current situation. They may say, "God, I will change my ways if you just let me live through this disease." This is more common among clients with religious beliefs.

- **Compensation**: The client will attempt to become stronger in one area to make up for a perceived or actual deficit in another area. This is common in men who were physically strong prior to a diagnosis of a debilitating illness.

- **Conversion**: The client may turn stress into complaints of physical problems. This is common among anxious middle-aged women.

- **Denial**: Similar to avoidance. Clients refuse to accept that they have an illness or injury. A life-changing event, such as a stroke or a motor vehicle accident, may be forgotten.

- **Dissociation**: The client feels dissociated from the person who is ill. She sees the sick party as someone outside herself.

- **Fantasy:** The client, unable to cope with the stress of reality, enters a world of fantasy. This is common among young children.

- **Idealization:** This involves seeing someone or a circumstance as being perfect. An example includes the husband of a client with a terminal illness stating that she is an angel. A second example is the family that feels as if their ill child can come home and everything will be perfect. This is common among family members of client's with a terminal diagnosis.

- **Projection:** The client cannot accept his feelings (usually negative feelings) and instead projects them onto others. He may say, "My wife is so frightened about what will happen to me."

- **Rationalization:** The client creates a rational reason why something has happened. She may say that her chronic cough is from being in the cold instead of being lung cancer.

- **Reaction Formation:** The client behaves in an opposite way to the way he really feels. A frightened client may appear to be overly brave and unconcerned about his diagnosis.

- **Regression:** The client regresses to an earlier state in order to avoid dealing with the current situation. This is common among children of five to ten years.

- **Repression:** The client hides his true feelings, even from himself. An example would be a husband who appears unconcerned about his wife's multiple sclerosis diagnosis.

Some of these coping mechanisms are also included in the five stages of grief — a subject discussed later in this chapter.

Adaptive versus Maladaptive Coping Mechanisms

The nurse must determine if the client's coping mechanism is adaptive or maladaptive. She must take into account the stage of a diagnosis. What is an appropriate coping mechanism in the first few weeks may not be appropriate later. The nurse can assist clients and families with inappropriate or maladaptive coping mechanisms to find better ways of dealing with their circumstances.

A client's first response to a serious diagnosis can be fear, despair, anger, or optimism. The nurse should be supportive and allow the client time to vent his feelings and ask questions. She should ascertain that he understands his diagnosis and prognosis as clients may not hear all that is said by the physician at such a stressful time.

The nurse should document the adaptive and maladaptive responses by the client and his family, as well as any teaching conducted.

Crisis Management

Nurses may find themselves involved in crisis intervention. This happens most frequently in emergency departments and psychiatric hospitals, but it can occur in any health-care or home setting. Every nurse must possess basic crisis intervention skills. These skills include:

- Stay firm and remain in control of the situation.
- Speak calmly to the person in crisis and ascertain her level of cognition.
- If the party seems to be hallucinating, delirious, or demented, attempt to calm the person by talking. Prepare for a physical force team intervention if needed. Contact security at your facility if available.

If the party is not hallucinating, delirious, or demented, try to ascertain what led to the crisis and what is needed to bring its resolution. If the party poses an immediate danger to you or others, let them know you are willing to work toward a resolution. Bring in assistance if at all possible in the form of manpower, security, or the police.

End-of-Life Care

- You may not have had adequate clinical experience with end-of-life care. Recognize that symptom management can be quite different than care for a client who is being healed and answer NCLEX questions accordingly.

General Principles of End-of-Life Care

The nurse must understand the principles of end-of-life care, including pain management, symptom management, and grief management for the client and family.

The Five Stages of Grief

Smart Strategies

- Expect to see one or more grief questions on the NCLEX. Know that grief can cause clients and loved ones to behave in ways that seem may unusual to people not in their situation. The nurse must remain nonjudgmental and look for ways to facilitate healthy grieving.

Dr. Elizabeth Kübler-Ross developed a theory about grief that bears her name. According to Kübler-Ross, we go through five stages of grief. Some clients will become stuck in one stage, hindering their healing. This model can be helpful in anticipating the needs of clients and their families who are facing a serious diagnosis.

1. Denial
2. Anger
3. Bargaining
4. Depression
5. Acceptance

The nurse can talk with the client and family about the stages of grief; enabling them to understand their moods and feelings and those of other family members. It is helpful for clients to understand that their feelings, while unique, have a universal theme and that it is part of their ultimate healing. The nurse should recommend support groups or counseling when needed.

Bereavement

Each person deals with bereavement in their own way. The nurse must offer support and remain nonjudgmental during the bereavement process. Allowing the family to talk about their feelings is therapeutic at these times.

Mental Health Concepts

Discussing Non-Adherence with the Client

Clients do not adhere to their prescribed treatment regimen for many reasons. Some common reasons include:

- They feel they cannot afford the treatment.
- They are frightened of the outcome.
- They are in denial that they have a problem that needs addressing.
- They do not wish to put forth the effort needed.
- They do not believe the caregiver or are suspicious of the medical profession in general.

- They have poor self-esteem.
- They feel they have a better way to handle the problem on their own.

Many clients never tell the physician or nurse that they are not following the prescribed treatment. It is important to question clients on this matter. Under direct questioning, they will frequently admit they are not taking their medication or following their diet. They should be queried on the reasons for the non-adherence. This should be documented and the physician made aware. Discuss the benefits of the treatment with the client and contract for adherence if possible. You may have to work out a trial program. For example, "Will you take your insulin as prescribed for two weeks and see how you feel? We can discuss this again at that time."

Managing Client Relapse

A client who has experienced relapse is frequently sad and frightened. Assisting them in regaining their self-esteem and getting back on track is imperative. Briefly discuss the relapse to see what insight they have learned from the experience and then move forward.

Promoting Client Independence

Promotion of client independence is an important topic on the NCLEX. Your nursing actions should always facilitate client independence as much as possible. Stroke clients and other clients who have sudden changes in their abilities must work on regaining their independence almost immediately, or an atmosphere of unhealthy dependence can develop. Assistive aids are frequently used by clients in these situations.

As a general rule, do not feed, bathe, or dress the client who can care for herself unless she medically needs to reserve her energy. Many times it would be quicker to perform a task yourself, but the nurse is taking away the client's independence by doing so. Always keep a client's independence on your mind.

Promoting Client Positive Self-esteem

Clients gain self-esteem by task performance and attempting to perform tasks. The care plan for the client may include task performance activities. The following is an example care plan.

Monday: The client will sit on the edge of the bed.
Tuesday: The client will stand briefly.
Wednesday: The client will walk to the chair with assistance.
Thursday: The client will walk to the chair with the nurse near.
Friday: The client will walk into the hallway with the nurse near.

The client should be aware of the plan and should be encouraged to vocalize their hopes and fears. Ideally, she will be a party in the plan development. True praise and encouragement should be given.

Mental Retardation or Developmental Disability

Mental retardation may also be referred to as intellectual disability.

Presentation: Intelligence Quotient (IQ) of 70 or less with behavioral manifestations

Profound Mental Retardation

Profound mental retardation is characterized by an IQ of 19 or less. 85 percent of clients with an intellectual disability are considered to have profound mental retardation.

Common characteristics of clients with profound mental retardation include:

- May speak a few words, if any
- May or may not be able to communicate a few basic needs
- Unable to perform activities of daily living
- Frequently institutionalized
- Unable to live independently

Severe Mental Retardation

Severe mental retardation is characterized by an IQ of 20 to 34. Ten percent of clients with an intellectual disability are considered to have severe mental retardation.

Common characteristics of clients with severe mental retardation include:

- May learn to speak enough to communicate basic needs
- Can eat and perform basic toileting
- Frequently institutionalized
- Unable to live independently

Moderate Mental Retardation

Moderate mental retardation is characterized by an IQ of 35 to 49. Four percent of clients with an intellectual disability are considered to have moderate mental retardation.

Common characteristics of clients with moderate mental retardation include:

- General intelligence level of a 7-year-old child
- Can perform skills with supervision
- Occasionally institutionalized, especially if a caregiver is not present
- Unable to live independently

Mild Mental Retardation

Mild mental retardation is characterized by an IQ of 50 to 70. 1 percent of clients with an intellectual disability are considered to have mild mental retardation.

Common characteristics of clients with mild mental retardation include:

- General intelligence level of an 11-year-old child
- Able to perform skills with or without supervision
- Rarely institutionalized
- May or may not live independently

Nursing interventions for clients with mental retardation include:

- Perform or assist with activities of daily living (ADLs) as needed.
- Monitor for appropriate diet and health decision-making.
- Monitor for low self-esteem.
- Provide positive reinforcement.
- Encourage self-care as much as possible.
- Keep a safe environment.
- Teach appropriate goal-setting for client and caregivers.

Psychopathy

You must be familiar with all the major types of psychopathy. Several of them are expanded upon here to assist test takers in understanding the depth of knowledge they should possess for each condition.

Separation Anxiety Disorder of Early Childhood

Presentation: Child is overly fearful of being out of the presence of primary caregiver

Nursing interventions for clients with separation anxiety disorder include:

- Caregiver education
- If child is to be hospitalized, allow family members to stay as much as possible.
- Provide support and distraction for periods away from family.

Attachment Disorder of Childhood

Presentation: Child avoids forming relationships with peers and others

Nursing interventions for clients with attachment disorder include:

- Encourage and reward play with others.
- Allow parallel play, eating, and learning to let child adjust to others being in his environment.
- Encourage child to verbalize fears and feelings.

Autistic Disorder

Presentation: A spectrum of disorders that includes Asperger's Syndrome

Nursing interventions for clients with attachment disorder include:

- Be consistent and help the child understand what to expect.

- Keep the child's room quiet and calm.
- Provide the family with adequate resources if this is a new diagnosis.

Religious and Spiritual Influences on Health

A client's religious or spiritual beliefs can have a powerful impact on her health. A person with an optimistic outlook for their recovery is more likely to have a successful recovery. A person who feels cursed may have a less fortunate outcome.

The nurse's role in a client's religious or spiritual influences should include:

- Accommodate the client's religious beliefs as much as possible. An example of this would be to allow for last rites and other formal and informal religious ceremonies

- The nurse must remain non-judgmental of religious beliefs other than her own.

- The nurse must attempt to accommodate reasonable dietary restrictions by working with the dietary department to facilitate nutritional meals that meet the client's needs.

- The nurse should make appropriate referrals for any ethical situations that arise. An example of this includes: A client refuses a needed blood transfusion on religious grounds. In emergency situations, the physician and possibly a court order could become involved. In non-emergent situations, a social worker or ethics committee could become involved. The nurse must advise her superior of any refusal of needed care, and she will be guided on the appropriate referrals to make.

Sensory and Perceptual Alterations

Clients with perceptual alterations require close assessment and monitoring. Such clients can easily harm themselves avoiding things they perceive. Monitor a hallucinating client to ensure their safety. The following steps should be abided by:

- Remove belts, sharp objects, over-the-counter medications, and any other objects the client could harm himself with.

- One-to-one monitoring may be ordered. An alternative may be to monitor with a camera. The client may attempt to jump out the window or drown in the bathtub.

- Auditory and visual hallucinations are frightening for the client. Reality orientation and support should be given. It does not help, however, to argue with the client. If he says that bugs are biting him, tell him that you do not see any bugs and that he is safe. Let him know that you have the situation under control. Occasionally, distraction will help. At times, monitoring the client's safety is the best form of support you can offer.

- It is okay to ask the client what he sees or hears. He may be afraid to talk about it, even though it will be therapeutic to discuss it. It will also allow you to make the physician aware of his symptoms. Do not diminish the client's concerns. The empathic nurse can imagine how the client must feel to be seeing monsters or devils coming at him.

Many conditions can lead to hallucinations. Some common ones include:

- Schizophrenia
- Other psychosis
- Effect of drugs
- Delirium

- Kidney failure
- End stage COPD
- Detoxification from drugs
- High fever
- Sleep deprivation
- Brain tumor
- Brain injury

Stress Management

Each client will have his own stress management tools. If these are not working appropriately, the nurse may need to educate the client of appropriate stress management.

Poor stress management techniques frequently seen in clients include:

- Alcohol or other substance abuse
- Verbal or physical abuse of family members

There are effective stress management techniques the nurse can teach a client. The nurse must carefully consider which stress management techniques the client will understand and utilize. Some examples include:

- Proper self-care, nutrition, and rest
- Relaxation techniques, such as meditation, deep breathing, or healthy diversions
- Exercise and hobbies
- Spending time in nature or with an animal

Support Systems

A client may have traditional or non-traditional support systems. These can include the following:

- Family members, both in and out of the household
- Significant others (both same sex and opposite sex)

- Friends
- Co-workers
- Pets
- People with whom the client shares similar interests
- People with the same disease or disorder as the client
- People who have recovered from the same disease or disorder the client is facing
- People from the client's place of worship
- Neighbors

The astute nurse will monitor the health of the client's support system and be alert for maladaptive relationships. Healthy support systems are to be encouraged and all support systems are to be respected. Make social work referrals when needed.

Therapeutic Communication

Boundaries of the Nurse-Client Relationship

The nurse must ensure that the boundaries of the nurse-client relationship are maintained. He should abide by the following ideals.

- Do not discuss your personal life with the client.
- Do not see the client as a potential relationship partner.
- Do not become overly involved in the client's relationships.
- Do not allow a parent-child-type relationship to develop.
- Do not allow a personal friendship to develop.
- Do not plan to meet or talk with the client after the client is discharged from care.
- Do not allow the client to become dependent on you, but not the other caregivers.
- Do not allow the client to "staff split."

If you feel uncomfortable with either your feelings or the behavior of the client, the client should be assigned to another nurse. Discuss the situation with your supervisor. Allowing the boundaries of the nurse-client relationship to become blurred is harmful to your client and may constitute abuse or malpractice.

Therapeutic Environment

Holding Impatient Community Meetings

Impatient community meetings can be an important tool to assist clients in preparing to deal with the outside world. During this time, they learn respect for others and the basics of human interaction.

General principles of a therapeutic milieu include:

- Each person in the milieu, both staff and clients, is to respect the other people in the milieu.
- Rules are adopted by the group and should be followed by all.
- The goals of the milieu must meet the needs of the group as a whole.

CASE STUDY: SANDY HARDING R.N., M.S.N., S.N.

Retiree of Colorado Northwestern Community College after a five year tenure as nursing instructor. She was a school nurse for 26 years in Craig, Colorado.

Students who pass the NCLEX on the first attempt have read the material assigned in their textbooks during nursing school, studied for all tests and quizzes, reviewed for the NCLEX during senior year, and have not waited until the last minute to review. They are critical thinkers, know what the questions are asking, and are able to generate possible answers in their minds and choose the correct answer from a list by eliminating wrong ones.

On the other hand, graduates who do not pass the first time are typically poor test takers in general, seldom read chapters assigned for class, and do little preparation for tests ahead of time. They tend to cram for exams and do not strive for retention of the material for future use as a nurse.

Four weeks prior to taking the NCLEX you should:

1. Review med-surg. nursing — this is the largest part of the NCLEX exam. Use the text and other resources to review. Focus on any topics that seem unfamiliar or that you feel unsure of, such as fluids and electrolytes.
2. Review leadership and management topics — these are also interspersed throughout the test.
3. Review pharmacological classifications, major categories of drugs, and possible side effects of those drugs. Know what conditions they are used for.
4. Review specialty areas such as obstetrics, pediatrics, and psychiatric nursing.
5. Meet with other students to review using games, flash cards, or case studies.

In studying for the NCLEX, graduates should focus on areas where they are deficient first. Hopefully, they have incorporated knowledge they have learned early in nursing school. They should use the table of contents in their textbooks to pinpoint topics they need to review. Standardized tests have areas listed which show deficiencies and the need for remediation.

Critical-thinking skills required on the NCLEX are innate to some degree, but are also learned during nursing school. Case studies, role play, and discussions all enhance these critical-thinking skills. Standardized testing covering all subjects during nursing school are also helpful in preparing for the NCLEX exam format.

CASE STUDY: SANDY HARDING R.N., M.S.N., S.N.

Study sessions at home should probably be no longer than two to three hours per day. If students begin reviewing early (at least one to two months in advance), it would be helpful. Longer sessions will probably not be retained. Working in a group setting with an NCLEX review book, flash cards, or games would be beneficial. NCLEX review classes, which are day-long classes, may also benefit some graduates.

It seems that the weakest points for graduates on the NCLEX are the questions about leadership and management. Students have also voiced a concern about the priority questions, which they have found to be difficult.

Ideally, candidates could work in the health-care field while preparing for the NCLEX, but to a minimum degree — not more than 24 hours per week. They may learn some useful skills and observe the leadership and management styles of RNs in the clinical setting. More hours than this will take away time that should be spent studying

When studying for the math questions, you should:

1. Review math calculation processes such as ratios.
2. Try to visualize an answer after reading the question and before looking at the answers provided.
3. Does the dosage or amount seem plausible? For example, with pediatric doses, does the child need multiple medicine cups or injections? If so, the dose is probably an overdose. In children, the dose is based on kg of body weight. Graduates should always check with other RNs if they have any questions as to the accuracy of their dosage calculation — especially with children.

Chapter 8

Basic Care and Comfort

Skills Checklist

I am unfamiliar	I am somewhat familiar	I am completely familiar	Skill
			Assist client with activities of daily living
			Provide palliative care
			Conduct an accurate calorie count
			Monitor client for dehydration and over-hydration
			Care for the client with a prosthetic limb
			Assess client's swallowing ability
			Insert, maintain, and remove a nasogastric tube
			Apply anti-embolism stockings

			Obtain client's height and weight
			Irrigate the client's bladder
			Provide incontinence care
			Insert, maintain, and remove a urinary catheter in a man, woman, and child
			Provide post-mortem care in the hospital and home-care setting.
			Care for a client with a traction device
			Care for client with osto-my appliance (urostomy, colostomy, ileostomy)
			Perform cast care
			Irrigate the client's eye or ear
			Care for a client using a sequential compression device
			Assess a client's gait, mo-tor strength, and overall mobility
			Feed client via tube feed-ing
			Provide client education regarding walking with a cane, crutches, or walker

Terms to Understand

I am unfamiliar	I am somewhat familiar	I am completely familiar	Term
			Body Mass Index
			Complementary and alternative therapies
			Food/medication interactions
			Non-pharmacological pain management
			Pain rating scale.
			Proper body alignment
			Special diets

Non-Pharmacological Pain Management

Complete the following quiz to test your knowledge of non-pharmacological pain management techniques.

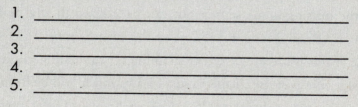

Quick Quiz #6

Can you name five non-pharmacological pain management techniques that you can utilize for your client?

1. _____

2. _____

3. _____

4. _____

5. _____

Complementary or Alternative Therapies

Smart Strategies

- Be aware that the general feeling gathered from the NCLEX developers is that complementary or alternative treatment methods are acceptable and to be encouraged.

Clients frequently seek out complementary and alternative therapies. Some of these are helpful, some are innocuous, and some are harmful. Determine why the client has explored these therapies. Common reasons include:

- It is less expensive than traditional care.
- They are suspicious of physicians, medicine, or "the establishment."
- A friend or family member tried it with success.
- It sounds less invasive than medications or surgery.
- They wish to use these therapies to complement traditional care.
- Their religious beliefs are congruent with an alternative therapy.
- Their religious beliefs forbid standard medical treatment.

Instituting Music Therapy

Music therapy can relax and lift the spirit of the client. It is frequently used in the nursing-home setting but can be utilized in any health-care setting. It is advantageous if one knows the type of music preferred by the client. If this is unknown, either soothing or stimulating music can be played, depending on the client's needs. Ideally, music will be from the era of the client's teens or twenties. Music is generally played from a radio near the client, and earphones are occasionally used. The client's hearing status should be taken into account when determining the appropriate volume level. Music therapy sessions generally last from 30 minutes to two hours, and are administered several days a week. A client's heart rate and blood pressure may be checked before and after the therapy sessions as an objective method of determining efficacy.

Instituting Relaxation Therapy

During relaxation therapy, the therapist creates a soothing environment of appropriate temperature and quiet noise level. The client is placed in a comfortable position and is encouraged to meditate or think of a peaceful scenario. The client may also be encouraged to think healing thoughts or to concentrate on their breathing and muscle relaxation. Light massage may be utilized. Relaxation therapy sessions generally last from 30 minutes to one hour and occur one or more times per week. Music may be added to the sessions.

Complementary or Alternative Therapies Generally Considered Helpful or Innocuous

The following therapies are generally considered safe:

- Chiropractic therapy
- Acupuncture
- Acupressure
- Magnet therapy (innocuous)
- Relaxation methods such as meditation and yoga
- Reiki

Complementary or Alternative Therapies Generally Considered Harmful or Risky

The following therapies are generally considered unsafe.

- Psychic surgery
- Surgery performed in Third-World countries

- Drugs that have not been approved by the FDA
- High-dose supplements
- Unregulated herbs

Any complementary or alternative therapy that is used in place of standard medical treatment can be harmful.

The client's physician should be made aware of any alternative therapies used by the client. The nurse should discuss the dangers of harmful alternative therapies with clients who are utilizing them or considering them.

Mobility and Immobility

Smart Strategies
- For the NCLEX, make sure you are familiar with the different body positions, their names, and the appropriate circumstance for each.

- Understand that clients need to be repositioned frequently and always kept in proper body alignment.

Positioning

Turn the bedridden client every two hours during the day and night. This should alternate left side, right side, and back, unless contraindicated. Good skin care and massage to bony prominences must be diligently performed to avoid skin breakdown. Use pillows for comfort and to maintain proper body alignment. Side-lying clients may need a pillow up against their back for support, and the arm may also need support.

Activity and Mobility

Keep clients as active as possible through walks (assisted, if necessary) and time spent in a chair. Utilize principles of active and passive range of motion. Encourage all clients to remain as active as possible to reduce the risk of skin breakdown, decreased strength, lung problems, and depression.

Safe Transfers from Bed to Chair or Bedside Commode

The nurse must know how to safely transfer a client from his bed to other places. Client safety should be foremost, with the nurse's safety addressed by having adequate help to move the client and applying ergonomic principles.

General Principles of Anti-Embolism Stockings

Anti-embolism stockings are appropriate for the postoperative client, the client who has just suffered a myocardial infarction, and the client who must remain in bed for an extended period of time. Many other types of clients also benefit from anti-embolism stockings. The following steps should be taken when applying anti-embolism stockings.

1. It is important to determine that the stockings are the correct size for the client.
2. Take one stocking and insert your hand until your hand is at the foot.
3. Holding the heel pocket, turn the stocking inside out.
4. Place over the client's foot and pull until heel is in heel pocket.
5. Continue to pull stocking on until just below knee for knee-high stockings or until gusset is at the level of the femoral artery for thigh-high stockings.
6. Pull the stocking at the toe to make sure the toes are comfortable.
7. Ensure that stocking is not bunched or overly tight.
8. Repeat with other stocking.
9. Place non-skid shoes on client. Do not allow client to walk without non-skid shoes due to the risk of falling.

General Principles of Sequential Compression Devices

Sequential compression devices are designed to avoid deep-vein thrombosis and lower extremity peripheral edema during periods of client immobility. The device applies squeezing pressure to the leg from lower to higher to promote venous return. It may squeeze at three to ten different places along the leg. The following steps should be taken to apply and maintain sequential compression devices.

- Apply the device to one leg through attached Velcro. Secure at each area with Velcro. The device should be snug, but not overly tight.

- Repeat with other leg.

- Set the machine as ordered and turn on. Settings may include total time in use, time between compressions, and amount of pressure applied.

- Remain with the client for several minutes to determine that no problems exist, such as extreme discomfort or a malfunction of the equipment.

Caring for a Pressure Ulcer

It is necessary to be familiar with the care of a pressure, or decubitus, ulcer. Many treatments exist depending on the area and grade of the ulcer. It is imperative to not allow the ulcer to become infected. The ulcer is measured at each treatment to determine if it is improving.

Caring for a Skin Rash

It is important to know the cause of a skin rash. It can be topical or part of a systemic issue, and it may or may not be contagious. Treatment frequently consists of a cream, ointment, lotion, or spray. The client must be discouraged from scratching the area. Rashes may itch, burn, hurt, or not have any feeling at all. An obvious rash can be embarrassing to a client.

Caring for an Incision

The nurse should know how to provide basic care for an incision. The goals are to promote healing, prevent infection, and prevent it opening.

Caring for a External Fistula

The nurse must know how to care for an external fistula, as well as the common causes of a fistula.

Caring for a Skin Graft

The nurse should be aware of the basics of caring for a fresh skin graft.

Non-Pharmacological Comfort Interventions

The nurse can aid in the client's healing by performing actions that do not include pharmacological agents. These actions include:

- Massage
- Warm bath
- Quiet conversation
- Assistance with problem-solving

Using the Pain Scale

Each facility may have its own pain scale, but a general rule is that pain is ranked from zero to ten, with ten being the worst pain imaginable. A happy/sad face scale is frequently used for children or adults who do not understand the number system. The purpose of the scale is to attempt to standardize the description of pain better than words such as "a little bit" or "a lot." This allows the nurse to know, for example, that the massage or the medication brought the pain from a nine to a three.

Non-verbal Signs of Pain

The nurse must be careful to assess pain in clients who are unable to articulate. Grimacing and wincing are good indicators of some level of pain, as are moans, screams, and groans. The nurse must do her best to find a way to communicate with the client to determine his pain level and treat it appropriately.

Nutrition and Oral Hydration

The nurse must understand the basics of human nutrition for all ages. All people need protein, carbohydrates, fats, vitamins, minerals, and water. The number of calories needed per day is dependent on the client's height, weight, age, health condition, and exercise level. Clients recovering from injury may have higher requirements. Clients who cannot meet their caloric needs through oral intake must be assisted via nasogastric tube, gastric tube, duodenum tube, or intravenously.

Clients with a small deficit in nutrition can be assisted through supplemental drinks, such as Ensure Plus®, that contain a high number of calories and balanced nutrition. These are frequently administered to nursing-home clients who do not eat their meals properly.

Client and family education must include the requirements needed for the client. Families may need specific information on cooking and food production. The nurse should discuss the client's needs and ask questions to ascertain that the family understands the instructions. Ideally, she will leave literature for later reference.

Nutritional Requirements

The table below lists the nutritional requirements for specified age groups. These calories are to be consumed on a daily basis.

Estimated Calories Needed by Gender, Age, and Activity Level				
Gender	Age (Years)	Sedentary	Moderately Active	Active
Child	2 - 3	1,000	1,000 - 1,400	1,000 - 1,400
Female	4 - 8	1,200	1,400 - 1,600	1,400 - 1,800
	9 - 13	1,600	1,600 - 2,000	1,800 - 2,200
	14 - 18	1,800	2,000	2,400
	19 - 30	2,000	2,000 - 2,200	2,400
	31 - 50	1,800	2,000	2,400
	51+	1,600	1,800	2,000 - 2,200
Male	4 - 8	1,400	1,400 - 1,600	1,600 - 2,000
	9 - 13	1,800	1,800 - 2,200	2,000 - 2,600
	14 - 18	2,200	2,400 - 2,800	2,800 - 3,200
	19 - 30	2,400	2,600 - 2,800	3,000
	31 - 50	2,200	2,400 - 2,600	2,800 - 3,000
	51+	2,000	2,200 - 2,400	2,400 - 2,800

Source: http://www.health.gov/Dietaryguidelines/dga2005/toolkit/healthfacts/nutrition.htm

Nutritional Requirements for Client's with Specific Circumstances

There are specific nutritional requirements for pregnant and lactating females. Their specific needs include:

- Foods high in protein, folic acid, iron, and calcium should be consumed by pregnant and lactating women.
- A prenatal vitamin should be taken daily by pregnant women.
- A multivitamin should be taken by lactating women.
- Alcohol should be avoided.
- Excessive caffeine should be avoided.

The chart below lists the specific caloric requirements for pregnant and lactating females. These additional calories are to be consumer per day on top of the recommended caloric intake listed in the previous chart.

Trimester	Extra Calories
1st	Same as non-pregnant
2nd	200
3rd	400
Lactating	300-500

There are specific nutritional requirements for diabetic clients. These clients should consume 1,200 to 2,000 calories per day, according to physician's orders. These clients should avoid concentrated sweets and goods with a high-glycemic index.

There are specific nutritional requirements for clients with heart disease. These clients should consume the same calories as a client without heart disease, unless weight loss is needed. These clients should eat a low-fat, low-cholesterol diet. They may also need to eliminate caffeine from their diet.

There are specific nutritional requirements for malnourished clients. Clients who are considered to be malnourished should increase their caloric intake by 25 to 50 percent more than a normal diet. The malnourished client should be sure to get enough protein in their diet and eat the proper amount of fats. They should take a multivitamin supplement and avoid excess alcohol.

There are specific nutritional requirements for clients with major burns. These clients should increase their caloric intake by 50 to 100 percent. They also will need extra protein, vitamin C, and zinc to aid in healing.

Palliative and Comfort Care

End-of-Life Physical Symptom Management

For the NCLEX, test takers should know how to provide symptom management for each of the following common end-of-life symptoms.

- Pain
- Delirium and agitation
- Dyspnea
- Respiratory secretions
- Anorexia, nausea, and vomiting
- Constipation

Personal Hygiene

All clients need proper personal hygiene. It is the responsibility of the nurse to see that each of her clients receives basic hygiene care, including a bath, shower or sponge bath, hair washing, hair combing, oral care, teeth brushing or denture care, and proper toileting or incontinence care. If the client requires assistance with these activities, the nurse can delegate this care for stable clients.

How to Give a Sponge Bath

The nurse should be familiar with the basics of giving a sponge bath. While technique varies, some of the basic principles follow.

- Respect the client's privacy and only uncover them as needed. Keep them safe from being seen by others.
- Keep them warm during and after the bath.
- Wash cleaner areas first.
- Do not leave soap on a client's skin.
- Do not over-scrub fragile skin.
- Moisturize skin after the bath.

How to Assist the Client with a Bath

Allow the client to perform all the tasks he can himself. However, be mindful of safety and stand nearby when needed. Have all the needed equipment handy so it is not necessary to leave the client at an inopportune time. If the client is bathing himself, ensure that the call light is in reach, or stay close enough to hear the client is he needs assistance. Give the client as much privacy as possible.

Assisting the Client with a Shower

Be familiar with the basics of showering a client. For the NCLEX, be prepared for safety questions, infection control questions, and self-esteem questions.

Assisting the Client with a Hair Shampoo

As a general rule, elderly clients may suffer from dry hair due to their bodies producing fewer natural oils. Be familiar with the basic techniques of shampooing hair in the bathtub, shower, and improvising in bed. Be aware that clients can have a stroke if their neck is hyper-extended for a lengthy period of time. Use the time shampooing to look for cancerous lesions in the scalp.

How to Dress the Client

Allow the client to pick her clothes and dress herself as much as possible. Consider safety concerns such as safe shoes for walking.

How to Groom the Client

The nurse must prioritize daily grooming for the client. Each client should have his face washed, teeth cleaned, and hair brushed for the day, in addition to other grooming tasks.

How to Perform Daily Oral Care for the Client

Be familiar with performing oral care on the client who can and cannot assist. Know how to clean and store dentures. Be aware that dentures are often accidentally discarded in the hospital setting.

How to Assist the Incontinent Client

Maintain the dignity of the client at all times. Gather necessary materials, wash your hands, don clean gloves, pull curtains for privacy, and explain to the client what you are about to do. Open the soiled brief, clean the client with wipes or a warm washcloth front to back, washing, rinsing, and drying if possible as you remove the soiled brief. Place a clean brief and use barrier creams or ointment if needed. Reposition the client, adjust the side rails if they have been moved, dispose of the soiled brief, remove your gloves, and wash your hands. Place water in reach, assure that the call bell is in reach, adjust the lights if necessary, and ask the client if she needs anything.

How to Perform Post-Mortem Care in the Health-Care Setting

It is necessary to be familiar with the basics of post-mortem care in the hospital and long-term care setting. The nurse must take into account the client and family's religious and cultural wishes as well.

How to Perform Post-Mortem Care in the Field (Including the Client Home)

If a death is anticipated, the nurse must have the proper supplies on hand to perform basic post mortem care. She must also know who to contact when death occurs.

Rest and Sleep

Adult clients need about eight hours of sleep each night. This can be difficult to achieve in the hospital setting, when physicians, lab workers, and X-ray technicians come and go at all hours. Special accommodations are occasionally made for clients who are staying in the hospital on a long-term basis to allow them to remain undisturbed during the night. All clients must be checked in the acute-care setting at least every 30 minutes and in the psychiatric and nursing-home setting every hour. It is possible for the nurse to check on the client without waking them.

Clients with insomnia may receive pharmacological intervention while in the hospital. This can lead to falls and disorientation, and these clients will require extra monitoring when the medication is initiated. Non-pharmacological interventions include a massage, warm bath, relaxing book, or quiet music.

CASE STUDY: DEBORAH L. FREYMAN R.N., M.S.N., M.A.

National Park Community College
Hot Springs, Arkansas 71913
dfreyman@npcc.edu

Ms. Freyman is a member of the ADN nursing faculty at
National Park Community College in Hot Springs, Arkansas.

Characteristics of students that are successful on NCLEX are those who:

- Do well with test taking in nursing school
- Study the content that is provided and apply the information to situations in clinical
- Practice NCLEX style questions whenever possible
- Have learned test-taking strategies throughout their nursing school
- Are not necessarily the best and the brightest, but have learned to apply critical thinking to the testing situation
- Have learned to control their testing anxieties
- Maintain a positive mind set when taking tests
- Have learned not to read into what the stem is asking

Characteristics of students that fail the NCLEX the first time are students who:

- Scraped by with a passing grade every semester
- Are unable to think critically in the testing situation
- Do not apply theory to clinical
- Have not learned successful testing strategies
- Have not learned to control test-taking anxieties
- Do not do extra NCLEX-style questions
- Read into the stem of the question, moving them away from the right answer

Four weeks prior to the NCLEX, you should:

- Ensure you have purchased a good NCLEX review book
- Divide out the book so that you cover all the questions by the time you test.
- Go over NCLEX questions every night. Ensure you review what you missed the previous night so you retain the new information.
- If you are driving to the test, have your tires checked to reduce the chance of a flat tire on testing day.

CASE STUDY: DEBORAH L. FREYMAN R.N., M.S.N., M.A.

On the morning of the NCLEX:

- Eat a good breakfast.
- Practice stress reduction techniques.
  Maintain a positive frame of mind
- Make sure you give yourself plenty of time to drive to
  the testing place so you are not hurried or late.

I believe students should review all the material to ensure it is fresh in their minds. I think using a NCLEX study guide will help reinforce the information they know and understand as well as identify areas they need to brush up on. There is no way nursing school can cover all the content that NCLEX questions may come from. Using a reliable, resourceful, and easy to follow study guide can assist the student in filling in the gaps. For length of study time, I think six hours at a time is the maximum for a well-structured learning environment.

NCLEX is application. The more the students can apply the information they have learned to real life situations, the more they remember. Working can help their confidence by increasing the amount of information they are able to apply. When the light bulb goes on for students, they are likely to feel more confident that they understand the information.

Students tend to read into the stem to help them figure out what is being asked. When students do this, they very frequently choose the wrong answer. Students need to practice NCLEX-style questions and not read into what is being asked.

I believe critical-thinking skills are both learned and innate. Some students just think critically without difficulty. They have demonstrated this ability throughout their schooling. Then there are the other students who have to learn to critical thinking. It is harder, but it can be done with practice. This second type of student really benefits from reviewing NCLEX style questions as much as possible.

For the math questions, trust in the math system you have been taught. Practice math questions before taking the NCLEX. Practice on the computer using the calculator to become familiar with it before testing.

Chapter 9

Pharmacological and Parenteral Therapies

Skills Checklist

I am unfamiliar	I am somewhat familiar	I am completely familiar	Skill
			Evaluate client need for "PRN" medications, including pain medication
			Evaluate medication orders for safety and efficacy
			Administer and monitor blood and blood products (Administer – RNs only, Monitor – RNs and LPNs)
			Prepare and administer oral medications
			Prepare and administer sublingual medications
			Prepare and administer buccal medications

			Prepare and administer intravenous medications (RNs only)
			Prepare and administer vaginal medications
			Prepare and administer intradermal medications
			Prepare and administer subcutaneous medications
			Prepare and administer intramuscular medications
			Prepare and administer rectal medications
			Prepare and administer otic medications
			Prepare and administer ophthalmic medications
			Prepare and administer topical medications
			Prepare and administer nasal medications
			Prepare and administer medications for inhalation
			Insert, maintain, and remove an intravenous line (Insert and remove – RNs only)
			Insert, maintain, and remove a peripherally inserted central catheter (PICC line) (RNs only)
			Maintain an epidural infusion (RNs only)

			Be able to count and waste narcotics per governmental and facility policy
			Access venous access devices (RNs only)
			Be able to administer sliding scale insulin
			Give fluids and medications via intravenous infusion (intermittent and continuous)
			Calculate IV drip rates
			Name and identify the veins appropriate for intravenous therapy
			Administer total parenteral nutrition (TPN) (RNs only)
			Give medications via IV piggy-back

Terms to Understand

I am unfamiliar	I am somewhat familiar	I am completely familiar	Term
			Contraindications to medications and medication incompatibilities
			Hickman catheter
			Port-a-cath catheter
			Side effects and adverse effects to medications
			Side effects and adverse effects to total parenteral nutrition (TPN)

			Reactions to blood products
			Six "rights" of medication administration
			Titration of medications

Blood and Blood Products

Smart Strategies

- Be prepared for questions about blood administration to appear on the test. You may not have had adequate experience with this in clinicals and may need to refresh your memory on both the method and the many problems that can occur during and after administration.

General Principles of Blood Administration

All human blood is type O, A, B, or AB. It is either Rh-positive or Rh-negative. Blood is typed and cross-matched prior to administration, and packed red blood cells and whole blood must be administered within 4 hours. Medications are frequently given prior to blood administration, including Benadryl® and Tylenol®.

The nurse may administer the following types of blood:

- Whole blood (infrequently used)
- Packed red blood cells
- Platelets
- Fresh frozen plasma
- Other types for special needs

Procedure for Hanging Blood or Blood Products (RNs only)

The nurse must know the procedures for hanging blood.

Quick Quiz #7

- What size catheter is used to administer blood products to an adult?

  _____

- Name 5 reactions to monitor for during blood administration.
  1. _____
  2. _____
  3. _____
  4. _____
  5. _____

- Name two reasons why clients may need blood.
  1. _____
  2. _____

- Name two reasons why clients may need platelets.
  1. _____
  2. _____

Monitoring the Client During Blood Infusion

It is necessary to understand the basic principles involved in monitoring a client during a blood transfusion.

Evaluating the Client Response to Blood Infusion

The nurse must be able to evaluate the client response to a blood infusion, including expected and unexpected responses.

Lab Work Values to Expect Post-Infusion

Following a blood transfusion, anticipate blood lab work to move closer to normal levels. Generally, it is necessary to give blood until levels are out of the panic range. Do not expect to continue to give blood until labs are in normal range.

Emergency Management of Adverse Effects of Blood Administration

The nurse must be familiar with managing adverse effects when administering blood.

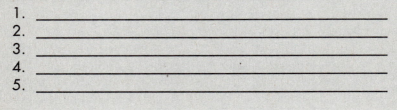

Quick Quiz #8

Name five things you must do before administering blood.

1. _____
2. _____
3. _____
4. _____
5. _____

Central Venous Access Devices (RNs only)

The nurse must be familiar with the basics of the various common central venous access devices.

How to Insert a PICC Line (RNs only)

It is imperative a nurse be fully trained before attempting to insert a PICC line. She must be monitored at least once throughout the procedure prior to inserting PICC lines on her own. Be aware of the basic procedures to inserting a PICC line.

Equipment Needed

The nurse should be able to identify the equipment needed to insert a PICC line.

Setting Up the Sterile Field

A sterile field is required for inserting a PICC line. Be sure to understand the basics of setting up the sterile field, including masks for the client and everyone participating.

Caring for a PICC Line

PICC line care varies by facility. It must be flushed at intervals and the site must be kept clean.

Caring for and Accessing a Port-A-Cath (RNs only)

The nurse must understand the basic principles of caring for a client with a port-a-cath. It is necessary to know how to access a port-a-cath for infusions and other needs.

Caring for and Accessing a Hickman Catheter (RNs only)

The nurse must understand how to care for a client with a Hickman catheter. It is necessary to know how to safely access a Hickman catheter.

Expected Effects and Outcomes of Medications Administered

The nurse must understand the expected effect of every medication that she administers. If she is unfamiliar with a prescribed medication, she must research it prior to administration. She must also educate the client on the expected effects of any new medications.

Medication Administration

Smart Strategies

- You may have learned of the "five rights of medication administration" while in nursing school. The NCLEX developers recognize six "rights," and you should answer the questions accordingly.

- Be prepared for questions related to how to administer medications. While the majority of medications are given by mouth, the test will test your knowledge of the other routes, as well.

Conversion Chart

It is necessary to be familiar with common equivalents when performing calculations on the NCLEX.

5 ml	1 teaspoon
15 ml	1 tablespoon
3 teaspoons	1 tablespoon
30 ml	1 ounce
2 tablespoons	1 ounce
1,000 ml	1 liter
1 grain	60 mg
1,000 mg	1 gram
1,000 grams	1 kilogram
1 kilogram	2.2 pounds

The Six Rights of Medication Administration

The six rights of medication administration include:

1. The nurse must administer the correct drug, as the names of many drugs are similar. The nurse must also be sure to give immediate release and not sustained release. Some facilities require two nurses

to check certain drugs, such as insulin, to be certain the correct drug is given.

2. The nurse must administer the right dose. The primary health-care provider's order must be legible and make sense for the client. Many facilities allow a 10 percent discrepancy in the dose. For example, if a physician orders 300 milligrams of aspirin for the client, and the nurse only has 325 milligram tablets available, it would be acceptable to administer what is available at many facilities.

3. The nurse must administer to the right client. Facilities vary in how they identify clients, but armbands are one of the safest methods. If necessary, ask a client their name. Do not say, "Are you John Doe?"

4. The nurse must administer the medication at the right time. Facilities differ in the amount of time the nurse has to administer a routine medication. Hospitals frequently allow a leeway of no more than 30 minutes before or 30 minutes after a drug is due for it to be administered in a timely manner. Nursing homes frequently allow an hour either way. Other medications must be given prior to, with, or after meals in order to be effective. PRN medications will have rules as to how often they can be given.

5. The nurse must administer the medication via the right route. Orders that do not explain any route are generally intended to be given orally (PO). Ask the pharmacist if necessary. It is imperative that medications be given by the correct route, as a dose that is appropriate orally may be lethal when given intramuscularly or intravenously.

6. The nurse must record the medication administration with the right documentation. This is a relatively new "right" and indicates

the importance of keeping a clear record of administration. If this is not done, a client can be overdosed on a PRN medication, or tomorrow's staff may not know how many milligrams of Coumadin the client was given.

Maintaining a Medication Administration Record

Regular Medications

Medication administration records vary widely according to the healthcare setting. The following are general rules on recording the administration of regular medication.

- The record must indicate every routine medication given. An administration time will be delineated.

- The nurse will place her initials on the record to acknowledge the administration, holding of the medication, or client refusal. Her full name must be elsewhere to indicate whose initials are on the record.

- Both prescription and non-prescription medications must be recorded.

- The medication administration record must be checked for accuracy on a consistent basis. At many facilities, routine orders expire and must be rewritten.

PRN Medications

The following are general rules for recording as-needed medications on the medication administration record.

- The record must indicate every as-needed medication given. The date and time are always recorded along with the nurse's initials.

- Both prescription and over-the-counter PRN medications must be recorded.

- Frequently, the reason for the administration is also recorded. Example: Acetaminophen is given for a headache with a pain rating of 6.

- Frequently, a follow-up is documented an hour (or some other specified time) later. Example: Acetaminophen is given for a headache. One hour later, the headache pain rating is a 1.

How to Phone in Prescriptions to a Pharmacy

To phone in a prescription to a pharmacy, have the following information available:

- Client's name
- Client's date of birth
- Name of drug
- Dosage instructions (Example: Take two 20 mg tablets three times a day with meals for ten days.)
- Total number of pills (or other) to dispense
- Number of refills
- Physician's name
- For controlled substances, the physician's DEA number will be needed. C-II controlled substances cannot be called in. A written prescription is required.
- In some circumstances, the client's address or insurance information may be needed.

Oral Administration

Oral administration is the most common method to administer drugs. Tablets, capsules, and liquids can be administered orally. It is important to be certain the client actually swallows the medication. In pediatric or psychiatric settings, the nurse may be expected to check the mouth of the client to determine compliance.

Some pills cannot be crushed or divided. Pills that fit this description include:

- Enteric-coated tablets
- Time-delayed tablets (frequently contain CR, ER, LR, or SR in the name)
- Drugs that have teratogenic or carcinogenic potential when crushed

Ask the pharmacist before crushing or dividing a tablet that is not scored.

Buccal Administration

These medications should be placed in between the cheek and the lower gum. It may be in solid form, or painted or sprayed on. This route allows for fast absorption of the medication.

Sublingual Administration

Sublingual administration can include small tablets and liquids. Reasons for sublingual administration include the fast absorption rate and the avoidance of the gastrointestinal tract.

Inhalation Administration

The nurse is expected to provide inhalation treatments in many settings. Be aware of the basic methodology of inhalation administration.

Nasal Administration

Be familiar with the administration of medication via nasal administration. Be aware that clients occasionally use nasal sprays more often than prescribed. Instruct clients of the reasons to follow the prescriptive orders of nasally administered drugs.

Ophthalmic Administration

It is necessary to know how to administer both eye drops and ointments.

Otic Administration

The following procedures should be followed when administering medication:

1. Eardrops should be room temperature or slightly warm, if indicated.
2. Have client lie with affected ear upward. Alternatively, have client sit with affected ear upward.
3. Shake bottle if indicated.
4. Grasp pinna and gently pull upward and back for an adult client, or downward and back for a pediatric client under 3 years of age.
5. Visualize the ear canal.
6. Place dropper over ear, not touching the ear canal, and administer the ordered number of drops.
7. Have client stay in place for five minutes.
8. Place sterile cotton in ear canal if indicated.
9. Perform the same procedure for other ear if ordered.

Topical Administration

Patches and Discs

Follow these steps to apply a drug patch or disc:

1. Look for the old patch (if one exists) and remove it.
2. Place the new patch onto clean, intact, non-oily skin in an appropriate place. For a demented client, you may wish to place it on the

back out of reach.

3. Write the date, time, and your initials on the patch.

4. Instruct the client of any special directions to care for the patch (bathing, avoiding sunlight, or how long to leave the patch in place).

Creams, Lotions, and Ointments

Follow these steps to correctly apply creams, lotions, and ointments.

1. Don gloves.

2. Apply a thin or thick layer to the affected area (according to the prescription).

3. Follow instructions as to whether to merely apply or to massage into the skin.

4. Apply a dressing if indicated.

5. Remove gloves and wash hands.

Sprays

Follow these steps to correctly apply sprays:

1. Apply a light coat of spray for two to ten seconds on the area to be treated, being careful to avoid you or the client breathing the fumes. Hold the spray close to the treatment area.

2. Allow the area to dry before putting clothes or bed linens on the area.

Note: Some authorities suggest applying a pair of gloves and washing the area with warm, soapy water, then rinsing and drying prior to administration of topical medications. Remove those gloves and wash hands before following the steps listed above.

Vaginal Administration

Suppositories, creams, and ointments may be administered vaginally. The client is frequently allowed to administer the medication herself with clean hands and a glove if the physician has ordered self-administration.

1. Place client in the Sims' position or the dorsal recumbent position.
2. Wash hands and don gloves.
3. Wash, rinse, and dry the perineum if needed. Remove gloves, wash hands, and apply fresh gloves.
4. Spread labia and administer medication three inches inside the vagina using your finger or an applicator.
5. Remove your finger or applicator from vagina.
6. Apply a pad if necessary for discharge.
7. Instruct client to remain flat in bed for 20 minutes.
8. Clean applicator if applicable.
9. Remove gloves and wash hands.

Rectal Administration

Rectal Suppositories

It is necessary to know how to administer a rectal suppository. Be aware that some suppositories are kept in the refrigerator prior to administration. It is also necessary to know the types of medications that are delivered by suppository.

Rectal Medicinal Enemas

It is necessary to know how to administer a medicinal enema. Be aware of typical amounts given and duration of time held before expelling.

Parenteral Medications

Parenteral administration involves administering medication by needle and syringe.

Be familiar with how to draw up medications from an ampule, a single dose vial, and a multi-dose vial. It is necessary to know how to safely mix medications in a syringe and use a cartridge for injection.

Intradermal Administration

Intradermal injections can be given on the inside forearm, outer aspect of upper arm, chest between clavicle and beginning of breast, or upper back on either side. If no site is mentioned, it is best to use the inner aspect of the forearm. Follow these steps for correctly administering intradermal injections.

1. Wash hands.
2. Prepare medication if needed, using a 1 ml syringe with a 26- or 28-gauge needle.
3. Don gloves.
4. Cleanse the site with an alcohol prep pad and allow to dry.
5. Remove cap and pull skin taut with non-dominant hand.
6. Hold needle with the bevel side up. Insert the needle 1/8 inch just beneath the skin, at a 10- to 15-degree angle.
7. Inject the medication slowly as a bleb forms.
8. Remove the needle as you inserted it.
9. Safely dispose of needle.
10. Do not dab the site unless blood is present. If it is necessary to clean with an alcohol prep pad, do so carefully.
11. Remove gloves and wash hands.
12. Place a circle around the bleb if needed.

Intramuscular Administration

Intramuscular injections can be administered into the deltoid muscle, ventrogluteal muscle, vastus lateralis muscle, dorsogluteal muscle, or rectus femorus muscle. Know the landmarks for each site and the appropriate usage of each site.

The standard administration procedures for administering intramuscular injections are as follows:

1. Wash hands.
2. Prepare medication using a 3 ml syringe and a 21, 22, or 23 gauge needle with a length of 1 inch, 1 ½ inches, or 2 inches. Remember to add .2 ml of air.
3. Place the client in an appropriate position.
4. Don gloves.
5. Cleanse the site with an alcohol prep pad and allow to dry.
6. Remove cap and pull skin taut with non-dominant hand.
7. Insert the needle at a 90 degree angle with your dominant hand.
8. Pull back on the plunger and observe for blood. If no blood appears, push the plunger down to administer the medication.
9. Remove the needle as you inserted it.
10. Safely dispose of needle. Depending on the site of the disposal, perform step 11 first.
11. Cleanse the area with an alcohol prep pad and massage the area or hold firm pressure if massaging is contraindicated.
12. Remove gloves and wash hands.

Quick Quiz #9

It is acceptable/not acceptable to reuse the same needle multiple times on the same client?

Z-track Administration

The nurse must be familiar with the administration of medicine via a Z-track injection. Complete the following quiz to test your knowledge on this procedure.

Quick Quiz #10

True or False Quiz Regarding the Z-track Injection

1. _____ The Z-track can be used for any medication.

2. _____ The Z-track should be used with a 2- or 3-inch needle.

3. _____ The Z-track is known to be more painful than a standard IM injection.

4. _____ You must change needles after drawing up the medication.

5. _____ It is appropriate to draw up .5 ml of air into the syringe.

6. _____ The skin should be pulled laterally and down 1 inch before drug is administered.

7. _____ The needle should be inserted at a 60-degree angle.

8. _____ You should not aspirate for blood when using the Z-track method.

9. _____ The needle should be held in place for ten seconds after the drug is administered.

10. _____ You should massage the area for ten seconds after drug administration.

Subcutaneous Administration

Appropriate subcutaneous injection sites include the side and back aspect of the upper arm, the side of the thighs, on the areas on either side of the umbilicus, and either side of the upper back. These injections must be made into subcutaneous fat. Understand which site to use for each medication and age. The standard administration procedures for administering subcutaneous injections are as follows:

1. Wash hands.
2. Prepare medication using a 2- to 3-ml syringe and a 25-, 26-, or 27-gauge needle with a length of ½ and 7/8 inch long.
3. Place the client in an appropriate position.
4. Don gloves.
5. Cleanse the site with an alcohol prep pad and allow to dry.
6. Remove cap and grasp one inch of fat with your non-dominant hand.
7. Insert the needle at a 45-degree angle with your dominant hand.
8. Pull back on the plunger and observe for blood. If no blood appears, push the plunger down to administer the medication.
9. Remove the needle as you inserted it.
10. Safely dispose of needle. Depending on the site of the disposal, perform step 11 first.
11. Cleanse the area with an alcohol prep pad and massage the area unless heparin was administered.
12. Remove gloves and wash hands.

Quick Quiz #11

The best place to inject subcutaneous heparin is

_____.

Intravenous Administration

"IV Push" Medications (RNs only)

It is necessary to be familiar with the basic rules for IV push medications. In most facilities, intravenous medications will only be administered through an existing intravenous line. Frequently, saline is administered first, followed by the medication, more saline, and sometimes heparin — the type suited for a "heparin lock." The site at which the medication is put into the line is cleansed with alcohol. Follow these basic principles for IV push medications.

- They are generally given slowly, over one to ten minutes. Be sure to follow both physician orders and the rules for administering the particular drug.

- Be certain to use the proper dose for intravenous use. Most drugs require a smaller dose when given intravenously as opposed to other routes.

- Be certain the drug is safe for intravenous administration. When in doubt, read a medical drug reference or call the pharmacist.

- Closely monitor the client during and after administration. Assume the drug may begin to work quickly, and be prepared. For example, a diuretic may cause the client to need to void quickly, and a sedative may cause the client to become drowsy quickly.

- Some intravenous medications should only be given when the client is wearing telemetry. Be aware of which drugs require close cardiac monitoring.

"IV Piggy-Back" Medications

It is necessary to understand the basics of giving an IV piggy-back medication — a medication that is given at the same location IV fluid has been given.

Calculating Drip Rates for Intravenous Medications

For the NCLEX, it is necessary to know how to correctly calculate drip rates for IV medications. IV medications are given via pump if at all possible, but may be given with an inline controller or merely by drip.

How to Insert a Peripheral Intravenous Line (RNs only)

The supplies needed for beginning a peripheral intravenous line will vary by facility, but frequently, facilities have a kit that contains most of the needed supplies. Know the basic rules for IV insertion.

It is necessary to know the appropriate veins for beginning a peripheral intravenous line on an adult and a child. Know where each vein is located. The NCLEX may contain a question that requires test takers to mark the spot where the cannula should be inserted. Bear in mind that dehydration or scarred veins can influence the vein choice in a given client.

How to Monitor and Care for Infiltration, Infection, or other Complications of Intravenous Therapy

Be aware of the signs and symptoms of infiltration and infection at an IV site, including the client's report of excessive pain in the absence of other symptoms.

Quick Quiz #12

Name three problems that may lead to IV infiltration.

1. _____
2. _____
3. _____

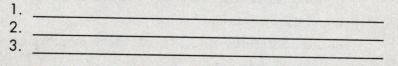

Quick Quiz #13

Name three problems that may lead to IV site infection.

1. _____
2. _____
3. _____

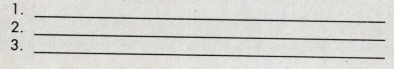

How to Care for an Infiltration

- The IV should be stopped and removed immediately.
- Follow physician orders regarding the placement of a warm or cool compress to the site, depending on the fluid that infiltrated.
- You will usually be ordered to elevate the extremity.
- The site should be checked regularly for at least 48 hours for potential complications.
- Place the replacement IV in another extremity if at all possible.

How to Operate an Infusion Pump

Know the basic principles of operating an infusion pump. Each brand of pump will vary somewhat. Make certain the drip rate is properly calculated. Use an infusion pump whenever possible, and do not bypass it. Bypassing the pump can lead to an uncontrolled delivery rate or a large amount of air going into the client's bloodstream. This is more critical for a pediatric client or when the IV line is going through a central catheter.

General Principles of Parenteral Fluid Therapy

- **Hypertonic Solutions**: Be able to name common hypertonic solutions and their indications.
- **Hypotonic Solutions**: Be able to name common hypotonic solutions and their indications.
- **Isotonic Solutions**: Be able to name common isotonic solutions and their indications.
- **Monitoring for Fluid Overload**: Know the symptoms of fluid overload and what to do when it occurs.

Take the following Quick Quiz to test your knowledge of fluid overload.

Quick Quiz #14

Name two categories of clients who are especially susceptible to fluid overload.

1. _____

2. _____

Epidural Administration of Medications

While you are not expected to know how to administer epidural medications, you should be aware of the issues involved in caring for a client receiving epidural medications.

Pharmacological Agents and Actions

- Know the indications, side effects, adverse effects, and contraindications for all the major drugs.
- Be able to recognize a dangerous dose of a drug; for example, morphine sulfate, 50 milligrams IV.
- Know the different categories of drugs and the major uses of each.
- Know the special nursing considerations for each common medication.

The nurse must have a basic understanding of all common prescription and non-prescription medications. She must be able to identify their pharmacological actions.

In addition to being familiar with the drugs below, it is necessary to understand the different categories of drugs, such as alpha blockers and ACE inhibitors. Know their indications, the means in which they work, and any important dosing information.

Below, you will find a list of common medications that you should be familiar with. The brand name of the medicine is indicated, as well as the generic name of the medicine contained within the brand name (in parentheses).

Analgesics and Anti-Inflammatory Medications

- Advil®, Motrin® (Ibuprofen)
- Aspirin
- Bextra®
- Celebrex™
- Codeine
- Darvocet® (Propoxyphene and acetaminophen)
- Demerol® (Meperidine)
- Dilaudid™ (Hydromorphone)
- Duragesic® (Fentanyl)
- Hydrocortisone
- Indocin® (Indomethacin)
- Methadone
- Morphine
- Percocet® and Oxycontin (Oxycodone)
- Prednisolone
- Prednisone
- Tylenol™ (Acetaminophen)
- Ultram® (Tramadol)
- VICODIN, LORTAB® (Hydrocodone bitartrate and acetaminophen)
- Vioxx™

Anti-Infectives

- AMOXICILLIN
- AMPICILLIN
- AZT, RETROVIR (ZIDOVUDINE)
- Bactrim, Septra® (Trimethoprim, sulfamethoxazole)
- CELCOR (Cefaclor)
- CIPRO (Ciprofloxacin)
- DIFLUCAN (Fluconazole)
- Erythromycin
- FLAGYL (Metronidazole)
- Gentamicin (Garamycin)
- INH (Isoniazid)
- Keflex® (Cephalexin)
- LEVAQUIN
- PENICILLIN
- TAMIFLU (Oseltamivir Phosphate)
- VANCOCIN (Vancomycin)
- Vibramycin® (Doxycycline)
- ZOVIRAX (Acyclovir)
- Zithromax® (Azithromycin)

Anticoagulants

- COUMADIN (Warfarin)
- Heparin

Cancer Medications

- 5-FU (Fluorouracil)
- Adriamycin (Doxorubicin)
- Cytoxan (Cyclophosphamide)
- Methotrexate
- Nolvadex® (Tamoxifen)
- Taxol® (Paclitaxel)
- VINCRISTINE

Cardiovascular Medications

- ACCUPRIL
- ALDACTONE
- ALTACE®
- BUMEX®
- CAPOTEN® (Captopril)
- COREG®
- CRESTOR
- DIOVAN®
- Hydrochlorothiazide
- HYTRIN®
- HYZAAR®
- INDERAL® (Propranolol)
- lISORDIL
- LANOXIN®, DIGITEK (Digoxin)
- LASIX (Furosemide)
- LIDOCANE®
- LIPITOR®
- Lisinopril
- LOPRESSOR®
- LOTENSIN®
- CARDIZEM® (Diltiazem Hydrochloride)
- CATAPRES® (Clonidine)
- CORDARONE®, PACERONE® (Amiodarone)
- COZAAR®
- NORVASC ®
- PLAVIX®
- PRAVACHOL®
- PROCARDIA® (Nifedipine)
- Quinidine
- RYTHMOL®
- TAMBOCOR®
- TENORMIN™ (Atenolol)
- Toprol (Metoprolol)
- Triamterene
- VASOTEC® (Enalapril maleate)
- Verapamil Hydrochloride
- ZOCOR®

Central Nervous System and Neurological Medications

- ARICEPT®
- COGENTIN®
- DILANTIN® (Phenytoin)
- Levodopa
- LUMINAL® (Phenobarbital)
- NEURONTIN® (Gabapentin)
- RITALIN®
- SINEMET® (Carbidopa/Levodopa)
- TEGRETOL® (Carbamazepine)

Diabetic Medications

- ACTOS™
- Avandia®
- GLUCOPHAGE® (Metformin hydrochloride)
- GLUCAGON
- GLUCOTROL® (Glipizide)
- Insulin (All common types)

Gastrointestinal Medications

- ACIPHEX™
- ANTIVERT® (Meclizine)
- BENTYL®
- CARAFATE®
- COMPAZINE™
- IMMODIUM
- NEXIUM™
- PANCREASE®
- PANCREATIN
- PEPCID® (Famotidine)
- PHENEGRAN (Promethazine)
- PREVACID®
- PRILOSEC®
- PROTONIX®
- TAGAMET® (Cimetidine)
- Zantac® (Ranitidine)

Genitourinary Medications

- CIALIS
- DETROL™
- FLOMAX®
- LEVITRA®
- MACROBID® (Nitrofurantoin)
- VIAGRA®

Hormones and Women's Health Medications

- ACTONEL®
- BONIVA®
- DEPO-PROVERA™
- Estradiol Patch
- EVISTA®
- Fosomax
- LEVOXYL®
- Norplant
- ORTHO-CEPT®
- ORTHO TRI CYCLEN®
- ORTHO NOVUM®
- PREMARIN®
- SYNTHROID®, LEVOTHROID®, LEVOTHYROXINE®
- Thyroid

Musculoskeletal Medications

- Baclofen
- Colchicine
- FLEXERIL®
- ROBAXIN®
- Soma (Carisoprodol)
- ZYLOPRIM® (Allopurinol)

Psychiatric Medications

- ADDERALL®
- AMBIEN®
- ATIVAN® (Lorazepam)
- CELEXA™ (Citalopram)
- CONCERTA™
- CYMBALTA®
- DEPAKOTE®
- DESYREL® (Trazadone)
- EFFEXOR®
- ELAVIL® (Amitriptyline)
- GEODON™
- HALDOL® (Haloperidol)
- KLONOPIN® (Clonazepam)
- LEXAPRO™ (Escitalopram)
- LIBRIUM™
- Lithium
- PAXIL®
- PROZAC® (Fluoxetine hydrochloride)
- RESTORIL® (Temazepam)
- RISPERDAL® (Risperidone)
- SEROQUEL®
- Sonata
- VALIUM® (Diazepam)
- VISTARIL® (Hydroxyzine)
- WELLBUTRIN®, Zyban
- XANAX® (Alprazolam)
- ZOLOFT®
- ZYPREXA®

226 Ways to Score Higher on Your NCLEX

Respiratory and Allergy Medications

- Advair Discus
- ALLEGRA™
- ATROVENT® (Ipratropium Bromide)
- Brethine
- COMBIVENT®
- Cromolyn Sodium
- FLONASE®
- NASONEX®
- PROVENTIL®, Ventolin (Albuterol sulfate)
- SEREVENT®
- SINGULAIR®
- THEO-DUR® (Theophylline)
- ZYRTEC®

Topical, Otic, and Opthalmic Medications

- CORTISPORIN®
- Timolol

Vaccines, Vitamins and Miscellaneous Medications

- ANTABUSE® (Disulfiram)
- Cyanocobalamin
- Ferrous Sulfate
- Folic Acid
- K-lor (Potassium)
- NARCAN® (Naloxone hydrochloride)
- Nystatin
- Predinisone
- Vitamin B12

Common Medication Contraindications

It is necessary to be familiar with all common contraindications to commonly used medications.

Pharmacological Interactions

Drugs frequently interact with each other. It is necessary to be able to identify well-known interactions.

Common Incompatibilities of Medications

Teaching Clients about Incompatibilities and Interactions of Prescribed and Over-the-Counter Medications

Clients must be educated about interactions of medications, including prescribed, over-the-counter, and complementary treatments.

The nurse should be familiar with the list of drugs that cannot be taken with grapefruit juice.

Pharmacological Pain Management

Smart Strategies
- Pain management is a big part of medical care. Be prepared to answer questions on the NCLEX regarding both chronic and acute pain management.

As-Needed Pain Medication versus Continuous Pain Management

Understand the basics of choosing between continuous pain management and intermittent medication use. Continuous pain management is commonly found in:

- Cancer care
- Palliative care
- End stage chronic obstructive pulmonary disease
- Burn care

Intermittent medication use is appropriate for:

- Post-operative surgical pain
- Post-injury pain
- Fractures

Dependence and tolerance of narcotics must be considered when choosing a pain management method. Pain management specialists are often called in to address these issues.

Principles of Administering Narcotics

The nurse must know the client's heart rate, blood pressure, and respiration rate prior to administering a narcotic. She must also know that the client is not about to engage in a dangerous activity, such as driving a car. She should know when the last dose was given. The nurse should monitor the client for both intended and potential adverse effects of the medication.

How to Count Controlled Substances

Each facility will differ in the methodology of counting narcotics. In general, the nurse should count any controlled substances for which she will be responsible, both before and after such responsibility. The count is then written and signed by two nurses. As medications are used, the count is adjusted accordingly. Which items are subject to count is controlled by each facility.

How to Waste Controlled Substances

The procedure for wasting controlled substances will vary by facility. At times, the nurse will administer only part of an ampule of medication and must waste the rest. Or the nurse might draw up an injection, only to have the client refuse it. Many policies require two nurses to watch and document the wasting of controlled substances.

Vital Sign Monitoring Prior to and During Pain Management

It is necessary to be familiar with safe vital sign parameters during narcotic administration.

Pain Management for Clients with Cancer

The nurse must understand the basics of providing pain management for clients with cancer.

Pain Management for Clients with Burns

It is necessary to understand the basics of providing pain management for clients with severe burns.

Pediatric Pain Management

Pediatric pain management can be frightening to the new nurse. It is necessary to understand common pediatric pain medications and doses.

Benefits and Drawbacks to Oral, Topical, Subcutaneous, Intramuscular, and Intravenous Administration of Pain Medications

The nurse must understand the benefits and drawbacks to each type of pain medication administration, as well as the common uses of each.

Care of the Client Receiving Epidural Pain Management (RNs only)

The nurse must be familiar with the basics of caring for a client receiving an epidural. If adequate experience was not received during clinical, study this topic for the NCLEX.

Care of the Client with a Patient Controlled Anesthesia (PCA) Pump (RNs only)

How to Program and Operate a PCA Pump (RNs only)

The nurse should understand the basics of operating a patient-controlled anesthesia (PCA) pump. It has a key and can be operated by the client. The nurse follows physician orders regarding the drug and the amount of each dose. There is also a lockout amount that must be logged into the pump. A sample order would be: Morphine IV PCA loading dose 4 mg, PCA – 2 mg every seven minutes, not to exceed 10 mg every two hours. A basal rate can be set in addition to the bolus. It is advisable for two nurses to check the settings when the pump is began, or if the settings are changed.

Total Parenteral Nutrition (RNs only)

General Principles of Total Parenteral Nutrition (TPN) (RNs only)

Total parenteral feeding bypasses the gastrointestinal tract. The formula is tailored to the client's weight, medical condition, and needs. TPN may be short or long term. It is utilized when giving several days of common intravenous fluid, such as D5 ½ NS with 40mEq KCl, would not suffice.

Contents of TPN (RNs only)

TPN contains the following ingredients:

- Water
- Dextrose (for carbohydrates)
- Amino acids (for protein)
- Lipid emulsion (for fat) — may be given separately
- Multivitamin infusion (for vitamins)
- Electrolytes and trace elements (for minerals)
- Insulin (optional)

Frequency and Duration of Administration of TPN (RNs only)

The physician or pharmacist will determine the frequency and duration of TPN.

How to Calculate Rates of TPN (RNs only)

The nurse should receive TPN already mixed and ready to use. It may be the nurse's responsibility to calculate the proper dose. The order may read: 1000 ml to be delivered over eight hours. This could be at a flat rate of 125 ml per hour. The nurse may need to cycle the infusion, for example, beginning at a lower rate and slowly moving to a higher rate, then back to a lower rate near the end of the infusion.

Orders can also involve giving so many milliliters per hour, based on the client's weight. Be careful computing TPN rates and check with the pharmacist, or have another nurse double-check your work if you have any questions.

Lipids may also be ordered, which can be given at the same time or at a different time.

Diseases and Disorders in Which Clients Commonly Receive TPN (RNs only)

- Anorexia Nervosa
- Complicated recovery from surgery or accident
- Anorexia due to chemotherapy
- Severe malnutrition with inability to eat
- Head trauma
- Severe burns
- Cancers or other disorders that do not allow the client to swallow

- Crohn's disease
- Severe pancreatitis
- Ulcerative colitis
- Disorders in which the bowel needs to rest

Glucose Monitoring and Other Monitoring During TPN Administration

The nurse should monitor the following during TPN administration:

- The client's blood glucose level must be closely monitored during TPN therapy. It is frequently checked every six hours, and a sliding scale insulin dose should be administered. Insulin may also be added to the TPN itself; the dose is commonly dependent on the client's previous blood glucose readings.

- The client's intake and output should be checked continuously.

- The client's weight, complete blood cell count, electrolytes, and blood urea nitrogen should be checked daily.

- Liver function tests, serum albumin, calcium, phosphate, magnesium, prothrombin time, and plasma and urine osmolality should be checked per physician order.

Monitoring for Side Effects and Adverse Effects During TPN

The client receiving TPN must be monitored for side effects and adverse effects. Be aware of the common problems for both new and long-term TPN users.

CASE STUDY: MARILYN HEHR R.N., M.S.N.

marilyn.hehr@cncc.edu
(970) 824-1120

Marilyn Hehr graduated from Swedish Hospital School of Nursing in Minneapolis, Minnesota, in 1966. After many years as a staff nurse, head nurse of labor and delivery, school health occupations instructor, and others, she went back to college and earned a Bachelor of Science in vocational/technical education from Valley City State University, Valley City, North Dakota, in 1998. Hehr and her husband moved to Colorado, where she worked at a local clinic and as the tobacco control coordinator for two counties.

Colorado Northwestern Community College then started a nursing program, and she began a career in nursing education. In 2006, Hehr became the director of the nursing program there and, in 2007, finished her M.S.N. at the age of 62. She enjoys nursing education and has always been a strong believer in life-long learning.

Students who pass the NCLEX on the first attempt:

- Consistently have good grades
- Study, and do not cram
- Take direction well
- Are self-confident

Characteristics of graduates who fail the NCLEX on their first attempt are:

- Have poor time management skills
- Crammers
- "Know-it-alls."
- Minimal grades throughout the program
- Satisfied with minimal grades

Four weeks prior to the exam, you should

- Choose a NCLEX study guide and use it faithfully for a specific amount of hours every day
- Postpone every social engagement for the next four weeks
- Make this the priority in your life

After a good night's sleep, eat a high-protein breakfast on the morning of the NCLEX. Take lemon water with you to hydrate. Relax now; the work is already done.

CASE STUDY: MARILYN HEHR R.N., M.S.N.

You should start studying with the deficiencies, but then review everything again. You should have four-hour study sessions with a one-hour break. Some people will say only two hours, but it is easy to get involved with taking all the breaks and watching the clock and forget about studying. For math anxiety, get a tutor and work with that person ahead of time.

I think most people use critical-thinking skills to some degree, but almost everyone can use a few tips on how to use them better and use them more purposely.

Students should not try to work in health care while studying for the NCLEX. They need to spend all of their waking hours preparing for this all-important test. A new position is far too stressful for the graduate to be able to do well at both.

Chapter 10

Reduction of Risk Potential

Skills Checklist

I am unfamiliar	I am somewhat familiar	I am completely familiar	Skill
			Take vital signs of an adult, child, or infant
			Evaluate client lab work
			Perform blood glucose monitoring
			Test oxygen saturation level
			Prepare a client for surgery
			Evaluate client risk for skin breakdown
			Logroll a client with a back condition
			Obtain wound culture
			Monitor client receiving conscious sedation (RNs only)

			Monitor fetal heart rate during labor
			Perform and evaluate an electrocardiogram (EKG, ECG) (Evaluate – RNs only)
			Test for occult blood
			Obtain peripheral blood sample
			Test for gastric pH level
			Care for client during surgery
			Obtain clean and sterile urine specimen
			Obtain stool specimen
			Perform urine specific gravity test
			Obtain blood sample from central venous catheter
			Care for client recovering from anesthesia
			Evaluate results of fetal ultrasound
			Monitor intracranial pressure
			Evaluate amniocentesis results
			Evaluate results of a fetal non-stress test
			Monitor wound drainage devices
			Know normal arterial blood gas (ABG) values
			Know common lab work values

			Monitor pulmonary arterial pressure
			Monitor pulmonary arterial pressure
			Know the signs and symptoms of internal and external bleeding
			Insert and monitor decompression tube
			Care for a client with a chest tube
			Monitor client for abnormal electrolytes, including hypoglycemia and hyperglycemia
			Perform a cardiac assessment
			Perform neurological checks
			Perform circulatory checks
			Perform a respiratory assessment
			Check peripheral pulses
			Care for client with alteration in vital signs
			Perform a bladder scan

Terms to Understand

I am unfamiliar	I am somewhat familiar	I am completely familiar	Term
			Aspiration
			Electroconvulsive therapy
			Fall risk assessment
			Insufficient vascular perfusion

			Suicide precautions
			System-specific assessments
			Thrombocytopenia
			Wound healing

Diagnostic Tests

Smart Strategies

- Understand how to perform diagnostic tests and what the results indicate.

How to Perform Glucose Monitoring

The nurse should be familiar with the various methods of nurse-performed glucose monitoring. Some basic steps include:

1. Wash hands.

2. Gather all the needed equipment, including a mini-sharps container if one is not already nearby.

3. Don gloves.

4. Follow the machine's directions for turning it on, making sure it is set for the proper code if applicable, and inserting a strip.

5. Cleanse the client's finger (avoiding the index finger if possible) or other site with an alcohol prep pad and allow to dry. Do not blow on it.

6. Stick the side of the finger with a sharp and turn the finger upside down. Lightly squeeze only if necessary. Allow one drop of blood to fall onto the strip.

7. Take a fresh alcohol pad and firmly press on the site as you await the results.

8. Ascertain that the site has stopped bleeding. If it has not, apply a cotton ball and adhesive bandage (or similar dressing).

9. Record the reading and throw away the sharp, strip, prep pad, and anything else contaminated with blood into the sharps container.

10. Remove gloves and wash hands.

11. If the reading was very high or low, according to parameters at your facility, take the reading again.

12. If the reading is again very high or low, call for a stat blood glucose to be drawn by the lab.

13. Treat client according to physician orders and facility policy once correct blood glucose level has been determined.

How to Perform Testing for Occult Blood

Perform occult blood testing according to facility policy. It may involve a one-time test or testing over the course of three days.

The client should avoid the following food for 72 hours prior to the occult blood test:

- Fruits: grapefruit, cantaloupe, and other melons
- Vegetables: horseradish, broccoli, cabbage, mushrooms, potatoes, turnips, radishes, cauliflower, cucumbers, carrots, artichokes
- Meats: All red meats, fish

Other things to avoid prior to occult blood testing include:

- The client must be instructed to avoid iron supplements, vitamin C supplements, aspirin, and other blood thinners for 72 hours prior to testing.

- They should not present for testing while they have bleeding hemorrhoids or during menstruation.

- The client should not use a toilet bowl that has been cleaned in the past several days when obtaining the stool sample.

How to Perform Gastric pH Testing

The nurse should be familiar with the basics of gastric pH testing. In general, a specimen will be obtained via NG or G-tube and place it on pH paper. This is usually to be read within 30 seconds. A normal gastric pH is 0 to 2. If the client is receiving acid-inhibiting medications, it may read 2 to 4. A reading over 6 indicates the tube may be in the lungs. A reading of 7.5 to 8 indicates it may be in the intestine.

How to Perform Urine-Specific Gravity Testing

It is necessary to be familiar with how to perform urine-specific gravity testing and what outcomes to expect. Be able to name the conditions an abnormal finding could represent.

How to Perform an Electrocardiogram (RNs only to evaluate)

The nurse should be familiar with the following tasks:

- How to hook up a client to an EKG

- How to read an EKG, both in terms of knowing how to measure each wave and knowing the common rhythms a nurse may encounter
- How to recognize a dangerous rhythm

How to Perform Fetal Heart Monitoring

Fetal heart monitoring is a specific task that the nurse may or may not have encountered in his or her clinicals. If the nurse is unfamiliar with the basics of fetal heart monitoring, the procedure should be studied. The NCLEX developers indicate that test takers should be prepared for questions on fetal heart monitoring.

How to Perform a Bladder Scan

A bladder scan reliably tests post-void residual urine in the bladder. It should be performed within 20 minutes of the client voiding.

Follow these steps to perform a bladder scan:

1. Have the client lie supine.
2. Place gel on the area above the pubic bone.
3. Place the flat scan probe head on the lower bladder directly above the pubic bone.
4. Take two to three readings.
5. Remove the gel from the client's skin with cloth or tissue.
6. Document your findings.

Fetal Non-Stress Test Results

The nurse must be familiar with the various fetal non-stress test results and the implications for the mother, fetus, and family.

Amniocentesis Test Results

The nurse must be familiar with different possible results from an amnio-centesis test and the implications for the mother, fetus, and family. Know the reasons that women undergo amniocentesis testing.

Fetal Ultrasound Test Results

The nurse should know the basics of fetal ultrasound, including types, fetal age at which each type is used, and the information that can be gathered from a fetal ultrasound test.

Laboratory Values

Smart Strategies
- Practice memorizing your lab values on flash cards. Ask your peers and allow them to quiz you.

Normal Laboratory Values

Activated Partial Thromboplastin Time (APTT)	25 – 38 seconds
Alanine Aminotransferase (ALT) (SGPT)	1 – 21 U/L
Albumin (Blood)	3.5 – 5.0 g
Ammonia	12 – 55 umol/L
Aspartate Aminotransferase (AST) (SGOT)	7 – 27 U/L
Bleeding Time	3 – 9.5 minutes
Bilirubin, Direct	Up to 0.4 mg
Bilirubin, Total	Up to 1.0 mg
Calcium	8.5 – 10.5 mg
Cholesterol (Total)	120 – 220 mg

Cholesterol High Density Lipo-protein (HDL)	> 40
Cholesterol Low Density Lipopro-tein (LDL)	< 130
Creatinine	0.6 – 1.5 mg
Erythrocytic Sedimentation Rate (ESR)	Male 1 – 13 mm/hr, Female 1 – 20 mm/hr
Glucose, Fasting	70 – 110 mg
Hematocrit	Male 45 – 52%, Female 37 – 48%
Hemoglobin	Male 13 – 18 g/dl, Female 12 – 16 g/dl
Hemoglobin A1C (HBA1C)	4 – 7%
International Normalized Ratio (INR)	Normal 0.8 – 1.2. Therapeutic for those taking anticoagulants 2.0 – 3.0. Therapeutic for those needing more blood thinning 2.5 – 3.5.
Magnesium	1.5 – 2.0 mEq/liter
Phosphorus	3.0 – 4.5 mg
Potassium (K)	3.5 – 5.0 mEq/liter
Prothrombin time (PT)	< 2 seconds deviation from control
Red Blood Cells (RBC)	3.6 – 5.0 million
Platelets	150,000 – 400,000
Protein, Total	6.0 – 8.4 g
Sodium	135 – 145 mEq/liter
Urea Nitrogen (BUN)	8 – 25 mg
White Blood Cells (WBC)	4,500 – 10,000
Diff: Bands	3 – 5%
Diff: Neutrophils	50 – 70%
Diff: Eosinophils	1 – 3%
Diff: Basophils	0.4 – 1.0%
Diff: Lymphocytes	25 – 35%
Diff: Monocytes	4 – 6%

Arterial Blood Gases (ABG)

ABG	Normal Value
pH	7.35 – 7.45
PO2	80 – 100%
PCO2	35 – 45%
SaO2	90 – 100%
HCO3	22 – 26mEq/L

Urine Values

Albumin	0 – 8 mg/dL
pH	5 - 7
Urine Specific Gravity	1.010 – 1.025

Therapeutic Drug Values

Digoxin	0.7 – 2.0 ng/ml
Lithium	0.6 – 1.2 mEq/L

Obtaining a Wound Culture Specimen

The nurse must know how to obtain an ordered wound culture specimen.

Obtaining a Specimen of Gastric Contents

It is necessary to know how to obtain a gastric contents specimen.

Obtaining a Sputum Specimen

The nurse must know how to obtain a sputum specimen. It helps to tell the client to "cough up" a specimen from deep within the chest, instead of merely spitting into the cup.

Obtaining a Clean-Catch Urine Specimen

It is necessary know how to obtain a clean-catch urine specimen from a man and a woman. Be able to list the indications for a clean-catch urine specimen.

Obtaining a Sterile Urine Specimen

You must know how to obtain a sterile urine specimen from a client with an existing catheter, as well as a client you will have to catheterize to obtain the specimen. Be able to list the indications for a sterile urine specimen.

How to Obtain a Stool Specimen

A stool specimen is generally obtained by the client passing having a bowel movement into a specified container. Wearing gloves, obtain approximately one ounce of stool with a stick (usually a wooden tongue depressor) and place in the appropriate specimen cup. If the stool varies in color or consistency, place some of all the different types of stool into the cup. The stool should not be contaminated with urine.

How to Perform Venipuncture

The nurse performs venipuncture in the home, long-term care setting, and physician's office. The nurse should understand the basic procedure for both safe collection and handling of the specimen. Know the standard needle size for adults and children, the veins used, and what to do if complications develop.

How to Obtain a Blood Specimen via a Central Line or Other Venous-Access Device

For the NCLEX, test takers are expected to know how to safely obtain a blood specimen from a central line and other access devices. The nurse should be careful not to allow:

- Air into the line.
- Bacterial contamination to enter the line.

Handling Blood Specimens

The nurse should be familiar with the different types of blood specimens and the appropriate handling of each — such as keeping the specimen on ice. Know how to label the specimen with the client's identity and how to mark as a biohazard.

Conscious Sedation (RNs only)

General Principles of Conscious Sedation (RNs only)

Conscious sedation is used for short-term surgical, diagnostic, or therapeutic procedures.

Registered nurses may administer conscious sedation in most, if not all, states.

The following steps should be taken to prepare the client for conscious sedation:

- Perform an assessment to determine the appropriate drug and dosage for the client.

- Ensure the appropriate staff members are available should a complication occur. These staff members should be skilled in airway management, cardiopulmonary resuscitation, and emergency intubation.

- Emergency supplies (a "crash cart") must be available, including airway and ventilation equipment, suction, defibrillator, 100-percent oxygen, and emergency resuscitative and antagonist medications.

A registered nurse or physician must stay with the client at all times. The person monitoring the client must not have other tasks that hinder his ability to do so.

The client must be monitored during conscious sedation in the following ways:

- Heart rate and rhythm
- Level of consciousness
- Oxygen saturation
- Blood pressure
- Respiratory rate

Alterations in Body Systems

Smart Strategies

- One of the most important responsibilities of the nurse is to recognize untoward changes in a client's condition. She must know which checks to perform and what the normal results are.

The nurse must monitor the client for an alteration in body system. The client may have a new ailment he is complaining of, or the nurse may notice a change in skin color, orientation, appetite, or other factor.

Performing Neurological Checks

Follow these steps to perform a neurological check:

- Assess the level of consciousness.
- Assess whether the client is oriented to person, place, and time.
- Check for PERRLA — Pupils equal, round, reactive to light and accommodation. Document the pupil size bilaterally.
- Check for equal handgrips and leg strength.

Many other neurological checks may be performed based on the client's condition.

Performing Circulatory Checks

Follow these steps to perform a circulatory check:

- Determine if radial pulses are equal and adequate.
- Determine if pedal pulses are equal and adequate.
- Place finger against nail bed for three seconds and release. Watch for length of time for capillary refill.
- Assess pitting and non-pitting edema.
- Monitor a casted extremity for adequate circulation.

Intake and Output

It is a frequent responsibility of the nurse to monitor the intake and output of the client. The physician may order "Intake and Output" or "Strict Intake and Output."

Intake includes:

- Intravenous fluids
- Water

- Liquids consumed during meals (including beverages, soups, ice cream, and so on)
- Tube feedings

Output includes:

- Urine (The number of voidings may be acceptable for regular output orders; if strict output is ordered the urine must be captured and measured. A catheter may be needed to measure the amount of urine voided.)
- Liquid stool
- Vomitus
- Any secretions or drainage
- Excessive perspiration (documented as objective finding, but not volume)

The number of stools is also documented.

Prevention of Contractures

The nurse is responsible for helping to prevent contractures. These can occur due to immobility or paralysis. The following are some of the ways to prevent contractures:

- Passive range of motion exercises
- Teaching the client active range of motion exercises
- Proper turning and repositioning of the client
- Keeping the client's body in proper alignment
- Using orthotic devices as needed to keep hands open, and so on
- Encouraging the client to walk, exercise, and use his hands
- Encouraging client independence in bathing, eating, and dressing
- Ensuring that the client's pain is under control so that he feels like moving around

Foot Care for the Client with Diabetes Mellitus

Foot care for clients with diabetes should be performed by a licensed health-care provider. The client should be instructed to keep her feet clean and free from infection. She should not go barefoot or wear sandals or flip flops that expose the feet to potential skin breakage.

Follow these steps to perform foot care for the diabetic client:

- Ensure that feet are clean and that footwear and socks are not restrictive.
- Carefully trim toenails straight across and file toenails. Clean all around nails.
- Moisturize the feet, but not between the toes.
- Make the client's physician aware of any open sores or other problem areas.

Potential for Complications from Diagnostic Tests, Treatments, and Procedures

The nurse should understand the common complications from various diagnostic tests, treatments, and procedures.

How to Establish Precautions to Prevent Falls

Many facilities have a worksheet to determine whether a client should be monitored for fall prevention. Some of the criteria used may be:

- Age
- Mental status
- History of falls
- Frailty or physical impairments
- Medications
- Incontinence

Clients subject to fall prevention methods may have some of the following actions performed:

- Different rules for side rails than the general client population
- Bed alarms
- A more frequent schedule for checking on the client
- Non-slip slippers or devices that facilitate walking
- Making sure the client can call for staff assistance, regardless of where he is

Client Elopement

The nurse must do everything in her power to avoid client elopement. This includes the following:

- Follow all facility protocols.
- Encourage open communication between yourself and clients so that they will come to you if they are having a problem.
- Foster an atmosphere of acceptance of client needs and feelings.
- Monitor agitated clients carefully.
- Be aware of which clients are wanderers and help them to stay involved in activities.
- If you feel that the facility does not have proper security measures in place, such as door alarms, make suggestions to management.

What to Do When a Client Elopes

Facility protocol must be followed when a client elopes. The police may need to be notified if the client poses a risk to themselves or to others. Indications for calling the police would be frailty of a client, confusion or disorientation, or potential for self-harm. The family is generally notified. Staff members should be diligent in searching for the client who is at risk of harm.

Care of the Client Undergoing Electroconvulsive Therapy

The nurse must have a basic understanding of the impact of ECT therapy on the client, such as temporary memory loss.

Pre- and Post-procedure Care

The nurse should be familiar with the steps taken prior to ECT therapy, including making sure there is an informed consent. The nurse must know how to care for a client who has just had ECT therapy.

Monitoring O2 Saturation

Pulse oximetry is a method of measuring the oxygenation of a client's hemoglobin. A sensor is placed on the client's finger, earlobe, or toe. It may be ordered continuously with alarms that alert the nurse to dropping values, or it may be ordered as a one-time procedure.

Normal and Abnormal Values of O2 Saturation

As a general rule, an oxygen saturation level of 95 to 100 percent is considered normal. Concern develops when the level dips below 90 percent. In a client with COPD, 88 to 90 percent may be a target range. Low oxygen levels indicate the need for supplemental oxygen.

How to Teach Cough and Deep Breathing Techniques

The nurse must be familiar with the reasons for coughing and deep breathing, and be able to teach the client how to perform the techniques. The client may need to brace any surgical wounds with a pillow.

Surgical Complications

Smart Strategies

- Unless your surgical clinical rotation involved clients who had complications, this may be a topic you do not feel comfortable with. Study your nursing notes and textbooks until you can name the major surgical complications and how each is resolved. Know what the nurse should do in each circumstance.

The nurse must be familiar with common surgical and post-surgical complications and their interventions.

Care of the Immediate Post-Operative Client

The nurse must understand the basics of care of the immediate post-operative client in the post-anesthesia care unit. In general, the nurse is responsible for assisting the client back to a state of awareness, a return to normal vital signs, and pain management. She must also monitor for hemorrhage and other post-operative complications. The client may be receiving supplemental oxygen and may be on telemetry or other specialized monitoring.

System Specific Assessments

Smart Strategies

- Know how to perform system specific assessments. Quiz yourself and your peers frequently on different body systems.

The nurse must be knowledgeable in performing system specific assessments.

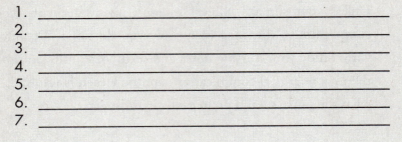

Quick Quiz #15

Name seven system specific assessments.

1. _____
2. _____
3. _____
4. _____
5. _____
6. _____
7. _____

Therapeutic Procedures

A large part of the nurse's role is to perform and assist with therapeutic procedures. Expect the NCLEX to test your knowledge of basic procedures.

How to Log-Roll a Client

Log-rolling is a means of transferring a client from one place to another such as a bed or exam table. This procedure may need to be performed on injured clients or if a client is unable to transfer themselves for another reason.

Follow these steps to log-roll a client:

1. Assemble at least three staff members.

2. Explain the procedure and instruct the client not to assist.

3. Reposition catheter tubing, ventilator tubing, intravenous lines, and any other tubing to prevent dislodging or overextension during the turning process.

4. Keep the bed flat and raise it to a high position.

5. Lower the side rails.

6. Position the client's arms so they will not be under the weight of the body when the roll occurs.

7. One staff member should stay at the head of the client and lead the others.

8. A second staff member should stand prepared to turn the client's upper body.

9. A third staff member should stand prepared to turn the client's lower extremities.

10. Place a pillow between the client's legs if not contraindicated.

11. The lead staff member should count "one, two, three," and the staff should all move in slow unison to log-roll the client onto his side.

12. Place pillows under the client if he is to remain on his side.

13. Position a pillow for the higher arm to rest upon and ensure that the lower arm is not in a bind.

14. Keep proper body alignment at all times.

15. Place bed back in low position, raise the side rails, and place the call light in reach.

Monitoring Continuous Bladder Irrigation

A three-way catheter is utilized to continuous bladder irrigation. The physician's order will specify the solution to be used, the volume of solution, and the rate of administration. The nurse must monitor the output for volume and character of urine.

How to Insert a Urinary Catheter in a Male or Female

The nurse must be familiar with the procedure for inserting a urinary catheter in a male or female, including choosing an appropriate size.

Indwelling versus In-and-Out Catheters

The nurse must know the reasons for indwelling catheters versus in-and-out catheters.

Indwelling catheters have a risk of infection that increases if they are left in place more than 30 days. They are used for clients who are incontinent, but have sores that need to heal or for whom frequent incontinence care is inappropriate. Many clients choose to have an indwelling catheter, rather than inserting a catheter every six hours.

In-and-out catheters are used for several purposes. These include checking residual and care of clients who cannot void without catheterization. Some clients who require catheterization would rather insert a catheter every six hours than wear an indwelling catheter. In-and-out catheters are also used for obtaining one-time sterile urine specimens. These types of catheters are usually smaller than indwelling catheters. They carry a different type of risk of infection, related to the frequency of their use and because they are often inserted by the client and are often non-sterile.

NG Tube Basics

The nurse must know how to insert a NG tube and the differences in placing one for suction versus placing one for feeding.

Checking Placement of a NG Tube

Facility policies differ regarding checking of NG tube placement. Check placement at least two different ways before using the tube.

Giving Medications Via a NG Tube

Giving medications via NG or G-tube can be complicated. The nurse must know which medications can be crushed. Ideally, the medication will be available in liquid form. The tube must be flushed, the medication given, and the tube flushed again. At many facilities, the nurse may not apply pressure to the NG tube, and the medication and rinse agent must be administered by gravity only. The client's head of bed should be kept elevated during and after the procedure.

How to Give Water and Nutrition Via a NG Tube

Water and nutrition can be given via NG tube indefinitely, but most clients will be given a G-tube if they will be receiving water and nutrition via this method on a long-term basis. The nurse must understand the basics of giving water and nutrition via the tube. This may be supplemental or it may be all the water and food that the client receives. Many clients receive feedings via an enteral feeding pump that is continuous or operates during the day only.

Suctioning Via a NG Tube

The nurse must be familiar with the basics of suctioning via a NG tube.

Continuous Suction versus Intermittent Suction

The nurse should know the reasons for continuous versus intermittent suction. Keep a record of the amount and character of fluid obtained via suctioning the NG tube.

Setting Up a Sterile Field in a Client's Room

The nurse must be able to set up a sterile field either in a hospital room or in the client's room at home. Strict procedure must be followed and the nurse must also know what materials to prepare.

Vital Signs

The nurse must be well-versed in obtaining vital signs via various equipment. She must also know normal vital sign ranges for age and diagnosis as well as what abnormal readings may indicate.

Temperature

The nurse must be familiar with the correct procedure for taking a temperature. While mercury thermometers are not frequently used, know that they must be left in place for about five minutes for an accurate reading.

Quick Quiz #16

Which client would not be expected to have a temperature of 100.0?

1. A client presenting with an earache.
2. A client seven months pregnant.
3. A client one day post surgery for an appendectomy.
4. A client with a new diagnosis of leukemia.
5. A malnourished client.

Heart Rate or Pulse

The nurse must be familiar with taking an apical and radial pulse. For a client with a dysrhythmia, count for a full minute to get an accurate rate.

Quick Quiz #17

Which client would not be expected to have a heart rate of 100?
1. An 18-month-old child.
2. A client taking theophylline for COPD.
3. A marathon runner getting a physical examination.
4. A client experiencing an anxiety attack.

Blood pressure

The nurse must be familiar with how to take the blood pressure of various age groups.

Quick Quiz #18

How high should you pump up the blood pressure cuff?

_____.

Respirations

The nurse must be familiar with taking an accurate respiratory count. Ideally, the client will not be aware the nurse is checking her respiration, as it can cause a variation in her breathing.

CASE STUDY: LYNN E. CAVANAUGH, R.N., B.S., M.S.

Lynn Cavanaugh has been an instructor at E.C. Goodwin Technical School in New Britain, Connecticut, for the past 17 years. She teaches fundamentals of nursing, pharmacology, life sciences, and medical-surgical nursing. She also serves as a clinical instructor in medical-surgical and geriatrics. Cavanaugh previously worked in acute care, home care, and long-term care. She received her Bachelor of Science and Master of Science from Central Connecticut State University.

CASE STUDY: LYNN E. CAVANAUGH, R.N., B.S., M.S.

Students who pass the NCLEX on the first attempt are self-starters, have good study skills, actively participate in learning, ask questions, seek clarification from instructors to formulate nursing judgments, and are consistently well-prepared for exams. Students who do not pass consistently do poorly on tests and also have poor recall of material presented in class, cannot correlate academic info with clinical situations, perform poorly in the clinical area, and cannot keep up with the volume of material presented.

Four weeks prior to the NCLEX, you should review notes from the program, concentrate on material you did poorly on during the program, and join a study group with peers who consistently passed courses during the program.

I would encourage graduates to review material covered early in the program, then content they had difficulty with. Critical-thinking skills, math skills, and prioritizing skills are usually students' weakest areas on the NCLEX. I think critical-thinking skills develop throughout a student's school years and are obviously enhanced by teachers who approach learning through critical-thinking exercises. Review math presented during pharmacology. Try to reword problems to clarify what is being asked, practice basic math skills, and ask "Does my answer make sense?"

I definitely think that working as a grad enhances the understanding of concepts taught in the program. Grads are often surprised at the amount of knowledge they have, and that becomes apparent only when working as a grad.

Chapter 11

Physiological Adaptation

Skills Checklist

I am unfamiliar	I am somewhat familiar	I am completely familiar	Skill
			Perform cardiopulmonary resuscitation (CPR) in the hospital and in the field on an infant, child, or adult
			Correctly use an automated external defibrillator
			Perform endotracheal suctioning
			Perform various types of wound treatment
			Monitor the prenatal client
			Care for a client with a tracheostomy
			Perform the Heimlich maneuver on an infant, child, or adult

			Perform a dressing change using sterile technique
			Provide emergency respiratory support in the hospital or in the field
			Assist a client with incentive spirometry
			Assist physician with debridement
			Care for the client undergoing radiation therapy
			Suction a client orally or nasopharangeally
			Perform peritoneal dialysis
			Care for a client undergoing phototherapy
			Provide emergency care for wound dehiscence or evisceration
			Monitor a client with an arterial line (RNs only)
			Care for a client on a ventilator or other assisted-breathing device
			Place client on telemetry and monitor reading
			Safely administer oxygen via nasal cannula or mask
			Assist physician with a biopsy
			Perform a gastric lavage (RNs only)
			Provide care to the post-operative client
			Care for a client with a pacemaker

			Care for client with an ostomy
			Assist physician with central line placement
			Care for a client with an implantable cardioverter defibrillator
			Perform chest physio-therapy
			Provide care to a client experiencing a seizure and postseizure
			Care for the client with increased intracranial pressure
			Recognize common cardiac rhythm abnor-malities
			Provide basic and com-plex care for the mater-nity client
			Care for the client in precipitous labor
			Remove sutures and staples
			Care for the client with an access device for he-modialysis
			Care for the client with an infectious disease

Terms to Understand

I am unfamiliar	I am somewhat familiar	I am completely familiar	Term
			Decreased cardiac output
			Disease management

			Eclampsia and pre-eclampsia
			Fluid and electrolyte imbalance
			Infection
			Pathophysiology

Principles of Phototherapy

Applications for phototherapy include newborn jaundice, eczema, psoriasis, acne, seasonal affective disorder, depression, and circadian rhythm issues. Different types of light work for different disorders. Be familiar with the basic principles of phototherapy.

Treating Increased Intracranial Pressure

Increased intracranial pressure is a medical emergency. The nurse must be familiar with the symptoms, the causes, the treatments, and the potential complications.

Care of the Client with a Chest Tube

The nurse must be diligent in caring for a client with a chest tube to avoid dislodgment. Drainage is measured on a routine basis.

Care of the Client with a Wound Drain

You must be familiar with the common types of wound drains and how to work with each one.

Quick Quiz #19

Name three common types of wound drains.

1. _____
2. _____
3. _____

Signs and Symptoms of Infection

Smart Strategies

- Infections cause many hospital deaths each year. Be prepared for questions regarding preventing and recognizing infections.

The nurse must know the signs and symptoms of infection, both local and systemic. These symptoms must be reported to the primary care provider so appropriate treatment can begin. Clients susceptible to infection should be educated on signs and symptoms.

Quick Quiz #20

Name three conditions that cause clients to be at a high risk of infection.

1. _____
2. _____
3. _____

Care of the Client with an Ostomy

Colostomy

The nurse must be familiar with the care of a client who has a new colostomy, as well as one whose colostomy is several years old. Be prepared for teaching questions regarding colostomies. Keep in mind that the nurse should help restore the client to the highest level of independent functioning possible.

Urostomy

The new nurse may or may not have had adequate experience caring for a client with a urostomy in clinicals. It is necessary know the basics of urostomy care. One important factor is emptying the bag on a regular basis.

Care of the Client who is Experiencing Seizures

Smart Strategies
- Be prepared for seizure-related questions on the NCLEX. You should know the types, correlating disorders, and common medications. You must also know what to do when a client experiences a seizure.

The nurse must be able to name the various types of seizures, their identifying symptoms, and how to care for a client who has both a brief and an extended seizure.

Seizure Precautions

The nurse must be familiar with seizure precautions for the hospitalized client.

Performing Peritoneal Dialysis

Follow these steps to perform peritoneal dialysis:

1. Wash hands.

2. Weigh client and record.

3. Warm bag or bottle.

4. Apply mask.

5. Add medications if ordered, and label bag or bottle appropriately.

6. Disinfect area where bag or bottle is spiked, then spike bag or bottle with IV tubing.

7. Prime tubing and hang bag or bottle on IV pole.

8. Place drainage bag lower than client's abdomen.

9. Open treatment supplies. Soak as many 4x4 gauze pads as you will need with hydrogen peroxide or sterile saline (per facility policy) and leave others dry.

10. Put on a clean gown.

11. Apply sterile gloves.

12. Remove and discard old catheter dressing. Examine site for signs of infection or dislodgement.

13. Remove sterile gloves, wash hands, and apply new sterile gloves.

14. Cleanse catheter insertion site with prepared gauze pads using a circular motion, going outward.

15. Apply antiseptic with dry gauze pads.

16. Apply catheter site dressing using sterile technique.

17. Remove gloves and wash hands.

18. Label dressing per facility policy (date, time, initials)

19. Apply sterile gloves.

20. Connect the end of the tubing to the abdominal catheter.

21. Clamp the tubing going from the abdominal catheter to the drainage bag.

22. Open dialysate solution tubing clamp. Allow first bag or bottle of fluid to drain into peritoneal cavity over a period of 10 to 15 minutes.

23. Allow fluid to remain in peritoneal cavity for 20 minutes or as specified by physician.

24. Monitor client's respiratory status.

25. Open clamp to drain bag and allow fluid to drain for time specified by physician. If fluid does not drain properly, reposition client and drain until only a slow drip remains.

26. Record amount of bag or bottle and amount collected in drainage bag.

27. Hang next bag or bottle and repeat process until ordered amount of bags have been hung.

28. Take vital signs every 30 to 60 minutes per facility policy.

29. Weigh client after procedure and record.

30. Empty drainage bag. Discard bag and tubing.

31. Cap peritoneal catheter.

32. Follow physician order's regarding post-dialysis lab work.

33. Clean up area.

34. Wash hands.

35. Document procedure, including appearance of dialysate return.

Monitor client's dressing site, respiratory status, mental status, and signs of electrolyte imbalance throughout procedure.

Performing Chest Physiotherapy

Chest physiotherapy is frequently performed with a small, handheld machine. The client is placed into the appropriate position, and the machine is held in different places for the prescribed amount of time.

Follow these steps to perform a manual chest physiotherapy:

1. Wash hands.

2. Place client in appropriate position for drainage of lung.

3. Make small cups with your palms.

4. Strike the area with the palms while holding the wrists stiff.

5. Alternate hands and continue for one to two minutes to each area.

6. If client is not on ventilator, ask them to take deep breaths in and slow breaths out.

7. Place hands on top of each other over the area.

8. During exhalation, shake the area by tensing your hands and arms. Only shake slightly, as in a small tremor.

9. Move hands to a slightly different place and repeat. Continue until area is covered (six to eight times).

10. Ask client to cough, or if client is unable or on ventilator, suction secretions.

11. Reposition client and repeat steps for each area.

12. Assess breath sounds.

13. Perform or assist with mouth care.

14. Elevate head of bed at least 45 degrees and turn client to side-lying position.

15. Wash hands.

16. Document procedure.

Teaching Your Client to Perform Incentive Spirometry

It is the responsibility of the nurse or the respiratory therapist to teach the client to perform incentive spirometry. It is commonly ordered postoperatively to help prevent pneumonia and other complications, and it is occasionally ordered for clients with pneumonia or other respiratory problems.

Care of the Client with a Tracheostomy

The following procedures should be followed to care for a client with a tracheostomy:

- Keep any small item that could end up in the tracheostomy away from the area.

- Keep emergency supplies available at all times.

- You must know the size of the client's tracheostomy.

- Check client's breathing sounds before and after care. Document these findings.

- Changing the inner cannula is generally performed every 24 to 48 hours.

- Never suction a tracheostomy for more than 15 seconds.

- The suctioning process should be intermittent, and the catheter should be rotated and kept in motion during the procedure.

- A tracheostomy with an inflatable cuff requires special instruction. Be careful not to overinflate the cuff, and follow all instructions regarding when the cuff should be inflated and deflated.

Suctioning a Tracheostomy

Follow these steps to suction a tracheostomy.

1. Hyperoxygenate the client.

2. Wash hands.

3. Open all equipment and sterile saline bottle.

4. Apply sterile gloves.

5. Remove appropriately sized suction catheter from packaging.

6. Dip tip of catheter in sterile saline.

7. Open the suction port.

8. Ask the client to take a deep breath if possible.

9. Insert cannula into trachea, stopping if resistance is felt. Do not use suction at this time.

10. Begin suctioning while slowly withdrawing the catheter. Rotate the suction catheter as you work.

11. Reoxygenate the client.

12. Rinse the catheter with sterile saline by suctioning the saline through the catheter.

13. Repeat procedure if needed.

14. Dispose of supplies, remove sterile gloves, and wash hands.

Cleaning the Inner Cannula

The inner cannula of a tracheostomy is generally cleaned every eight hours. The trach dressing will be changed at that time or more often if wet. The following is a general list of tasks performed when cleaning the inner cannula. Procedures may vary by facility, and it is better to be familiar with the following steps, rather than memorize them.

1. Wash hands.

2. Hyperoxygenate the client.

3. Suction the airway to remove secretions.

4. Wash your hands.

5. Place the client in high fowler's position.

6. Apply clean gloves.

7. Open the tracheostomy care kit.

8. Remove and discard the current dressing.

9. Remove gloves and wash hands.

10. Apply sterile gloves.

11. Set up sterile field.

12. Place sterile drape over client.

13. With non-dominant hand, pour sterile saline into one basin and a mixture of hydrogen peroxide and sterile saline into the other basin.

14. Remove the inner cannula with the same hand and place into the hydrogen peroxide and sterile saline mix.

15. With the dominant hand, dip the applicators and gauze in the hydrogen peroxide and sterile saline mix, and clean around the trach site.

16. With the dominant hand, dip fresh applicators and gauze in the sterile saline basin and rinse around the trach site.

17. Using the non-dominant hand, pick up the inner cannula and scrub it clean inside and outside with the brush and the hydrogen peroxide and sterile saline mixture.

18. Rinse the inner cannula in the sterile saline.

19. Dry the inner cannula with the pipe cleaner or other available apparatus on the inside. Leave saline on the outer part of the inner cannula.

20. Reinsert cannula with the non-dominant hand and lock it into place.

21. Take forceps and apply a sterile drain sponge to the trach site. Put it in place from the bottom.

22. Thread fresh ties through the flange holes and tie them.

23. Cut and remove the old ties.

24. Discard materials and gloves.

25. Wash hands.

26. Visually inspect area for foreign objects that could be pulled into tracheostomy.

The following Web site contains a great deal of helpful information regarding tracheostomy care if you feel you need to review in greater detail: **www.tracheostomy.com/resources/pdf/TrachHandbk.pdf**

Removing Wound Sutures

Follow these steps to remove wound sutures:

1. Wash hands.

2. Apply clean gloves and remove dressing (if applicable). Assess site for drainage or infection. If present, contact physician before continuing.

3. Remove gloves. Wash hands and apply sterile gloves.

4. Clean the suture line with a swab and antimicrobial solution, beginning at the center and working outward.

5. Use smooth forceps to lightly pull one part of the suture upward. With scissors, cut the stitch as close to the skin as possible.

6. Pull the stitch out in a manner so that no part of the stitch above the skin goes below the skin.

7. Carefully remove all stitches in this manner.

8. Disinfect the area.

9. Apply sterile wound strips if ordered.

10. Apply wound dressing.

11. Remove gloves and wash hands.

12. Document procedure.

Removing Wound Staples

Remove wound staples in the following manner:

1. Wash hands.

2. Apply clean gloves and remove dressing (if applicable). Assess site for drainage or infection. If present, contact physician before continuing.

3. Remove gloves. Wash hands and apply sterile gloves.

4. Clean the suture line with a swab and antimicrobial solution, beginning at the center and working outward.

5. Place the lower part of the staple remover under a staple at one end of the suture line and slowly press the device closed.

6. When the ends of the staple have left the skin, slowly remove the staple and discard in a sharps container.

7. Remove every other staple in this manner.

8. Remove the remaining staples.

9. Apply sterile wound strips if ordered.

10. Apply wound dressing.

11. Remove gloves and wash hands.

12. Document procedure. Some facilities may require you to document the number of staples removed.

Monitor the wound for dihensensce during the procedure and stop immediately if it occurs. Place sterile gauze or 4x4s soaked in sterile saline on the wound, instruct the client to remain still, and call the physician.

Checking a Pacemaker

While pacemakers vary greatly, for the purposes of the NCLEX, test takers should know the basics of check a client's pacemaker.

Fluid and Electrolyte Imbalances

Signs and Symptoms of Fluid Imbalance

The nurse should be able to identify the signs and symptoms of fluid imbalance, both in the new client and the client receiving intravenous fluids.

Common Interventions to Address Fluid Imbalance

It is necessary to be able to name the common interventions that address both the dehydrated client and the over-hydrated client.

Illness Management

Smart Strategies

- It is the nurse's responsibility to manage the chronic illness of the client. She must understand the disease course and educate the client and family regarding this.

Both chronic and acute diseases must be actively managed.

When educating a client or family member about illness management, adhere to the following principles:

- Educate the client regarding the disease progress and the expected outcome.

- Teach the client how to administer any medications including when to take them.

- Tell the client when they need to call the physician or seek emergency care.

- Advise the client of any dietary or exercise restrictions.

- Assess the client's level of understanding by asking for a return demonstration.

- Assess the client's level of compliance.

- Give written or other permanent instructions, as well as a way to contact a medical professional with any questions.

Chronic Diseases

Many chronic diseases and disorders have illness management models. Some of the more common ones include diabetes, heart disease, and chronic obstructive pulmonary disease.

Diabetes

The client with type I or type II diabetes understands that his disease must be actively managed for the rest of his life. Diabetes is a disorder that requires management by the client themselves — more so than most disorders. The client must adhere to the following principles:

- Know what, how much, and when to eat.

- Know how to test their blood sugar and to be alert to dangerous symptoms of hyperglycemia and hypoglycemia.

- Know how to administer oral medications or insulin. The insulin may be given by injection or any number of new pumps or other devices.

- Seek regular medical care.

- Be careful to avoid infection.

- Avoid stressors as much as possible.

- Remain physically active.

Heart Disease

The client with heart disease must actively manage his own care. He must adhere to the following principles:

- Eat a low-fat, low-saturated-fat diet.
- Exercise regularly as allowed.
- Take all medications as prescribed.
- Manage angina and know when to take nitroglycerin and when to seek medical help.
- Maintain a healthy, low stress lifestyle.

Chronic Obstructive Pulmonary Disease

The client with chronic obstructive pulmonary disease must adhere to the following principles:

- Take oral medications and inhalers as ordered. Do not take more than prescribed.
- Follow instructions for improving lung function.
- Do not smoke or be around others that smoke.
- Measure your oxygen level with pulse oximetry if required.
- If ordered, utilize oxygen continuously, at night, or as needed. Do not use a higher level than ordered.
- If needed, keep a supply of oxygen and equipment with you at all times.
- Always follow safety precautions with oxygen.
- Learn breathing techniques to assist with times of difficult breathing.

Acute Diseases

When handling a client with an acute disease, the nurse must monitor whether the client is becoming more or less stable. She must understand the typical progression of the disease process and know exactly what symptoms to monitor. It is important to educate the client and family on the disease process.

Infectious Disease

Client education should focus on the following:

- Keep any external infection sites clean.
- It is important to follow the prescribed medication regimen.
- Follow a healthy diet with adequate protein, vitamin C, and zinc.
- Watch for and report signs or symptoms of a worsening condition, including fever, redness, swelling, or pain.
- Follow appropriate precautions to avoid the spread of the disease.
- Take frequent rest periods.

Human Immunodeficiency Virus (HIV) and Acquired Immunodeficiency Syndrome (AIDS)

Client education should focus on the following:

- Follow all instructions for medications.
- Avoid persons with active infection.
- Follow a healthy diet to keep immune system as healthy as possible.
- Avoid undue stress.
- Keep all physician appointments and lab work appointments.
- Immediately report signs or symptoms of infection to physician.

Ask the physician what symptoms to monitor.

Tuberculosis

Client education should focus on the following:

- Take all medications as prescribed.
- Keep all physician appointments.

Infectious Diseases that must be reported to the CDC include:

- Acquired Immunodeficiency Syndrome (AIDS)
- Anthrax
- Botulism
- Brucellosis
- Chancroid
- Chlamydia trachomatis
- Cholera
- Coccidioidomycosis
- Congenital rubella syndrome
- Congenital syphilis
- Cryptosporidiosis
- Diphtheria
- Encephalitis: California, eastern equine, St. Louis, western equine
- Escherichia coli
- Gonorrhea
- Haemophilus influenzae: invasive disease
- Hansen's disease
- Psittacosis
- Rabies: animal
- Rabies: human
- Hantavirus: pulmonary syndrome
- Hemolytic-uremic syndrome following diarrhea
- Hepatitis A
- Hepatitis B
- Hepatitis C
- Human immunodeficiency virus infection: pediatric, under 13 years of age
- Legionellosis
- Lyme disease
- Malaria
- Measles (Rubeola)
- Meningococcal disease
- Mumps
- Pertussis
- Plague
- Poliomyelitis: paralytic
- Streptococcus pneumoniae: drug-resistant
- Syphilis
- Tetanus
- Toxic shock syndrome
- Trichinosis

- Rocky Mountain spotted fever
- Rubella
- Salmonellosis
- Shigellosis
- Streptococcal disease: invasive, group A
- Streptococcal toxic shock syndrome
- Tuberculosis
- Typhoid fever
- Yellow fever
- Varicella (chickenpox) (recommended, not mandatory)

Emergency Procedures

Smart Strategies
- Be familiar with emergency procedures for all common life-threatening circumstances. It is important to know the steps taken and in what order.

- Know how to care for emergencies both in the hospital and in the field.

Procedures relative to medical emergencies vary greatly depending on location. A client who unexpectedly experiences cardiac arrest in his home will be treated with different equipment and by different personnel than a client who "codes" in the hospital. The nurse must be prepared to perform cardiopulmonary resuscitation (CPR) at any time. At the most basic, one experienced person is needed to initiate CPR until help arrives.

General Principles of Medical Emergencies

Smart Strategies
- On the NCLEX, the ABCs of emergencies are likely to be utilized in test questions. Extend the ABCs to non-emergent client care as well.

The following information is intended to serve as a review. For discrepancies or questions, refer to the latest information available by your facility, your state Board of Nursing, the American Red Cross, or the American Heart Association.

For medical emergencies, the nurse must follow the ABCs:

1. Airway
2. Breathing
3. Circulation

Performing CPR on an Adult

The following steps should be followed when performing CPR on an adult:

- Open airway by performing the head tilt-chin lift.
- Assess for breathing. If no breathing, continue.
- Health-care providers give two rescue breaths at one second per breath.
- Check the carotid pulse. If no pulse, begin compressions.
- Give chest compressions, at the nipple line with the heel of one hand. Keep the other hand on top of the compressing hand. Use a compression to ventilation ratio of 30:2.

CPR requirements for a child, infant, and newborn vary somewhat. You should be familiar with all methods.

CPR Procedures: Differences Between Hospital Care and Care in the Field

CPR in the hospital is greatly enhanced by ambu bags, fellow staff, emergency drugs, and defibrillators. In the field, one must perform alone or with minimal assistance. When possible, remember the basics of calling for help before you begin procedures.

Performing the Heimlich Maneuver

The nurse must know how to perform the Heimlich maneuver on an adult and a child. Be familiar with the parameters by which the maneuver should be performed.

Using an External Defibrillator (RNs only)

Health-care providers with access to an automatic external defibrillator should use it as soon as possible, whether in the hospital or in the field.

Emergency Treatment of a Wound Evisceration or Dehiscence

It is necessary to know how to provide emergency care for a client with a wound evisceration or dehiscence. The nurse is often the first to come across such an emergency in a postoperative client and must be prepared to act immediately.

Emergency Ventilator Placement

The nurse must know how to assist in emergency ventilator placement for a client in acute distress.

Pathophysiology

Pathophysiology refers to the body being in an unhealthy state. This can occur from poor lifestyle choices, heredity, injury, age, or an unknown reason. Meeting the basic needs of the body allows it to remain at the healthiest point possible. Basic needs of the body include:

- Fresh air
- Nutritious food in an appropriate amount
- A safe, clean, comfortable environment free of infectious or disease-carrying agents
- Fresh water
- Proper sanitation
- Freedom from excessive stressors
- Adequate sleep in a dark, quiet room
- Freedom to exercise

When the body enters an unhealthy state, modern medicine attempts to correct the situation. First, knowledge of what has caused the poor health is ascertained if possible. For example, someone with emphysema should stop smoking immediately. Second, knowledge of the disease is used to correct the unhealthy state. Medication or surgery is frequently utilized. Third, the patient is stabilized and headed toward recovery if possible. Advice is given to restore and maintain health.

Radiation Therapy

Radiation therapy is most commonly used to treat various types of cancer. General principles of radiation therapy include:

- This therapy contains ionizing radiation.

- The goal is to kill or retard the growth of cancer cells. Healthy cells are also damaged or killed during this procedure.

- Radiation may come from alpha, beta, or gamma rays.

- Radiation may be given internally or externally.

- Internal radiation is sealed so that it does not contaminate body fluids. It is placed for a period of time at the area of the cancer.

- External radiation is aimed directly at the area of the cancer.

- Radiation therapy is given for a period of time, such as three days a week for eight weeks. The client's progress is then evaluated. More radiation therapy may then be ordered. There is generally a maximum total amount of radiation that can be given.

Principles of safe administration of radiation include:

- Pregnant staff members must stay away from radiation sources.
- A device, such a special badge, may be provided to measure exposure to radiation.
- Alpha and beta rays can be blocked by rubber gloves.
- Gamma rays can be blocked by thick lead or concrete.
- Exposure should be limited by time and by distance.
- Any staff members working around radiation must be thoroughly trained in both everyday procedures and emergency procedures.

Cancers commonly treated with radiation therapy include:

- Multiple myeloma
- Breast cancer
- Primary and metastatic brain tumors
- Primary and metastatic spinal cord tumors
- Biliary tract cancer
- Colon cancer
- Rectal cancer
- Anal cancer
- Prostate cancer
- Uterine cancer
- Cervical cancer
- Lung cancer
- Esophageal cancer
- Stomach cancer
- Pancreatic cancer
- Gallbladder cancer
- Liver cancer
- Vaginal cancer
- Brain cancer
- Neck cancer
- Hodgkin's disease
- Non-Hodgkin's lymphoma
- Soft-tissue sarcomas
- Bone sarcomas

Nursing interventions for clients receiving radiation therapy include:

- Instruct client on what to expect during and after radiation therapy.

- Monitor or restrict visitors for clients receiving internal radiation.

- Treat skin complaints such as burning, redness, itching, or sloughing.

- Use a bed cradle if needed.

- Cover exposed areas with a sterile dressing.

- Keep damaged skin free from soap or other chemicals.

- Teach client to avoid sunlight, heat, cold, or restriction to skin damaged by radiation.

- Administer anti-emetics prior to meals.

- Make meals small and attractive. Open the lid of the tray outside of the room to avoid odors, which can be nauseating.

- Administer antidiarrheals as needed.

- Monitor electrolytes if the client has persistent diarrhea.

- Encourage a high-protein diet if client becomes anemic.

- Assess for bleeding and teach client how to avoid injury and bleeding if the client develops thrombocytopenia.

- Keep the client from sources of infection if the client develops leukopenia.

- Monitor the client's lab values for signs of impending anemia, thrombocytopenia, or leukopenia.

Review of Diseases and Disorders

Smart Strategies

- Know your diseases and disorders. Spend more study time on the common ones.

- Think of client conditions in terms of what the nurse will be doing for the client.

- When studying diseases, it may help to ask yourself what you would include or expect to see on the nursing care plan for a client with the particular disease.

The nurse should be familiar with the etiology, presentation, and treatment for all common diseases and disorders. This list is provided to give test takers a beginning point for review purposes. It is not meant to be inclusive. Highlight any conditions you do not feel comfortable with and devote study time to those areas. Within this list, some diseases and disorders have been expanded to provide test takers with additional information. These expanded sections are highlighted for your reference.

Diseases and Disorders of the Nervous System

Alzheimer's Disease

Brain Aneurysm

Brain Tumor

Cluster Headache

Encephalitis

Epilepsy

Parkinson's Disease

Severed Spinal Cord

Stroke

Huntington's Disease (Huntington's Chorea)

Meningitis

Migraine Headache

Multiple Sclerosis

Myasthenia Gravis

Traumatic Brain Injury

Trigeminal Neuralgia

Diseases and Disorders of the Eye

Blepharitis

Cataracts – *Expanded*

Quick Facts About Cataracts:

- Can occur at any age from newborn to senility
- Most common in the elderly
- Can occur in one or both eyes
- Most people have mild cataracts by age 70

Presentation: Early: Painless, blurred vision, reduced visual acuity. Late: blurred vision degenerating to blindness, lens opaqueness, absent red reflex.

Treatment: Lens replacement surgery

Pre-operative nursing interventions include:
- Obtain IV access
- Administer a sedative
- Give medication to reduce intraocular pressure
- Instill eye medications for mydriasis, vasoconstriction, and paralysis

Post-operative nursing interventions include:
- The client may be wearing an eye patch
- Instill ophthalmic antibiotics and steroids
- Position the client on the non-operative side, and later in semi-Fowler's position
- Administer mild analgesics
- Explain and enforce activity restrictions
- Monitor for infection and bleeding

Conjunctivitis – *Expanded*

Quick Facts about Conjunctivitis

Inflammatory Conjunctivitis

Etiology: Occurs in response to exposure to allergens or irritants

Presentation: Tearing, itching, bloodshot eyes, edema, and burning

Treatment: Corticosteroid and vasoconstrictive ophthalmic drops or ointment

Infectious Conjunctivitis

Etiology: Occurs in response to a bacterial or viral organism

Presentation: Tearing, bloodshot eyes, edema, and watery or mucus-filled discharge

Treatment: Antibiotic ophthalmic ointment or drops. The drainage may be cultured. Care must be taken not to spread between persons or eye-to-eye.

Common type: Bacterial conjunctivitis (pink eye). This frequently occurs among school-aged children.

Diabetic Retinopathy

Glaucoma – *Expanded*

Quick Facts About Glaucoma

- Results from increased intraocular pressure (IOP)
- Several types exist — some occur slowly and some are emergencies
- More common in the elderly
- 10 percent of persons over 80 affected

Presentation: Determined by ophthalmic examination, decrease in visual fields, some types are painful, reddened sclera, nonreactive pupil, halos around lights

Treatment:

Medical Treatment
- Medical treatment is attempted first.
- Nursing interventions in medical treatment
- Administer ophthalmic beta-blockers and miotics
- Administer IV osmotics in emergency situations

Surgical Treatment
- Laser surgery may be required if medical treatment does not adequately reduce IOP.

Post-operative nursing interventions include:
- The client will be wearing an eye patch
- Administer ophthalmic steroids
- Position client on non-operative side
- Monitor for choroidal hemorrhage — symptoms include pain and decreased vision
- Macular Degeneration
- Retinal Tear

Diseases and Disorders of the Ear

Hearing Loss

Labyrinthitis

Meniere's Disease – *Expanded*

Quick Facts About Meniere's Disease:

- Usually occurs in the third, fourth, or fifth decade of life
- Clients frequently need to lie down from extreme vertigo
- May effect one or both ears

Presentation: Tinnitus, hearing loss, and vertigo. Nausea and vomiting may occur. Attacks last several hours and may abate for weeks. Eventual hearing loss occurs.

Nursing interventions include:
- Sodium-restricted diet
- Fluid-restricted diet
- Educate client about smoking cessation
- Administer antiemetics, antihistamines, diuretics, and antianxiety medications

Otitis Media – *Expanded*

Quick Facts About Otitis Media

- Can occur at any age
- Most common in children
- Usually caused by infection leading to inflammation
- Eustachian tube and mastoid also affected
- The tympanic membrane may rupture

Presentation: Pain, fullness, loss of hearing, fever, malaise, mild vertigo. Otoscopic examination may reveal a red tympanic membrane.

Treatment:

Non-surgical nursing interventions include:

- Place client on bed rest.
- Application of heat or cold may be ordered; heat must never be applied without physician order
- Administration of oral or IV antibiotics
- Administration of analgesics, decongestants, antihistamines, and antipyretics

Surgical interventions include:

- Myringotomy

Pre-operative nursing interventions include:

- Administer oral or IV antibiotics
- Prepare external canal by cleaning with povidone-iodine

Post-operative nursing interventions include:

- Change dressing every 24 hours or as ordered
- Administer oral or IV antibiotics
- Keep ear dry

Hematological Diseases and Disorders

Aplastic Anemia

Folic Acid and Vitamin B12 Deficiency Anemia

Hemophilia

Hodgkin's Lymphoma and Non-Hodgkin's Lymphoma

Iron Deficiency Anemia

Leukemia

Polycythemia Vera

Sickle Cell Anemia

Thrombotic Thrombocytopenic Purpura

Musculoskeletal Diseases and Disorders

Amputations

Bone Fractures

Carpal Tunnel Syndrome

Malignant Bone Tumors

Muscular Dystrophy

Osteomyelitis

Osteoporosis – *Expanded*

Quick Facts About Osteoporosis

- Most often found in the spine, hips, and wrists
- Half of all women over 65 have osteoporosis
- 20 percent of osteoporosis sufferers are men

Presentation: Fractures, back pain, kyphosis, and shortened height

Treatments for osteoporosis include:

- Calcium with Vitamin D
- Estrogen
- Bisphosphonates
- Calcitonin
- Weight-bearing exercises
- Orthotic appliances
- Paget's Disease
- Scoliosis

Gastrointestinal Diseases and Disorders

Appendicitis – *Expanded*

Quick Facts About Appendicitis

Presentation: Pain, tenderness, rigidity at McBurney's point in the lower right quadrant, nausea, vomiting, anorexia, rebound tenderness, and elevated white blood cell count

Nursing interventions include:
- Maintain NPO status
- Start an IV and administer fluids
- Administer analgesics only after diagnosis is made
- Keep head of bed elevated
- Avoid application of heat, laxatives, or enemas

Post-operative nursing interventions include:
- Monitor suture line and drains if present
- Administer analgesics
- Administer intravenous or oral antibiotics

Cholecystitis

Choleliathisis

Cirrhosis

Colon Polyps

Colorectal Cancer – *Expanded*

Quick Facts About Colorectal Cancer

- Most common type is adenocarcinoma
- Most frequent metastasis site is the liver
- The vast majority of victims are over 50 years of age.
- May be caused by a high fat diet
- More common in black Americans

Presentation: Changes in the stool, rectal bleeding, pain, narrowing of stools, and abdominal distention

Non-surgical nursing interventions include:
- Prepare client for radiation therapy
- Administer chemotherapy

Pre-operative nursing interventions include:
- Administer oral or IV antibiotics
- Prepare bowel with clear liquid diet, laxatives, enema, and/or a large quantity of GoLYTELY®
- Make sure client has IV access
- Place a nasogastric tube
- Prepare client for the possibility of a colostomy

Post-operative nursing interventions include:
- Perform colostomy care if indicated
- Monitor for fever, drainage at surgical site, and infection
- If drains have been placed, monitor closely
- Administer analgesics

Crohn's Disease

Diverticulitis

Diverticulosis

Fecal Incontinence

Food Poisoning

Gastric Carcinoma

Gastric Ulcers – *Expanded*

Quick Facts About Gastric Ulcers
- Frequently caused by helicobacter pylori bacteria

- May lead to hemorrhage
- May be related to use of non-steroidal anti-inflammatory drugs
- Can occur at any age
- Most common in elderly clients

Presentation: Dyspepsia and pain in upper left quadrant

Medical interventions include:

- Triple drug therapy — an antibiotic (amoxicillin or tetracycline), metronidazole, and bismuth
- Antisecretory or hyposecretory medications
- Antacids
- H2- receptor antagonists

Gastroenteritis – *Expanded*

Quick Facts About Gastroenteritis

- Causes significant watery diarrhea and/or vomiting
- Can quickly lead to dehydration in young children and the elderly
- Caused by a bacterial or viral organism

Presentation: Watery diarrhea, vomiting, dehydration, abdominal distention, nausea, and cramping

Nursing interventions include:

- Replace lost fluids via oral route or IV
- Advance client from liquids to bland foods to a normal diet
- Monitor client for dehydration
- Administer anti-infectives and anitperistaltic agents
- Follow precautions to avoid spread of organism

Gastroesophageal Reflux Disease (GERD) – *Expanded*

Quick Facts About GERD

Presentation: Regurgitation and dyspepsia

Medical interventions include:
- Antacids
- Histamine receptor antagonists

Post-operative nursing interventions include:
- Suction oral secretions
- Maintain NPO status.
- Maintain nasogastric tube
- Monitor suture line and clean as ordered
- Administer analgesics
- Keep head of bed elevated

Client education topics to relieve GERD include:
- Sleep with head elevated
- Stop smoking
- Limit spicy and acidic foods
- Avoid eating near bedtime
- Maintain a normal weight

Helminthic Infestation

Hepatitis (all types)

Hiatal hernia

Hemorrhoids

Irritable Bowel Syndrome – *Expanded*

Quick Facts About Irritable Bowel Syndrome

- Women are affected twice as often as men
- May be stress related

Presentation: Constipation mixed with diarrhea (soft, watery stools with mucus), abdominal pain, and bloating

Nursing interventions include:

- Encourage a high-fiber diet and adequate fluid intake
- Encourage client to avoid foods that precipitate attacks, including caffeine and alcohol
- Teach relaxation techniques

Liver Cancer

Malnutrition

Obesity

Pancreatic Cancer

Pancreatitis (Acute and Chronic)

Stomatitis

Ulcerative Colitis – *Expanded*

Quick Facts About Ulcerative Colitis

- Occurs more often in persons of Jewish descent
- Women are more likely to be affected
- Occurs most often in late adolescence to early adulthood
- Occurs in late fifties to early sixties
- Over 20 percent of victims will require a colectomy

Presentation: Tenesmus, abdominal pain, fever, abdominal distention, bloody diarrhea or stools with mucus, and passing of colon tissue

Nursing interventions include:

- Administer corticosteroids, anti-inflammatory drugs, and salicylates
- Keep client NPO during severe flare-ups
- Administer total parenteral nutrition (TPN)
- Advance to a low-fiber diet

Surgical interventions include:

The outcome of colectomy surgery may be a permanent ileostomy with pouch, "continent" stoma, or anastamosis, in which the ileum is connected to the anal canal.

Diseases and Disorders of the Endocrine System

- Cushing's Syndrome
- Diabetes Insipidus
- Diabetes Mellitus Type I
- Diabetes Mellitus Type II
- Hyperparathyroidism
- Hyperthryoidism
- Hypoparathyroidism
- Hypopituitarism
- Hypothryoidism
- Thyroid Cancer

Diseases and Disorders of the Integumentary System

- Acne
- Basal Cell Carcinoma
- Burns
- Decubitis Ulcers
- Eczema
- Malignant Melanoma
- Parasitic Infestations
- Pruritis
- Psoriasis
- Pyelonephritis
- Squamous cell carcinoma

Psychiatric Disorders and Conditions

- Amnesia
- Anxiety
- Depression
- Obsessive-Compulsive Disorder
- Panic Disorder
- Paranoid Personality Disorder

- Borderline Personality Disorder
- Hypochondriasis
- Manic Depression
- Phobias
- Posttraumatic Stress Disorder
- Schizophrenia
- Social Anxiety Disorder

Diseases and Disorders of the Urinary System

- Bladder Cancer
- Cystitis
- Diabetic Nephropathy
- Glomerulonephritis (Acute and Chronic)
- Kidney Disease
- Renal Failure (Acute and Chronic, including dialysis)
- Urinary incontinence

Diseases and Disorders of the Reproductive System

- Amenorrhea
- Benign Prostatic Hypertrophy
- Breast Cancer
- Cervical Cancer
- Chlamydia
- Dysmenorrhea
- Endometrial Cancer
- Epididymitis
- Erectile Dysfunction
- Genital Herpes
- Gonorrhea
- Menopause with Excessive Symptomology
- Orchitis
- Ovarian Cancer
- Penile Cancer
- Pelvic Inflammatory Disease
- Polycystic Ovary Syndrome
- Premenstrual Syndrome
- Priapism
- Prostate Cancer
- Prostatitis
- Syphillis
- Testicular Cancer
- Uterine Prolapse
- Vaginal Cancer
- Vaginitis

Diseases and Disorders of the Respiratory Tract

- Acute Respiratory Distress Syndrome
- Asthma
- Chronic Bronchitis
- Cystic Fibrosis
- Emphysema
- Epistaxis
- Influenza
- Laryngitis
- Lung Absess
- Obstructive Sleep Apnea
- Orophyrangeal Cancer
- Pharyngitis
- Pnuemonia (All Types)
- Pneumothorax
- Primary Pulmonary Hypertension
- Pulmonary Embolism
- Respiratory Failure
- Rhinitis
- Sarcoidosis
- Sinusitis
- Tonsillitis
- Tuberculosis

Diseases and Disorders of the Cardiac System

- Abdominal Aortic Aneurysm
- Atherosclerosis
- Arteriosclerosis
- Cardiomyopathy
- Congestive Heart Failure
- Coronary Artery Disease
- Dysrhythmia
- Endocarditis
- Pericarditis
- Peripheral Arterial Disease
- Peripheral Venous Disease
- Shock (All Types)

Immune System Diseases and Disorders

- Allergy
- Cancer (All Types Not Mentioned Elsewhere)
- Fibromyalgia
- Human Immunodeficiency Virus and Acquired Immune Deficiency Syndrome
- Gout
- Infection (All Types Not Mentioned Elsewhere)
- Lupus
- Lyme Disease
- Osteoarthritis
- Rheumatoid Arthritis

Systemic and Other Diseases and Disorders

- Heatstroke
- Hypercalcemia
- Hyperkalemia
- Hypernatremia
- Hypocalcemia
- Hypokalemia
- Hyponatremia
- Metabolic Acidosis
- Metabolic Alkalosis
- Respiratory Acidosis
- Respiratory Alkalosis

Other Health Issues

- Circumcision
- Mental Illness (All Major Types)
- Surgery
- Transplantation

Diseases and Conditions Encountered More Often or First Diagnosed in Pediatric Populations

- Acute Glomerulonephritis
- Autism
- Celiac Disease
- Cerebral Palsy
- Cleft Lip and Palate
- Cystic Fibrosis
- Down's Syndrome
- Encephalitis
- Hemophilia
- Hirschsprung's Disease
- Hydrocephalus
- Hyperbilirubinemia
- Intussusception
- Lymphoma (Hodgkin's and Non-Hodgkin's)
- Meningitis
- Nephrosis
- Phenylketonuria
- Prematurity
- Osteogenic Sarcoma
- Pediculosis
- Reye's Syndrome
- Rheumatic Fever
- Scoliosis
- Sickle Cell Anemia
- Spina Bifida
- Tay-Sachs Disease
- Tetralogy of Fallot
- Wilm's Tumor

Conditions Found in the Childbearing Client

Abruptio Placentae

Dystocia

Eclampsia and Pre-Eclampsia

Ectopic Pregnancy

Hydatidiform Mole

Placenta Previa

Spontaneous Abortion

Conclusion

Smart Strategies

- Walk proudly into the examination room and know that you will walk out proudly as well. You have chosen an honorable profession, and you should allow the confidence that carried you through nursing school to carry you through the NCLEX exam, as well.

I hope you feel confident and ready to pass the NCLEX and begin your long-anticipated nursing career. Nursing school prepared you well and, with this competent review, you are ready to score highly on the exam.

I wish you much success in your nursing career and encourage you to be a student of lifelong learning. May you touch many lives during your nursing career.

Appendix A

Common Abbreviations

Abbreviation	Meaning
ABG	arterial blood gas
ac	before meals
ACE	angiotensin converting enzyme
ADH	antidiuretic hormone
ADL	activities of daily living
ad lib	as desired
AED	automatic external defibrillator
AFP	alpha-fetoprotein
AIDS	acquired immunodeficiency syndrome
ALS	amyotrophic lateral sclerosis (a form of muscular dystrophy)
ALT	alkaline phosphatase
ARDS	adult respiratory distress syndrome
AST	aspartate aminotransferase
AV	atrioventricular
ax	axillary temperature
bid	two times a day
BLS	basic life support
BMR	basal metabolic rate

BP	blood pressure
BPH	benign prostatic hypertrophy
bpm	beats per minute
BUN	blood urea nitrogen
C	Celsius
c̄	with
Ca	calcium
CABG	coronary artery bypass graft
CAD	coronary artery disease
CAPD	continuous ambulatory peritoneal dialysis
CBC	complete blood count
CCU	coronary care unit
CDC	U.S. Centers for Disease Control and Prevention
CHF	congestive heart failure
CK	creatine kinase
Cl	chloride
cm	centimeter
CMV	cytomegalovirus
CNS	central nervous system
CO	carbon monoxide
CO2	carbon dioxide
COPD	continuous obstructive pulmonary disease
CPAP	continuous positive airway pressure
CPK	creatine phosphokinase
CPR	cardiopulmonary resuscitation
CRP	c-reactive protein
C & S	culture and sensitivity
CSF	cerebrospinal fluid
CT	computerized tomography
CVA	cerebrovascular accident
CVP	central venous pressure
cu	cubic
DC	discontinue
DIC	disseminated intravascular coagulation

dl	deciliter
DNR	do not resuscitate
DPT	diphtheria, pertussis, tetanus vaccine
DVT	deep vein thrombosis
D/W	dextrose in water
Dx	diagnosis
ECG	electrocardiogram
EKG	electrocardiogram
ECT	electroconvulsive therapy
EEG	electroencephalogram
EMG	electromyography
ESR	erythrocyte sedimentation rate or sed rate
ESRD	end stage renal disease
ET	endotracheal tube
F	Fahrenheit
FBS	fasting blood sugar
FFP	fresh frozen plasma
FUO	fever of undetermined origin
G	gram
GB	gallbladder
Gfr	glomerular filtration rate
gm	gram
gr	grain
gtt	drop
GU	genitourinary
H	hour
HCG	human chorionic gonadotropin
HCO3	bicarbonate
Hct	hematocrit
HDL	high density lipoprotein
Hg	mercury
Hgb	hemoglobin
HIV	human immunodeficiency virus
HR	heart rate

H2O	water
Hx	history
IABP	intra-aortic balloon pump
I&O	intake and output
IDDM	insulin dependent diabetes mellitus
IPPB	intermittent positive pressure breathing
IUD	intrauterine device
IVP	intravenous pyelogram
K+	potassium
kg	kilogram
Kvo	keep vein open
L, l	liter
LA	left atrium
lb.	pound
LBBB	left bundle branch block
LDL	low-density lipoproteins
LOC	level of consciousness
lt	left
LV	left ventricle
MAO	monoamine oxidase
Mcg	microgram
MD	muscular dystrophy
MDI	metered dose inhaler
mEq	milliequivalent
Mg	magnesium
mg	milligram
MI	myocardial infarction
ml	milliliter
mm	millimeter
MMR	measles, mumps, rubella
MS	multiple sclerosis
NIDDM	non-insulin dependent diabetes mellitus
Na+	sodium
NaCl	sodium chloride

neuro	neurological
NG	nasogastric
noc	at night
NPO	nothing by mouth
NS	normal saline
NSAID	nonsteroidal anti-inflammatory drug
NST	non-stress test
O2	oxygen
OR	operating room
os	mouth
OTC	over-the-counter
oz	ounce
P	after, post
P	pulse
P	Phosphorus
PAC	premature atrial complexes
PaCO2	partial pressure of carbon dioxide in arterial blood
PaO2	partial pressure of oxygen in arterial blood
PAD	peripheral artery disease
Pap	papanicolaou
pc	after meals
PCA	patient (client) controlled anesthesia
PCO2	partial pressure of carbon dioxide
PE	pulmonary embolism
PEEP	positive end-expiratory pressure
PERRLA	pupils equal, round, reactive to light and accommodation
PET	positron emission tomography
pH	hydrogen ion concentration
PID	pelvic inflammatory disease
PKU	phenylketonuria
PMS	premenstrual syndrome
PO, po	per os (by mouth)
PO2	partial pressure of oxygen
PPD	positive purified protein derivative

PRN, prn	as needed
pro time	prothrombin time
PSA	prostate-specific antigen
psi	pounds per square inch
PT	physical therapy
PT	prothrombin time
PTCA	percutaneous transluminal coronary angioplasty
PTT	partial thromboplastin time
PUD	peptic ulcer disease
PVC	premature ventricular contraction
Q	every
qh	every hour
qid	four times a day
R	respirations
R	rectal temperature
RA	rheumatoid arthritis
RBBB	right bundle branch block
RBC	red blood cell
RDA	recommended daily allowance
Rh+	an antigen that may be on a blood cell
Rh-	an antigen that may be on a blood cell
R/O, r/o	rule out
ROM	range of motion
rt	right
Rx	prescription
$\bar{s}$	without
SA	sinoatrial
SaO2	systemic arterial oxygen saturation
sed rate	sedimentation rate
SIDS	sudden infant death syndrome
SL	sublingual
SOB	shortness of breath
$\bar{\bar{s}}$	one half
SS	soap suds

stat	immediately
STD	sexually transmitted disease
sx	symptoms
T	temperature
tabs	tablets
TB	Tuberculosis
TBS	tablespoon
TED	antiembolism stockings
TENS	transcutaneous electrical nerve stimulation
TIA	transient ischemic attack
TIBC	total iron binding capacity
TID	three times a day
TPN	total parenteral nutrition
TSH	thyroid-stimulating hormone
tsp	teaspoon
TURP	transuretheral prostactectomy
UA	urinalysis
ung	ointment
URI	upper respiratory infection
UTI	urinary tract infection
VF	ventricular fibrillation
Vfib	ventricular fibrillation
VPC	ventricular premature complex
VS, vs	vital signs
VT	ventricular tachycardia
WBC	white blood cell
wt	weight

Appendix B

Practice Test One

Try this 75-question practice test. The results and rationales follow. The answers are numbered 1,2,3,4, just as you will encounter on the NCLEX. Time yourself on the test to get a feel for how long it takes you to answer the questions, but do not rush your answers.

1. The nurse must check the client's chart for _____ before inserting a feeding tube.

    1. Drug allergies
    2. Advance directives
    3. X-ray results
    4. A dietician consult

2. The physician orders an enema for a weak, elderly client. She says, "No!" when the nurse explains the procedure. What is the appropriate response for the nurse?

    1. Physically place her in position and give her the enema, knowing that she needs the procedure.

2. Call the physician and relay her refusal.
3. Record the refusal in the nurse's notes and pass it along during report.
4. Ask the patient why she is saying no and discuss the need for the procedure.

3. Which client would most likely benefit from having a case manager?

1. A healthy, 70-year-old widowed man
2. A college student newly diagnosed with diabetes
3. An attorney who is pregnant for the first time
4. A 6-year-old child who has just been diagnosed with bone cancer

4. Which issue would least likely be addressed at a client's interdisciplinary team meeting?

1. Her post-chemotherapy laboratory values
2. Her appetite
3. The fact that her son has not come to visit her since admission
4. Her friendship with her roommate

5. The nurse is assigned a client with a type of insulin pump the nurse is unfamiliar with. Her best strategy is to:

1. Say nothing and hope she can figure it out.
2. Ask the client how to operate the pump.
3. Tell her superior she is unfamiliar with the pump.
4. Ask her peers if they have ever worked with the pump.

6. The nursing-home staff nurse is asked to conduct a staff development conference for new, unlicensed assistive personnel to discuss what vital sign findings they should report to the nurse immediately. Which of the following should the nurse definitely not include in the criteria?

1. A pulse rate below 50
2. A systolic blood pressure above 160
3. A respiratory rate above 16
4. A temperature above 100 degrees

7. The medical-surgical nurse has been sent to a conference to learn how to use a new pain management pump. She is now to teach others how to use the pump. Who should she expect to educate at the in-service? Mark all that apply.

1. The other nurses on her floor
2. The unlicensed, assistive personnel
3. The nurse manager of the medical-surgical unit
4. The respiratory therapists
5. The physical therapists

8. An agency nurse arrives for duty on the medical-surgical unit. After taking report, the staff nurse notices her taking pills in a break area. An hour later, the agency nurse is slurring her words and laughing inappropriately. What should the staff nurse do first?

1. Ask the nurse why she is laughing.
2. Ask the other staff nurses if they have noticed the behavior.
3. Contact her supervisor and tell her exactly what she witnessed.
4. Call the agency and report the nurse.

9. Which statement about alternative therapies by the client requires follow-up by the nurse?

1. I eat a balanced vegetarian diet and it helps my arthritis.
2. I drink an ounce of hydrogen peroxide each morning to prevent the cancer that killed my mother.

3. I get reiki treatments in addition to physical therapy for my back pain.

4. Aromatherapy helps to reduce my stress levels.

10. The nurse should check the client's respiratory rate prior to the administration of which type of medications?

   1. Cholesterol-lowering medications
   2. Insulin
   3. Otic medications
   4. Narcotics

11. The nurse is conducting an osteoporosis screening. Which of the following clients is not at high risk of osteoporosis?

   1. A 70-year-old Caucasian female
   2. A 50-year-old heavy smoker
   3. A 56-year-old thin, Asian female
   4. A 45-year-old vegan who does not exercise regularly
   5. A 50-year-old black female bodybuilder

12. The nurse is caring for a client with seasonal affective disorder. Which of the following treatments should she be expecting to educate the client about? Select all that apply.

   1. Hypnotic medication
   2. Phototherapy
   3. Antidepressant medication
   4. A 30-minute daily walk outdoors
   5. Psychotherapy

13. The nurse is asked to assist with a biophysical profile (BPP) ultrasound of the fetus of her client. She knows that the test consists of which of the following components? Select all that apply.

    1. Fetal motion
    2. Non-stress test
    3. Amniotic fluid volume
    4. Fetal muscle tone
    5. Fetal breathing

14. The nurse is accepting a fecal occult blood sample from a client in the physician's office. The client is asked what he has eaten for the last three days. Which of the following foods would alert the nurse to repeat the test if there is a positive result?

    1. White rice
    2. Milk
    3. Cantaloupe
    4. Chocolate candy

15. The nurse is looking over the medications she will be administering to clients for the day. She should assess the hearing of the client receiving which of the following drugs?

    1. Gentamicin
    2. Lanoxin
    3. Penicillin
    4. Thorazine

16. An obstetrical client is scheduled for an amniocentesis. Her husband asks about the purpose of the test. The nurse explains that, for a pregnancy of 16 weeks, the test will show which of the following? Select all that apply.

1. The sex of the fetus
2. Chromosomal defects
3. The size of the fetus
4. Neural tube defects
5. The blood type of the fetus

17. The nurse is preparing a client for peritoneal dialysis. Which of the following is normally indicated?

    1. Performing a mini-mental status examination
    2. Serving the client lunch
    3. Warming the dialysate
    4. Placing the client in high-Fowler's position

18. The history of which of the following clients raises concern about latex allergy? Select all that apply.

    1. A three month old infant undergoing surgery for a fracture.
    2. A 50-year-old woman undergoing her seventh reconstructive surgery following a burn.
    3. An avid gardener hospitalized for a fall with head trauma.
    4. A man of Asian descent who is allergic to bananas.
    5. A carpenter undergoing surgery for a herniated disc.

19. A client is admitted with a fever of unknown origin, currently at 103 degrees. She is diaphoretic, pale, and listless. Which of the following measures should you include in her plan of care?

    1. A low-fat, low-calorie diet.
    2. Restricting visitors.
    3. Keep her on bed rest only.
    4. Change her linens frequently.

20. The nurse is describing the steps involved in a Schilling test to a client. Her daughter states, "This sounds like a lot of trouble. Why is this necessary anyway?" How should the nurse respond?

   1. This test will measure her ability to produce vitamin B12.
   2. This test will measure her ability to absorb vitamin B12.
   3. This test will measure her ability to digest vitamin B12.
   4. This test will measure her ability to excrete vitamin B12.

21. It is 6:00 p.m. Which statement by a client requires the immediate attention of the nurse?

   1. "I haven't passed water all day."
   2. "I'm starving; is my dinner tray coming?"
   3. "I'm so bored, I could scream."
   4. "I'm feeling sleepy."

22. The psychiatric nurse is helping to plan a group therapy session. How many clients should she place into one session?

   1. Three
   2. Four
   3. Seven
   4. Eleven

23. A 26-year-old female presents to the emergency department complaining of a stiff neck, fever, and vomiting. What should the nurse anticipate?

   1. The physician sending the client home with pain medication, an anti-emetic, and an anti-pyretic
   2. The physician ordering a blood test for encephalitis
   3. The physician ordering an MRI of the brain
   4. The physician ordering the client activated charcoal

24. The client is an 8-year-old child who has just had a myelogram. Which of the following should the nurse not do?

1. Have the child lie flat for four hours.
2. Encourage the child to drink fluids.
3. Ask the child to attempt to void if he does not void within eight hours.
4. Give the child acetaminophen for pain.

25. The nurse is teaching the newly diagnosed diabetic client how to give herself an insulin injection. Which statement(s) by the client indicate the need for further teaching?

1. I am so scared of shots; I hope I can do this.
2. It is hard to inject my own arms; I will use my abdomen and thighs.
3. If I run out of my insulin, I can use my husband's.
4. I am glad my insulin will be safe out of the refrigerator for a few hours so that I can take it to work.
5. I will keep snacks handy in case my blood sugar gets low.

26. A 4-year-old child is ordered Lanoxin 0.12 mg per day by mouth. The bottle contains Lanoxin 0.05 mg per milliliter. How much solution should the nurse prepare?

_____.

27. Which dinner would be most appropriate for a 10-year-old child with third-degree burns to his legs?

1. Cheeseburger, baked beans, peaches, vanilla milkshake
2. Vegetable soup, crackers, banana, milk
3. Chicken taco, tomatoes, apple, vegetable juice
4. Pureed ham, pureed green beans, applesauce, and grape juice

28. A 45-year-old male client is hospitalized with chronic granulocytic leukemia. Which of the following is least likely to be in the client's plan of care?

    1. A regular diet including three meals a day with ad lib snacks.
    2. Bed rest with bathroom privileges.
    3. Assistance as needed with bathing, shaving with a manual razor, and teeth brushing.
    4. A visit from a representative of the hospital's cancer support group.

29. A 70-year-old client has presented to the physician's office with herpes zoster. He states that he is miserable due to the itching. Which of the following should the nurse instruct him to do? Select all that apply.

    1. Apply cold compresses three times a day.
    2. Carefully remove the scabs as soon as they appear.
    3. Do not disturb the lesions at all.
    4. Apply rubbing alcohol twice a day to the area and the surrounding skin.
    5. Avoid eating dairy products until the lesions are completely gone.

30. Which of the following clients should the nurse place in semi-Fowler's position?

    1. A 90-year-old client with decubitus ulcers
    2. A 10-year-old client with ascites
    3. A 50-year-old client preparing for a lumbar discectomy tomorrow
    4. A 20-year-old client with a compound comminuted fracture of the fibula and tibia

31. The client is suffering a personal crisis. What is it most important for the nurse to convey to the client?

1. It is everyone's responsibility to deal with crisis.
2. The nurse will handle the crisis for the client.
3. If the client does not think about the crisis, it will go away.
4. The client has the skills and ability to deal with the crisis.

32. An 18-year-old client is admitted with preeclampsia. Which of the following should alert the nurse to a possible impending seizure?

1. Periorbital edema
2. 2+ proteinuria
3. Urinary output of 100 milliliters per hour
4. Severe epigastric pain

33. A female client with diverticulitis is about to be discharged. The nurse has educated her about following a low-residue diet. Which of the following foods can she eat at home?

1. Pinto beans
2. Blueberries
3. Cantaloupe
4. Prune juice

34. A client is admitted to the psychiatric unit with obsessive-compulsive disorder. He compulsively washes his hands. He is to be treated with exposure response prevention therapy. The nurse should anticipate which of the following?

1. Explaining to the client that one 30-second hand washing is adequate
2. Showing the client that other people only wash their hands one time
3. Having the client dirty his hands and not allowing him to wash them

4. Allowing the client to wash his hands a prescribed number of times per day

35. A client is admitted to the medical floor with hepatitis A. Which of the following symptoms should the nurse expect the client to exhibit? Select all that apply.

1. Anorexia
2. Severe headache
3. Chills
4. Tenderness over the liver
5. Leg tremors

36. An agency nurse advises the charge nurse that she has never cared for an ileostomy before. Her client has ileostomy care ordered during her shift. Which response by the charge nurse is appropriate?

1. Ask the client's wife if she can show you how it is done.
2. Read the procedure in the policy manual and follow the instructions.
3. I will perform the procedure myself.
4. I can perform the procedure at 2:30. You should be prepared to observe.
5. See if another nurse can do it for you.

37. The client presents to the gynecologist's office for an annual appointment. Her husband angrily asks the nurse why the client has not become pregnant. The nurse sees on the client's chart that she has been receiving monthly birth control pills for the last three years. How should the nurse respond to the client's husband?

1. "You would have to ask your wife that question."
2. "There are many reasons that people do not become pregnant.

Perhaps the physician can help you with that question."
3. "People only get pregnant when it is God's will."
4. "How many children would you like to have?"

38. A client asks the nurse if she must take her medications forever. Observing her medication list, she relates that the client will probably take which of the following medications indefinitely?

1. Lanoxin
2. Lexapro
3. Ampicillin
4. Robaxin

39. A client calls the crisis hotline and states that he is about to kill himself. Which of the following statements would be an inappropriate response by the nurse?

1. "Tell me what has been happening in your life."
2. "You know better than to do that; what would happen to your children?"
3. "I want you to promise me that you will not kill yourself for the next 24 hours."
4. "How long have you been feeling this way?"

40. An inpatient client is being prepared for external beam therapy. Which of the following precautions should the nurse place the client under?

1. Contact isolation precautions
2. Absolutely no visitors
3. Universal precautions
4. No pregnant or child visitors

41. The nurse would anticipate a diagnosis of cryptorchidism in a client of which of the following ages?

    1. 4 months of age
    2. 5 years of age
    3. 18 years of age
    4. 72 years of age

42. A client is admitted to the intensive care unit with acute glomerulonephritis. The nurse should anticipate which of the following treatments? Select all that apply.

    1. Fluid restriction
    2. Peritoneal dialysis
    3. Intravenous antibiotics for strep infection
    4. Intravenous antihypertensives
    5. Oral muscle relaxants

43. The nurse should be alert for which adverse reaction in a client taking corticosteroids?

    1. Congestive heart failure
    2. Strabismus
    3. Hypoglycemia
    4. Hyperkalemia

44. A child with rubeola is in the pediatric clinic. The child's mother is concerned about whether her other children, all unvaccinated for religious reasons, have been exposed to the virus. The nurse replies that the incubation period for rubeola is:

    1. 3 to 4 days
    2. 5 to 6 days

3. 8 to 12 days
4. 14 to 21 days

45. Which finding in a laboring client would cause the nurse to become concerned about uteroplacental insufficiency?

    1. She begins talking incoherently.
    2. Fetal monitoring shows late decelerations.
    3. Her serum albumin is low.
    4. She is suffering from chills.

46. The nurse should measure an infant's chest circumference when he exhales. Where should the nurse place the measuring tape?

    1. One inch above the nipples
    2. Across the nipples
    3. One inch below the nipples
    4. At the widest point

47. The nurse is to administer 30 ml per hour of D5 ½ NS to a 10-year-old child via an intravenous line with a pediatric microdrip chamber. Calculate how many drops per minute he should set the infusion pump at. Respond with a whole number.

    _____ drops per minute

48. A young woman is in the emergency room, screaming in pain from suspected appendicitis. Which of the following statements by the client brings concern to the nurse?

    1. "I need pain medicine, now!"
    2. "My mother had this same pain, and it was her appendix."

3. "Hey, it suddenly feels better."
4. "Bring a bag; I'm going to be sick."

49. The nurse has created a care plan for a client with severe dehydration. Her nursing diagnosis is "Deficient fluid volume related to caregiver neglect." What criteria should she use to determine achievement of the goal of correcting the issue?

   1. The client has gained three pounds.
   2. The client has moist mucous membranes.
   3. The client states she is not thirsty.
   4. The client is able to walk without assistance.

50. The nurse is at a park when an elderly man suddenly collapses. He is not breathing and has no pulse. She instructs someone to call 911 and begins cardiopulmonary resuscitation. The ratio of chest compressions to breaths in one-person adult CPR is:

   1. 5:1
   2. 5:2
   3. 15:1
   4. 15:2

51. The nurse is at a restaurant when a middle-aged woman begins to choke. She is coughing and pounding on the table. Her friend reaches to perform the Heimlich maneuver. What should the nurse do first?

   1. Ask if a doctor is in the restaurant.
   2. Call 911.
   3. Stop the person who is about to perform the Heimlich maneuver.
   4. Ask what the woman was eating.

52. The nurse is discharging a client who has suffered an aortic aneurysm and now has an artificial graft replacing part of her aorta. What should he be sure to include in the client's discharge instructions?

    1. Never go into a swimming pool.
    2. Do not exert your heart beyond 120 beats per minute.
    3. Advise the physician before you have any major dental work.
    4. Do not hold your breath for longer than 20 seconds.

53. An elderly client has been told that she must lose 50 pounds. She asks the nurse to recommend some exercises for her to follow. The nurse appropriately gives the client which of the following options? Select all that apply.

    1. Jogging
    2. Aquatic exercise
    3. Brisk walking
    4. Yoga
    5. Mild aerobic activity in a supervised class

54. The nurse is monitoring a client in the post-anesthesia care unit. She is aware that clients recover from general anesthesia in a particular order. Put the steps in the correct order.

    1. The client regains his ability to control his behavior and to reason.
    2. The client experiences muscular irritability.
    3. The client shows recognition of pain.
    4. The client is delirious and restless.

    First: _____

    Second: _____

    Third: _____

    Fourth: _____

55. The nurse is caring for a post-operative adult client. Which of the following pain management orders should cause the nurse to call the physician for clarification?

1. Demerol 100 mg IV every 4 hours PRN
2. Morphine sulfate 4 mg IV every 4 hours PRN
3. Codeine sulfate 60 mg PO every 4 hours PRN
4. Ibuprofen 600 mg PO every 6 hours PRN

56. The nurse is teaching a health promotion class. She instructs her students that which of the following disorders has more male victims prior to age 50, and more female victims after age 50?

1. Obsessive-compulsive disorder
2. Bell's palsy
3. Osteoarthritis
4. Myasthenia gravis

57. The nurse receives an order to place a nasogastric tube in a newly admitted client. He knows that NG tubes are inserted for the following reasons: Select all that apply.

1. Pre-operatively before coronary artery bypass graft surgery
2. For relief of severe nausea
3. To evacuate gastric contents
4. To check the client's gag reflex
5. To provide nutritional support through the gastrointestinal tract

58. The nurse is to record the intake and output of her client. Record the total intake for the day shift. Record a whole number.

Breakfast
Orange juice, 4 ounces
Coffee, 6 ounces

Lunch
Milk, 8 ounces
Soup, 240 milliliters
JELL-O,® 120 milliliters

Water Pitcher
½ pitcher consumed; total pitcher volume is 480 milliliters

Intake: _____ milliliters

59. The nurse notes that her client has an erythrocyte sedimentation rate of 55 mm/hr. A student nurse asks her what an elevated ESR indicates. She replies with which of the following explanations:

1. An elevated ESR indicates infection or inflammation somewhere in the body.
2. It is a harmless finding that is computed when a CBC is ordered.
3. An elevated ESR indicates mononucleosis.
4. An elevated ESR indicates malnutrition.

60. The nurse is caring for a client with advanced lung cancer. She knows that all of the following groups of syndromes are associated with lung cancer except the following:

1. Thrombophlebitis, scleroderma, proteinuria, and arthralgia
2. Cushing's syndrome, gynecomastia, arterial thrombosis, and acanthosis nigricans
3. Seizures, edema, polycythemia, and anemia
4. Tonsillitis, Bruton's agammaglobulinemia, lipoma, and Broca's aphasia

61. The psychiatric nurse is giving a 20-year-old client her first dose of Risperdal. She must take which of the following precautions: Select all that apply.

1. Place the client on seizure precautions.
2. Monitor the client's temperature at least every eight hours for the first three days.
3. Check the client's blood sugar or blood glucose level at least weekly.
4. Instruct the client not to take oral contraceptives.

62. The nurse has responded to an alert of cardiopulmonary resuscitation in progress. He is asked to prepare epinephrine for injection for intracardiac injection. What dosage does he anticipate being asked to prepare?

1. 0.25 mg
2. 0.5 mg
3. 2.5 mg
4. 2.6 mg

63. The nurse receives her client's lab work results. She knows that a low pH, elevated $PaCO_2$, low PaO_2, and elevated $K+$ level indicate which of the following conditions?

1. Respiratory acidosis
2. Respiratory alkalosis
3. Metabolic acidosis
4. Metabolic alkalosis

64. The nurse is suctioning a client with a tracheostomy in the intensive care unit. She is aware that suctioning can lead to vagal stimulation, which can cause which of the following conditions? Select all that apply.

1. Hypotension
2. Heart block
3. Ventricular tachycardia
4. Bradycardia
5. Asystole

65. The nurse is caring for a client with severe emphysema and congestive heart failure. Which choice represents the best lunch for her client?

1. A peanut butter sandwich on whole-wheat bread, boiled egg, and peaches
2. Barbecued chicken, French fries with ketchup, and coleslaw
3. Tuna casserole, fried mushrooms, baked beans, and chocolate cake
4. Chicken noodle soup, crackers, and bananas

66. A client has a new order for Pancrease. The nurse has instructed the client about the medication. Which of the following statements by the client indicates a need for further education by the nurse?

1. "I will take it with 8 ounces of water."
2. "I will report ongoing nausea or diarrhea to my doctor."
3. "I will report if my stools become frothy or foul-smelling to my doctor."
4. "I will not crush the medicine."

67. A client is admitted to the intensive care unit with a diagnosis of septic shock. The nurse anticipates administering all but which of the following medications:

   1. Vasopressors
   2. Antibiotics
   3. Diuretics
   4. Thrombolytics

68. The nurse has received a client who has just had a thyroidectomy. Which of the following should she incorporate into the client's care plan? Select all that apply.

   1. Keep the client supine for at least eight hours.
   2. Be alert for signs of thyroid storm.
   3. Keep a tracheotomy tray and calcium gluconate nearby.
   4. Assess for hypercalcemia.

69. The nurse has received report on four clients. Which client should consume three liters of fluid per day?

   1. An adult with renal calculi
   2. An adult with mild congestive heart failure
   3. A child who is to undergo eye surgery tomorrow
   4. An adult with poorly controlled diabetes mellitus

70. The nurse is preparing to administer Synthroid to a client. She notes the vital signs provided to her by the unlicensed, assistive personnel. Which of the following findings should cause her to hold the medication and contact the physician?

   1. A temperature of 100.2
   2. A pulse of 112

3. A blood pressure of 150/92
4. Respirations of 22

71. The nurse is educating a group of mothers about rheumatic fever. All of the following statements about rheumatic fever are true except which of the following?

    1. Rheumatic fever occurs within weeks after an infection of group A beta-hemolytic streptococcus.
    2. Rheumatic fever can ultimately damage the heart.
    3. The child with rheumatic fever can go to school but should not actively play.
    4. The child who has had rheumatic fever should continue to take penicillin for years afterward.

72. The nurse is teaching a class about diabetes. She is asked how to prevent lipodystrophy. A correct response is:

    1. "Rotate your injection sites to prevent lipodystrophy."
    2. "Eat a balanced diet and do not become overweight to prevent lipodystrophy."
    3. "Include sit-ups or other abdominal exercises in your workout to avoid lipodystrophy."
    4. "Take your medication regularly so that you do not become hyperglycemic and eventually develop lipodystrophy."

73. The client has been receiving 125 ml per hour of D5 ½ NS for the last eight hours. Record the total intake as a whole number.

_____ milliliters

74. The staff education nurse is asked to provide a review of cardiac conduction for new nurses. She places the conduction steps in the following order: Place each of the steps in order.

1. Internodal pathways
2. AV node
3. Purkinje fibers
4. Bundle of His
5. Bundle branches
6. SA node
7. Bachmann's bundle

75. The nurse is teaching a breastfeeding class. Which of the following should she include in a discussion about how to avoid mastitis?

1. Keep the nipples covered at all times with a clean pad or cloth other than when breastfeeding.
2. Wash the nipples and the entire breast with mild soap and water. Avoid antibacterial soap.
3. Make sure the baby has released the nipple before pulling away.
4. Change the breast pads twice a day.

Answers and Rationale for Practice Test One

1. **Correct Answer:** 2. *Rationale:* If an advance directive is in place, it could prohibit the use of a feeding tube.

2. **Correct Answer:** 4. *Rationale:* The nurse must recognize the client's refusal and make sure she understands the procedure and the need for it. She must not go ahead and perform the procedure or she could be committing battery. She should not simply record the refusal until she has clarified the situation. She should not notify the physician until she has clarified the situation.

3. **Correct Answer:** 4. *Rationale:* The family of a child newly diagnosed with cancer is suddenly in a new situation. They are dealing with chemotherapy, radiation, and hospitalizations. They must encounter many new people, places, and environments. A case manager can help them navigate the multiple appointments and let them know what to expect.

4. **Correct Answer:** 4. *Rationale:* The client's laboratory values, appetite, and family situation are all appropriate topics for an interdisciplinary meeting. While the roommate situation may be discussed, it is not as important to the client's well-being as the other topics.

5. **Correct Answer:** 3. *Rationale:* If a nurse is unfamiliar with equipment she is expected to use, she must notify her superior so she can be taught the correct procedure, or the client can be assigned to a different nurse.

6. **Correct Answer:** 3. *Rationale:* A respiratory rate above 16 is not an abnormal finding. A normal respiratory rate is 16 to 20 breaths per minute. The other answers represent abnormal findings and should be reported to the nurse.

7. **Correct Answers:** 1 & 3. *Rationale:* She will educate all nursing personnel who need to understand the pump, including her nurse manager. Unlicensed, assistive personnel and staff from other departments will not be using the pump.

8. **Correct Answer:** 3. *Rationale:* The correct procedure is to notify her superior and to relate the objective facts. She must protect the clients in the care of the agency nurse, so not reporting the situation would not be an option. It is not her responsibility to call the agency that sent the nurse.

9. **Correct Answer:** 2. *Rationale:* The other answers are most likely harmless, while drinking hydrogen peroxide can be dangerous.

10. **Correct Answer:** 4. *Rationale:* Narcotics can suppress respirations and a client's current respiratory rate must be noted prior to their administration to avoid respiratory depression.

11. **Correct Answer:** 5. *Rationale:* Some of the risk factors for osteoporosis include advanced age; not getting enough exercise; or being Caucasian, Asian, thin, a smoker, or vegan.

12. **Correct Answers:** 2, 3, 4, & 5. *Rationale:* These are all common treatments for SAD. Hypnotics are not normally indicated because the client is more likely to be sleeping too much instead of not enough.

13. **Correct Answers:** 1, 2, 3, 4, & 5. *Rationale:* All of the answers are correct components of the BPP.

14. **Correct Answer:** 3. *Rationale:* Clients should not consume cantaloupe prior to taking the fecal occult blood test, as a false positive result can occur.

15. **Correct Answer:** 1. *Rationale:* Gentamicin can be ototoxic, and the client's hearing status should be monitored.

16. **Correct Answers:** 1, 2, & 4. *Rationale:* The sex of the fetus, chromosomal defects, and neural tube defects can be discovered through amniocentesis at 17 weeks. It does not involve measuring the fetus or learning the blood type.

17. **Correct Answer:** 3. *Rationale:* Dialysate should be warmed to avoid discomfort to the client. A mini-mental status examination is not required prior to the dialysis. The client should be supine or in low-Fowler's position. Lunch does not affect peritoneal dialysis.

18. **Correct Answer:** 1 & 4. *Rationale:* A history of multiple surgeries increases the client's risk of latex allergy. Clients who are allergic to

bananas, apricots, avocados, grapes, guava, hazelnuts, kiwi, peaches, potatoes, and tomatoes are at increased risk for latex allergy.

19. **Correct Answer:** 4. *Rationale:* The client is in active diaphoresis, and wet linens will make her more uncomfortable. There is no special need for a restricted diet or visitor restrictions. There is no justification for requiring bed rest, and it could increase the discomfort of a listless client.

20. **Correct Answer:** 2. *Rationale:* The Schilling test comprises several stages designed to diagnose pernicious anemia by measuring the client's ability to absorb vitamin B12.

21. **Correct Answer:** 1. *Rationale:* A client who has not voided by 6:00 may have an inability to void and could have too much urine stored in their bladder. The needs of the hungry, bored, or sleepy client should be addressed, but they are not immediate needs.

22. **Correct Answer:** 3. *Rationale:* An ideal group therapy session consists of six to eight clients. Clients placed into very small groups can feel self-conscious and not contribute, while clients in large groups can miss out on significant interactions, and the more timid members will tend to not participate.

23. **Correct Answer:** 4. *Rationale:* The client has classic symptoms of encephalitis. Sending the client home without testing would not be the best approach to care. An MRI of the brain would not be the first step in obtaining a diagnosis. Activated charcoal is not indicated given the client's symptoms.

24. **Correct Answer:** 1. *Rationale:* The post-myelogram client must be kept sitting up or lying with his head elevated at least 60 degrees. He should not lie flat in bed for at least eight hours. Fluids should be encouraged. The client should be encouraged to void if he does not within eight

hours. The administration of acetaminophen is not contraindicated after a myelogram.

25. **Correct Answer:** 3. *Rationale:* Clients must not take the medication of another. It could be a different medication or a different dose. It is natural for a newly diagnosed client to be afraid of getting a shot. Many clients cannot comfortably give themselves an injection in the subcutaneous fat of their arms and choose to exclusively use their abdomen and thighs. Insulin can safely stay out of the refrigerator a few hours (and many brands can stay unrefrigerated indefinitely). Clients taking insulin should always keep snacks handy for hypoglycemic episodes.

26. **Correct Answer:** 2.4 milliliters. If 0.5 mg = 1 milliliter, then 1.2 mg = 2.4 milliliters.

27. **Correct Answer:** 1. *Rationale:* A child with serious burns will need a high-protein, high-calorie diet. This diet contains the most protein and calories. Pureed foods are not indicated with burns to the legs.

28. **Correct Answer:** 3. *Rationale:* The client is likely to have thrombocytopenia due to his chronic granulocytic leukemia and should not be shaving with a manual razor. The client's diet, activity level, and need for a support group cannot be ascertained from the question and the other answers may or may be appropriate to the client, leaving the shaving issue as the most likely to apply to the client who is hospitalized with leukemia.

29. **Correct Answer:** 1. *Rationale:* Cold compresses will ease the burning pain of herpes zoster. The scabs should not be removed by the client. The lesions can be touched to apply a cold compress. Rubbing alcohol is not indicated for herpes zoster. There is no reason to avoid dairy products.

30. **Correct Answer:** 2. *Rationale:* The client with ascites can breathe eas-ier in semi-Fowler's or high-Fowler's position. A client with decubitus ulcers should generally be side-lying, as ulcers are most often present on the buttocks. A client requiring disc surgery will most often be lying supine or on his side. Semi-Fowler's position places extra strain on the lumbar area. A client with a comminuted leg fracture will usually be lying with the leg elevated.

31. **Correct Answer:** 4. *Rationale:* The first answer sounds judgmental and is unhelpful to the client's situation. The second answer is incorrect because the nurse cannot take care of the crisis for the client, although, she may be able to assist. The third answer is incorrect because it is likely to be untrue.

32. **Correct Answer:** 4. *Rationale:* Severe epigastric pain is indicative of a potential seizure in a client with preeclampsia. The other symptoms may or may not be present but do not directly correlate with seizure risk.

33. **Correct Answer:** 3. *Rationale:* The other foods are contraindicated on a low-residue diet.

34. **Correct Answer:** 3. *Rationale:* The method utilized in exposure re-sponse prevention therapy involves exposing the client to what they fear (dirt or germs) and not allowing him to remove the object of fear (by not letting him wash his hands).

35. **Correct Answers:** 1, 3, & 4. *Rationale:* Anorexia, nausea, vomiting, dyspepsia, chills, and tenderness over the liver are all early symptoms of Hepatitis A.

36. **Correct Answer:** 4. *Rationale:* Having the nurse observe the procedure will prepare her to perform it with supervision and then solo in the fu-ture. Simply reading the manual and performing it is not appropriate, as nurses should watch new procedures and then perform them under

supervision prior to performing them solo. It is not appropriate to expect the agency nurse to find another nurse to perform the procedure.

37. **Correct Answer:** 2. *Rationale:* The nurse should factually state that many factors can be involved in a client not becoming pregnant. Beyond that, she should defer the situation to the physician. She should make the physician aware of the circumstances so that she can prepare an appropriate response. Telling the husband to ask the client would violate the client's privacy. Inserting your religious views into the situation is never appropriate. Ignoring the question by changing the subject is not the best response.

38. **Correct Answer:** 1. *Rationale:* The need for Lanoxin is unlikely to change as heart rhythm problems generally stay the same or worsen. An antidepressant is generally taken for a period of months, not forever. An antibiotic is generally taken for a number of days only. A muscle relaxant is generally not taken indefinitely.

39. **Correct Answer:** 2. *Rationale:* Guilt and condescension are not appropriate responses. The client may feel that his children would be better off if he died. Ascertaining what has been happening in the client's life and how long he has been contemplating suicide are appropriate. Contracting with the client is a good response after a rapport has developed.

40. **Correct Answer:** 3. *Rationale:* The client undergoing external beam therapy does not need any special precautions, as the radiation comes from an external source and is not within the client. She should be placed on universal precautions as all other clients.

41. **Correct Answer:** 1. *Rationale:* Cryptorchidism is a condition in which a male infant is born with an undescended testicle. This condition frequently corrects in the first few months after birth. If it does not cor-

rect, surgery is usually performed between the ages of four months and two years of age. Uncorrected cryptorchidism can lead to infertility.

42. **Correct Answers:** 1, 2, 3, & 4. *Rationale:* The client, ill enough to be admitted to the intensive care unit, will most likely be on fluid restriction. The client may require temporary dialysis as the kidneys and heart may be compromised. Antihypertensives are indicated if the blood pressure is elevated. Streptococcal infection is a common precursor to acute glomerulonephritis. Muscle relaxants are not indicated for acute glomerulonephritis.

43. **Correct Answer:** 1. *Rationale:* Congestive heart failure is a known adverse reaction to corticosteroid therapy. Strabismus is not an adverse reaction of corticosteroids. Corticosteroids can cause hyperglycemia and hypokalemia.

44. **Correct Answer:** 3. *Rationale:* The incubation period for rubeola is 8 to 12 days.

45. **Correct Answer:** 2. Rationale: Uteroplacental insufficiency manifests as late decelerations because there is a decreased blood flow and oxygen transfer to the fetus during contractions. Incoherent speech, low serum albumin, and chills are not indicators of uteroplacental insufficiency.

46. **Correct Answer:** 2. *Rationale:* Chest circumference should be measured at the nipples.

47. **Correct Answer:** 30. *Rationale:* For a pediatric microdrip infusion, the number of milliliters per hour equals the number of drops per minute.

48. **Correct Answer:** 3. *Rationale:* When a client with suspected appendicitis has severe pain and the pain suddenly disappears, the nurse should suspect that the appendix may have ruptured. The other responses are normal findings.

49. **Correct Answer:** 2. *Rationale:* The goal is to safely rehydrate the client. Moist mucous membranes indicate proper hydration. Weight gain alone does not indicate proper hydration. Lack of thirst is not a good indicator. The ability to walk alone is not an indicator.

50. **Correct Answer:** 4. *Rationale:* The correct ratio of compressions to breaths in one-person adult CPR is 15:2.

51. **Correct Answer:** 3. *Rationale:* The Heimlich maneuver should only be performed if the victim cannot make any sounds at all due to complete airway obstruction. Coughing or speaking indicates that some air exchange is occurring.

52. **Correct Answer:** 3. *Rationale:* The client with an artificial graft may need prophylactic antibiotics prior to dental work to avoid the risk of systemic infection.

53. **Correct Answers:** 2, 3, & 5. *Rationale:* Brisk walking, aquatic exercises, and supervised, mild aerobic activity are all healthy activities for weight loss in elderly clients. Unsupervised jogging is not recommended for an elderly client who is not accustomed to exercise. Yoga is a healthy exercise, but does not facilitate weight loss as well as the other activities.

54. **Correct Answer:** 2,4,3,1. *Rationale:* Muscular irritability is the first sign of a return to consciousness, followed by delirium and restlessness, followed by showing signs of recognition of pain and, finally, the ability to control one's behavior and reason.

55. **Correct Answer:** 1. *Rationale:* A normal dosage range for Demerol IV post-operatively is 12.5 to 25 mg. A 100 mg dose IV could be dangerous to the client. The other responses are within normal ranges for post-operative pain management.

56. **Correct Answer:** 3. *Rationale:* More males have osteoarthritis prior to age 50, but after age 50, osteoarthritis strikes women more often. Obsessive-compulsive disorder and Bell's palsy strike men and women equally. Myasthenia strikes men more frequently after age 40.

57. **Correct Answers:** 2, 3, & 5. *Rationale:* NG tubes are placed to relieve severe nausea, evacuate the gastric contents, and provide nutritional support through the gastrointestinal tract. NG tubes are not placed prior to CABG surgery. They are not used to test the gag reflex.

58. **Correct Answer:** 1,140 milliliters. *Rationale:* Each ounce equals 30 milliliters. Half of the pitcher is 240 milliliters.

59. **Correct Answer:** 1. *Rationale:* The erythrocyte sedimentation rate indicates infection or inflammation somewhere in the body. While it is true that it is never discovered why an ESR is elevated, it is not considered a harmless finding. While it may be elevated in mononucleosis, an elevation does not necessarily indicated mononucleosis. It is not indicative of malnutrition.

60. **Correct Answer:** 4. *Rationale:* Lung cancer can lead to all the syndromes mentioned except tonsillitis, Bruton's agammaglobulinemia, lipoma, and Broca's aphasia.

61. **Correct Answers:** 1, 2, & 3. *Rationale:* Seizure precautions should be instituted on a client newly receiving Risperdal. The client's temperature should be monitored due to the risk of neuroleptic malignant syndrome. The client's blood sugar should be monitored due to the risk of development of diabetes mellitus. All women of childbearing age should be using some form of birth control while taking Risperdal.

62. **Correct Answer:** 2. *Rationale:* The correct dosage of epinephrine for intracardiac injection during cardiac arrest is 0.5 mg. It is injected into the left ventricular chamber and can be repeated every 5 minutes.

63. **Correct Answer:** 1. *Rationale:* A low pH, elevated PaCO2, low PaO2 and elevated K+ level indicate respiratory acidosis.

64. **Correct Answers:** 1, 2, 3, 4, & 5. *Rationale:* Vagal stimulation can cause hypotension, heart block, ventricular tachycardia, bradycardia, and asystole.

65. **Correct Answer:** 1. *Rationale:* By process of elimination, choice number 1 is best. Choice number 2 is too high in sodium and the meal is too heavy (high in calories) for a person who is having difficulty breathing. Heavy meals can further impede comfortable breathing. Choice number 3 is also a heavy meal. Choice number 4 is high in sodium. Commercial soups can be very high in sodium. Choice number 1 has moderate sodium and calories.

66. **Correct Answer:** 3. *Rationale:* Foul-smelling, frothy stools are normal when taking Pancrease and do not need to be reported. The medication should be taken with 8 ounces of water and should not be crushed. Nausea and diarrhea are common side effects of Pancrease and can usually be managed.

67. **Correct Answer:** 4. *Rationale:* Thrombolytics are not indicated for septic shock. The client may require vasopressors to increase his blood pressure, antibiotics to fight his infection, and diuretics to keep his urine output above 20 milliliters per hour if fluid resuscitation is successful.

68. **Correct Answers:** 2 & 3. *Rationale:* The client must be monitored for thyroid storm. A tracheotomy tray must be kept nearby in case of respiratory distress. Calcium gluconate must be readily available for emergency intravenous administration. The client should be kept in Fowler's position, not supine, to promote venous return and to keep pressure off the incision. The client should be monitored for symptoms

of hypocalcemia, not hypercalcemia. This could occur if the parathyroid glands are nicked or otherwise damaged during surgery.

69. **Correct Answer:** 1. *Rationale:* An adult with renal calculi should consume 3 liters of fluid per day to facilitate passing the stones. An adult with congestive heart failure should be on fluid restriction or normal fluids. A child should not normally consume three liters of fluid per day. Diabetes mellitus is not an indication for increased fluids.

70. **Correct Answer:** 2. *Rationale:* Tachycardia is a sign of thyroid toxicity. The physician should be notified prior to administering the Synthroid.

71. **Correct Answer:** 3. Rationale: The child with rheumatic fever should be on bed rest until the fever resolves and the erythrocyte sedimentation rate returns to normal. Rheumatic fever can lead to rheumatic heart disease. The child with rheumatic fever should take penicillin for five years or throughout their teens, whichever is longer.

72. **Correct Answer:** 1. *Rationale:* Lipodystrophy can occur from multiple injections into the same site or a very close site.

73. **Correct Answer:** 1,000 milliliters. *Rationale:* 125 x 8 = 1,000.

74. **Correct Answer:** 6,7,1,2,4,5,3. *Rationale:* The electrical impulse begins at the SA node and travels to Bachmann's bundle, through the internodal pathways, the AV node, the Bundle of His, the bundle branches, and finally to the Purkinje fibers.

75. **Correct Answer:** 3. *Rationale:* The nipple and areola can be irritated if the suction on the breast is not released prior to pulling away. This can lead to mastitis. The breasts should not be continuously covered. The nipples should be exposed to air for a while each day. Breast pads should be changed more frequently than twice a day.

What Your Score Means

Score of 60 – 75.

You have a good grasp of the information and how to take the NCLEX. Look at the questions you missed to ascertain if you missed them accidentally, if you almost selected the right answer, or if you totally missed them. Take notes of the questions you missed other than accidentally, and study those topics in-depth. If you missed more than two questions accidentally, practice reading questions more carefully and taking your time to answer. You may wish to read all the questions and answers twice before answering.

Score of 40 -59.

Look at the questions that you missed to determine if you are missing memorization questions or critical-thinking questions. If you missed mostly memorization-type questions, write down the topics you need to study and spend a good deal of time on them. If you missed critical-thinking questions, reread the questions and compare your answer to the correct answer. Discuss the question with a peer if you need to. Spend some time trying to learn how your critical-thinking skills can improve. Write down the topics you feel weak in and study them in-depth.

Score of 0 – 40.

You may not be ready to take the NCLEX. Continue to review this book and all your materials from nursing school. Take practice tests whenever you have the opportunity to see if your score is improving. If, after a great deal of studying, you still score poorly, consider one-on-one tutoring for assistance in uncovering your deficits. Remember that you successfully graduated nursing school and the problem lies in testing, not in your intelligence. Do not hesitate to get the help you need to pass.

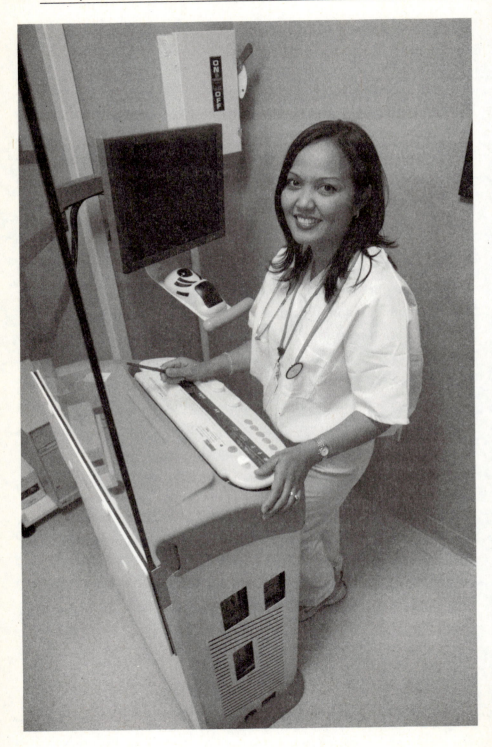

Appendix C

Practice Test Two

Try this 75-question practice test. The results and rationale follow. The answers are numbered 1,2,3,4, just as you will encounter on the NCLEX. Time yourself on the test to get a feel for how long it takes you to answer the questions, but do not rush your answers.

1. The nurse is preparing to teach a sexual education class to female teens. She will explain that cervical mucus serves all but which function?

    1. To deter unhealthy sperm from entering the cervix
    2. To act as a bacteriostatic agent
    3. To provide an alkaline environment for sperm, which offers protection from the acidic vagina
    4. To lubricate the vaginal canal

2. The obstetrical nurse is asked by a young pregnant client when her fetus' heart will begin to beat. Which answer is appropriate?

    1. "Every fetus is different. It could happen anywhere from four weeks to seven weeks."

2. "Because this is your first child, we anticipate the heart beat beginning at six weeks."

3. "Your fetus will develop a heartbeat during the fourth week."

4. "Your fetus began having a heartbeat in the second week."

3. The nurse had admitted a 30-year-old client with dumping syndrome. She knows that his diet should follow which of the following principles? Select all that apply.

1. Drink at least one cup of liquid with each meal.

2. Eat five or six small meals each day, rather than large meals.

3. Follow a diet high in insoluble fiber.

4. Try to avoid sweets and milk.

5. Eat a diet relatively high in protein.

4. A client in the coronary care unit is developing worsening hyperkalemia. The nurse knows that he must monitor the client for which of the following potential complications?

1. Hypokalemia

2. Dysrhythmia with cardiac arrest

3. Acute respiratory distress syndrome

4. Hyperglycemia

5. The intensive care unit nurse has a 40-year-old client experiencing thyroid storm. She expects to perform all but which of the following functions:

1. Give large doses of antithyroid drugs.

2. Administer acetaminophen.

3. Apply a warming blanket.

4. Administer intravenous sodium iodide.

6. The nurse is caring for a client with chronic hypothyroidism. All but which of the following manifestations would he recognize as typical?

   1. Impotence, dyspnea, and weight gain
   2. Intolerance to heat, increased urine output, and diarrhea
   3. Depression, paranoia, and hoarseness
   4. Slurred speech, hearing loss, and an enlarged heart

7. The nurse is preparing to educate a group of retirees about renal cell carcinoma. She may include which of the following facts? Select all that apply.

   1. Renal carcinoma is most common in persons 70 years of age and older.
   2. Hematuria is a common early sign.
   3. In renal carcinoma, healthy kidney cells are replaced by cancer cells.
   4. Renal carcinoma may cause men to experience nipple darkening and breast enlargement.
   5. A nephrectomy may be performed as management of renal carcinoma.

8. The emergency department nurse is expecting a client who was removed from a burning house. He has experienced severe burns and inhalation of smoke and hot air. She knows that respiratory insufficiency is a cause or contributor to death in similar cases:

   1. 10 percent of the time
   2. 25 percent of the time
   3. 77 percent of the time
   4. 90 percent of the time

9. The nurse is employed at a minority outreach center with a large African-American population. He is aware that the leading causes of death for African-Americans in 2000 were as follows: Place these most common causes of death in order.

   1. Diabetes mellitus
   2. Heart disease
   3. Cancer
   4. Unintentional injuries
   5. Cerebrovascular diseases

10. The nurse is caring for a 45-year-old female burn client. He is introducing a new pressure garment to the client and describing its use. The nurse is aware that the garment must be worn 23 hours a day for the next twelve months and that many clients complain that they are itchy and warm. He explains that the pressure garment will assist in all but which of the following:

    1. It will inhibit venous engorgement to parts of the body with lowered lymphatic outflow.
    2. It will assist in the prevention of contractures.
    3. It will assist in reducing hypertrophic scarring.
    4. It will substitute for performing range-of-motion exercises.

11. The nurse is admitting a client with fat embolism syndrome. She knows that some of the causes of this condition include: Select all that apply.

    1. Bone fracture
    2. Sickle cell anemia
    3. Emphysema
    4. Pancreatitis
    5. Diabetic coma

12. The maternity nurse is caring for a client with pregnancy-induced hypertension. What should she recognize as predisposing factors in the client's history? Select all that apply.

    1. Multiple fetuses
    2. Renal disease
    3. Vascular disease
    4. Adolescence
    5. Third pregnancy of 25-year-old client

13. Which two clients on the medical-surgical floor should the registered nurse assign to the licensed practical nurse? Select two answers.

    1. A client who had an abdominal hysterectomy one day ago
    2. A client who has just been diagnosed with diabetes mellitus
    3. A client with multiple decubitus ulcers requiring frequent treatments
    4. A client with severe asthma
    5. A client with a high fever of unknown origin

14. The neonatal nursery nurse is checking the vital signs of a newborn. Which of the following normal ranges is incorrect?

    1. Skin temperature of 96.8 to 97.7 degrees Fahrenheit
    2. Respirations of 30 to 60 per minute
    3. Blood pressure of 90 to 80 systolic and 60 to 50 diastolic
    4. Heart rate of 120 to 150 beats per minute

15. The normal neonate exhibits which of the following reflexes? Select all that apply.

    1. Sucking and rooting
    2. Pincer grasp
    3. Blink and tonic neck

4. Moro and step
5. Babinski

16. Which of the following facts about the umbilical cord should the newborn nursery nurse include in her teaching plan? Select all that apply.

    1. The umbilical cord should fall off in 7 to 14 days.
    2. The area must be kept moist at all times.
    3. The cord should be cleaned at least two to three times a day.
    4. If the cord has not fallen off in two weeks, you should begin to carefully loosen it.
    5. The umbilical cord contains thousands of nerve endings.

17. The client mentions practicing a complementary therapy for her arthritis and asthma. She asks for the nurse's opinion of complementary therapy. The most appropriate response would be:

    1. They are only harmful if you eat or drink something. Otherwise, they are all right.
    2. They are very useful.
    3. Which therapies do you use? As long as they are not harmful, they can be healing or relaxing. Do not use them in place of the treatment prescribed by your physician and always let your physician know that you use them.
    4. If they are a part of your religious practices, they are acceptable.

18. A client in a physician's office states that she takes three high-dose Vitamin-A pills each day to prevent cancer. The most appropriate response by the nurse would be:

    1. If you eat carrots each day, you should not need to take vitamin A. What made you think to take that many pills each day? Why are you so worried about getting cancer?

2. Vitamin A is a water-soluble vitamin and cannot hurt you, but you are wasting your money.

3. If you are just taking vitamin A, then you are not getting your other vitamins and minerals. You need to take a supplement that contains all the vitamins and minerals.

4. If a person eats an adequate diet with lots of variety, they should not need to take a vitamin supplement. If the physician determines that you need more than the average amount of a particular nutrient, she will alert you to take a supplement. Otherwise, it is not recommended to take more than 100 percent of the U.S.-recommended daily allowance (RDA) of any nutrient each day. I will ask the physician to discuss your current regimen with you.

19. The nurse has been asked to conduct a smoking cessation session. Which of the following statements should she include in her teaching plan? Select all that apply.

1. Chewing tobacco is a good alternative to smoking cigarettes.
2. Nicotine is a stimulant that leaves the user feeling depressed and fatigued when it wears off.
3. Nicotine is approximately as addictive as cocaine.
4. When clients are stressed, nicotine needs are reduced due to enhancement by corticosterone.
5. The use of nicotine patches, gum, and similar items, when combined with a counseling and support program, can be an effective means of smoking cessation.

20. The nurse works in a foot care clinic, caring for clients with a variety of illnesses. Place the symptoms under the most common type of leg ulcer for that symptom. This is a drag-and-drop question such as the type you may find on the NCLEX.

	Arterial	Venous	Ulcer
1. Intermittent claudication			
2. Foot cold			
3. Brown pigmentation			
4. Pulses decreased or absent			
5. Granulation tissue common			

21. The nurse is caring for a client on the neurological floor. She knows that an extramedullary spinal cord tumor characterized by neurological and sensory dysfunction, motor weakness present in the thoracic area, and amenable to surgical excision is known as a:

1. Hemangioblastoma
2. Schwannoma
3. Meningioma
4. Neurofibroma

22. A client has just been diagnosed with a malignant astrocytoma. The client's wife states, "I'm just glad it was not something serious." The most appropriate response by the nurse is:

1. A malignant astrocytoma can be quite serious. I will ask the doctor to discuss the diagnosis, prognosis, and treatment plan with you.

2. I agree. His condition is highly treatable with a low mortality rate.

3. Your husband will most likely make it through this, but he may be in pain for the rest of his life.

4. You are in denial, which is a natural reaction. Would you like to speak with our chaplain or a grief counselor?

23. An elderly client hospitalized for pneumonia uses her call light. When the nurse enters the room, she notes the client has slurred speech. She

manages to tell the nurse that she is experiencing double vision, vertigo, and numbness in her arm and hand. The nurse immediately suspects:

1. A stroke
2. A transient ischemic attack
3. A stroke or a transient ischemic attack
4. A side effect from medication for pneumonia

24. A nurse witnesses a woman being struck by an automobile that does not stop. The woman is flung into a nearby yard. She is conscious and repeating over and over that she cannot move her legs. After calling 911, the next response by the nurse should be:

1. Ask the woman to move each leg to determine the extent of damage.
2. Carefully move the woman's legs on at a time to see if she has sensory function.
3. Keep the woman still and observe for any bleeding.
4. Elevate the woman's legs to prevent further trauma.

25. A 25-year-old woman is suffering neutropenia after chemotherapy for cancer. Her absolute neutrophil count is 440. The oncology nurse knows that the client's risk of infection is:

1. Extremely high
2. High
3. Normal
4. Low

26. A client has been on the medical-surgical unit for five days. The client does not speak, and no one knows the identity of the client. He appears to be in his 50s and is unkempt and irritable. The day shift nurse

begins to notice that the client always eats the food on one side of his plate only. What does the nurse suspect?

1. Homonymous hemianopia due to a prior stroke
2. A psychiatric deficit due to homelessness
3. Recent history of a blow to the head
4. Attention-seeking behavior

27. A teen boy is sent to the school nurse after it is discovered that he has marks on his neck. The child admits to the nurse that he has been participating in erotic asphyxiation. He tells the nurse that it is safe as long as he does not pass out. The best response by the nurse would be:

1. Sniffing fumes from a bag tied on your head can be deadly. You must stop doing this immediately.

2. Cutting off the oxygen to your brain in any matter is very dangerous. You and any other participants must stop immediately.

3. It is an accepted sexual practice if you do not pass out.

4. This is unacceptable behavior. I am calling your parents right now.

28. The nurse is caring for a home-health client suspected of having Parkinson's disease. Place the signs of Parkinson's disease in order as to when they appear.

1. Akinesia
2. Tremors
3. Bradykinesia
4. Rigidity

29. The nurse is educating a group of new child-care workers. When discussing sudden infant death syndrome, she tells them which age groups

are at the highest risk? Place the following ages in order from highest risks for SIDS to lowest risk.

1. 3 months
2. 2 weeks
3. 5 months
4. 9 months

30. A 4-year-old client with phenylketonuria has just received food from home brought by her grandparents. The nurse knows that which of the following foods may be consumed on her diet:

1. Plain boiled chicken
2. Diet caffeine-free soda
3. Honey
4. Fat-free ice cream

31. A 6-year-old child is admitted to the pediatric intensive care unit after being dared by his brother to consume a bottle of acetaminophen. He was found by his parents six hours after the late night ingestion of 20 325 mg pills. The nurse anticipates the client to exhibit which of the following symptoms:

1. Right upper quadrant pain
2. Severe headache
3. Moderate grade fever
4. Coughing

32. The mother of a child in a hip spica cast inquires why she was told to feed the child small, frequent meals. The best explanation for the nurse to give is:

1. We do not want her blood sugar to fluctuate while she is in the cast.

2. Small frequent meals will encourage her to sleep more.

3. Eating frequently will help her keep her strength up.

4. Eating large meals can cause the abdomen to swell, thus causing the cast to feel tight and uncomfortable.

33. The nurse is caring for a 3-year-old child who is significantly underdeveloped for his age. The nurse should suspect which of the following?

1. Child abuse

2. Diabetes mellitus

3. Heart disease

4. A psychiatric disorder

34. The oncology nurse is caring for a client with pancreatic cancer. She expects that the client may receive which of the following treatments? Select all that apply.

1. Whipple's operation

2. Blood transfusions

3. Orlistat

4. Pancrease

5. Chemotherapy drug combinations

35. The parent of a teen client takes you aside and asks you if her child will become addicted to the narcotic pain medication he has been prescribed for a leg fracture. The best response would be:

1. It is impossible to become addicted to a drug if you take it as prescribed.

2. He might become addicted; I would not let him have the medication.

3. If he becomes addicted, you can send him to rehabilitation.

4. It is unlikely, but possible, that he could become addicted. He should take the medication for only as long as it is needed.

36. The nurse is preparing to draw a blood sample from a home-health client. Which of the following steps in her procedure are incorrect? Select all that apply.

    1. She uses a 14-gauge needle.
    2. She uses a blood pressure cuff as a tourniquet.
    3. She asks the client to hold his breath as she inserts the needle.
    4. She inserts the needle at a 30-degree angle.
    5. She holds pressure for 30 seconds after the procedure.

37. The nurse has received an order to begin passive range of motion on a comatose client. He understands that range-of-motion activities will:

    1. Help to prevent decubiti
    2. Help to prevent contractures
    3. Improve blood circulation
    4. Help to prevent fractures

38. When performing an assessment of the circulatory system, the nurse may use Doppler equipment to assess which of the following?

    1. Pedal arterial blood flow
    2. Pedal venous blood flow
    3. Pedal capillary refill
    4. Babinski reflex

39. The nurse is caring for a client with low testosterone. She instructs him that his testosterone medication can cause all but which of the following side effects:

    1. Nausea
    2. Fluid retention
    3. Rash

4. Hypocalcemia
5. Dizziness

40. The psychiatric nurse is caring for a teenaged client who has been tak-ing caffeine pills for four months. He has been hospitalized for two days. The main concern of the nurse is:

    1. To monitor the client's visitors to make certain they do not give him more caffeine
    2. To keep him away from the coffee and coke products
    3. To monitor him for symptoms of withdrawal
    4. To test him for illegal substance use

41. A nurse and an unlicensed assistant are preparing to assist an elderly client with a shampoo using a shampoo board. Which temperature is appropriate for the water?

    1. 95 to 100 degrees Fahrenheit
    2. 105 to 110 degrees Fahrenheit
    3. 115 to 120 degrees Fahrenheit
    4. 125 to 130 degrees Fahrenheit

42. The nurse is caring for newborns in the nursery. Which baby has mea-surements that are out of the range of normal?

    1. Paul, with a head circumference of 14 inches
    2. Sandra, with a length of 20.5 inches
    3. Fred, with a weight of 8.5 pounds
    4. Jason, with a length of 23 inches

43. A staff nurse overhears an unlicensed assistant tell an elderly client, "You don't know what you're doing. Let me finish, or I will make things

very hard for you." She knows that the assistant is having marital and financial problems. What should the nurse do?

1. Speak with the assistant immediately and tell her to never speak that way to a client again.
2. Recognize that the assistant is having problems and mention counseling opportunities to her.
3. Report the situation to her superior and keep the assistant away from the client by either sending her home or reassigning her until the issue can be dealt with by the superior.
4. Talk with the client and explain that the assistant did not mean what she said.

44. A newly diagnosed diabetic is improving after being admitted in a diabetic coma. The nurse overhears her say, "I cannot wait to get home and eat what I want again." What actions by the nurse are appropriate? Select all that apply.

1. Make the physician aware of the comment.
2. Ask the dietician or diabetes educator to speak with the client.
3. Remind the client about a healthy diet and the ramifications of maintaining a poor diet.
4. She should not do anything. The information was overheard and it is a violation of the client's rights to discuss it.

45. A 30-year-old female client approaches the nurse's station and asks what day it is. The nurse is aware that the client is receiving electroconvulsive treatment. She recognizes that the most likely reason for the client's question is:

1. Electroconvulsive therapy commonly causes temporary memory loss.
2. Antidepressant medication commonly causes temporary memory loss.

3. Depressed clients frequently seek attention.

4. Depression frequently brings on dementia for clients in their 30s.

46. The nurse is caring for a client with a hydatidiform mole, a form of gestational trophoblastic disease. The client and her husband are frightened and have asked the nurse for full information about the condition. The nurse should include which of the following statements in her education? Select all that apply.

1. A suction dilatation and curettage will be performed, or you could develop choriocarcinoma.

2. You should not attempt pregnancy for three years.

3. There is a 50 percent chance that the hydatidiform mole is benign.

4. Risk factors for this condition include a poor diet deficient in protein.

5. You may be given methotrexate to help prevent choriocarcinoma.

6. You will need close follow-up for a year or two.

47. The psychiatric nurse is caring for a client with severe hypochondriasis. He knows that typical treatments for the condition include all but which of the following:

1. Serotonin reuptake inhibitors

2. Group therapy

3. Tricyclic antidepressants

4. Cognitive behavioral therapy

48. The emergency room nurse has received an 8-year-old child with stridor, heavy drooling, complaints of difficulty swallowing, and extreme restlessness. The nurse knows that the symptoms are consistent with:

1. Asthma

2. Epiglottiditis

3. Respiratory syncytial virus (RSV)
4. Epilepsy

49. The hospital's nurse executive is looking over incident reports from the previous month. She realizes which of the following cases could lead to a charge of assault and battery:

1. A nasogastric tube was placed in a client without informed consent.
2. An elderly client writhed in bed until she dislodged her urinary catheter, causing urethral damage.
3. A client demanded a drug that the physician refused to give her. She called her attorney from her hospital bed.
4. A client refused surgery and went home against medical advice.

50. A 55-year old client is to receive four liters of D51/2 NS with 20mEq of KCl over the course of 24 hours. At what rate should the IV pump be set? Use a whole number.

_____ ml per hour

51. A client with panic attacks refuses to leave her room on the psychiatric floor. The nurse has encouraged her to visit the dayroom and walk in the halls, to no avail. The nurse should try which of the following procedures: Select all that apply.

1. Tell her that if she does not come out, she will have to take more medication.
2. Tell her that the other clients are asking why she does not come out.
3. Compromise with her to come out accompanied by the nurse for five minutes and then take part in an activity she likes to do in her room.

4. Have her come out of the room at night when the dayroom is empty to explore the area.

5. Tell her that lunch will be served in the dayroom and that if she wants to eat, she must come to the dayroom.

52. The nurse is speaking with a spouse of a client with a paraphilia. She is angry and asks how her husband turned out this way. The nurse explains some of the known contributing factors to developing paraphilias, which include all of the following except:

1. Sexual trauma, emotional trauma, or childhood incest
2. Closed head injury or a central nervous system tumor
3. A personality disorder or social stressors
4. Having a lot of knowledge about sex

53. The nurse is caring for a healthy newborn. Which of the following findings should be of concern to the nurse? Select all that apply.

1. The infant's diaper has dark red spots on it.
2. The infant has a black, tarry stool.
3. The nurse can see 1 to 3 millimeter white papules on the palate of the infant's mouth.
4. The infant does not void for 18 hours.
5. The infant's apical heart rate is 100.

54. A client in the outpatient clinic has just been diagnosed with ringworm. He asks the nurse what ringworm is. The nurse should reply:

1. It is a tiny worm that burrows under the skin.
2. It is a fungus.
3. It is a tiny worm inside the intestine that can grow to several feet long.
4. It is a worm that is caught from animal contact.

55. Which of the following scenarios should cause the nurse to suspect Munchausen syndrome by proxy?

   1. A sick child is not taken for medical care despite a fever of 103 degrees.
   2. A child presents to the emergency room with a broken arm.
   3. A child is taken to the emergency room six times in a 12-month period with vomiting and diarrhea.
   4. A child tells the nurse that she is forced to go to school when she has a cold.

56. A neonate is diagnosed with necrotizing enterocolitis. The frantic parents ask the nurse to explain the condition. The nurse may give all but which of the following explanations:

   1. It occurs when blood is shunted away from the intestine to the brain and heart. This can occur due to shock, asphyxia, prematurity, respiratory distress syndrome, or fetal distress.
   2. A common virus can attack the ulcerated area, causing sepsis.
   3. It is characterized by an area of ischemia causing an infraction of the affected area of the bowel. It can cause ulceration and inflammation.
   4. Some of the bowel may need to be removed because the bowel can perforate with a risk of death.

57. A long-term psychiatric client exhibits involuntary movements of the face, tongue, and extremities. The nurse knows this is a permanent extrapyramidal condition resulting from long-term administration of psychiatric medications, known as:

   1. Tardive dyskinesia
   2. Dystonic reaction

3. Neuroleptic malignant syndrome
4. Akathisia

58. The nurse is teaching a class for parents who have children with phenylketonuria. She instructs that a child with phenylketonuria should avoid which of the following in his diet:

1. Tea, coffee, cocoa, sugar, and mushrooms
2. Dried peas and beans, organ meats, and oats
3. Eggs, meat, poultry, fish, cheese, breads, nuts, and legumes
4. Citrus fruit, watermelon, cruciferous vegetables, and beans

59. The nurse is caring for a client with a feeding tube. He knows that signs of feeding intolerance include the following: Select all that apply.

1. Bradycardia
2. Nausea, vomiting, and diarrhea
3. Glycosuria
4. Gastric residual above 120 milliliters
5. Aspiration and abdominal distention

60. The nurse has been to an in-service teaching her how to use a new transcutaneous electrical nerve stimulator (TENS). She knows that TENS units should not be used in clients with:

1. Diabetes
2. A herniated cervical disc
3. A pacemaker
4. Cerebral palsy

61. A client in the intensive care unit is under close observation for hyper-volemia. The nurse knows that hypervolemia may manifest in all but which of the following ways:

    1. Frothy or pink-tinged sputum
    2. Hypotension
    3. Neck vein distention
    4. Rales

62. The nurse is teaching a class about drugs commonly used to treat the various types of shock. She includes all but which of the following drugs:

    1. antibiotics, sodium nitroprusside, and digitalis
    2. nonsteroidal anti-inflammatories and Phenergan
    3. dopamine and dobutamine
    4. isoprotenerol, corticosteroids, and norepinephrine

63. The nurse is caring for a client who is terminally ill with breast cancer. She notes that the client seems depressed. The nurse realizes that, according to the Kübler-Ross model of grief, the stages of grief are the following: Place the stages in the correct order.

    1. Acceptance
    2. Depression
    3. Anger
    4. Denial
    5. Bargaining

64. A geriatric client is ordered to take iron supplements for mild anemia. The nurse advises her to take the medication with which beverage for maximum absorption?

    1. Whole milk
    2. Skim milk

3. A full glass of water

4. Orange juice

65. The nurse is preparing to teach a class of expectant, first-time parents. She may include all but which of the following statements:

1. When weaning from breastfeeding, it is best for the infant to stop all at once.

2. It normally takes 6 weeks for the mother to return to her pre-pregnancy weight.

3. The mother may resume sexual intercourse when her lochia has stopped and, if she has an episiotomy, the pain has resolved.

4. One of the benefits of taking a folic acid supplement during pregnancy is to help prevent hemorrhage during delivery.

66. A 4-year-old child is newly diagnosed with a seizure disorder. Her father asks the nurse if she will have normal intelligence in school. The correct response from the nurse should be:

1. "The seizure disorder should not affect her intelligence."

2. "She will be of normal intelligence, but she will need to be in special classes."

3. "You can expect her to be a grade level behind."

4. "Most children with seizure disorder have a 10-point deficit in IQ level, but it varies from child to child."

67. An infant has just had surgical repair of a myelomeningocele. The nurse can expect to perform which of the following actions when caring for the infant: Select all that apply.

1. Keep the infant's legs in an abducted position as much as possible.

2. Explain to the parents that the infant may need physical therapy at home.

3. Insert a feeding tube for nutrition and hydration.

4. Monitor the child for a bulging fontanel.

68. A client with Parkinson's disease has just been prescribed Levodopa. The nurse should include which of the following statements in her client education: Select all that apply.

1. Your urine and sweat may be darker than usual.
2. Take the medication on an empty stomach.
3. Take a vitamin supplement that contains B vitamins daily.
4. Side effects can include anorexia, nausea, and vomiting.

69. A family asks the nurse about the symptoms of early-stage Alzheimer's disease. The nurse includes the following:

1. A loss of sense of humor, a lack of energy, and a loss of spontaneity
2. Restlessness, impaired judgment, and poor impulse control
3. Indifference to food, urinary incontinence, and inability to communicate
4. Wandering, repetitive behavior, and voracious appetite

70. The nurse must monitor the operative client for malignant hyperthermia:

1. Immediately after induction of anesthesia
2. During the surgical procedure
3. After the anesthesia has been stopped
4. At all of the above times

71. Four surgeries are planned for the operating room on a particular day. Place the clients in order according to who is at the highest risk for malignant hyperthermia. Begin with the client at highest risk.

    1. A 20-year-old female undergoing an abdominal hysterectomy whose brother developed malignant hyperthermia during battle
    2. A 5-year-old male undergoing surgical removal of a tumor
    3. A 60-year-old female undergoing exploratory brain surgery
    4. An 80-year-old male undergoing a transurethral prostatectomy with spinal anesthesia

72. The nurse has been ordered to perform the Romberg test. He should collect which of the following supplies:

    1. A cup of water and a box of tissues
    2. An ear speculum and a small basin
    3. A pair of clean scissors and a pen and paper
    4. None of the above

73. The nurse is performing routine tracheostomy care. She is aware that overinflating the cuff can cause all but which of the following complications:

    1. Tracheal necrosis, tracheal stenosis, and tracheomalacia
    2. Tracheitis, bleeding, and cuff herniation
    3. Tracheoabdominal fistula, dysphagia, and psychogenic shock
    4. Tracheoesophageal fistula, tracheoinnominate artery fistula, and tracheal erosion

74. The nurse receives report in the intensive care unit and learns that her client's Glasgow Coma Scale is 7. She knows that this most likely means:

    1. Her client is at risk of imminent death.
    2. Her client is comatose.

3. Her client is septic.

4. Her client will soon be discharged to the medical floor.

75. The nurse is conducting a neurological examination. For which client is Babinski's sign a normal finding?

1. A 12-month-old female with blindness

2. A 35-year-old male with Parkinson's Disease

3. A 70-year-old female with schizophrenia

4. An 85-year-old healthy male

Answers and Rationale for Practice Test Two

1. **Correct Answer:** 1. *Rationale:* Cervical mucus is bacteriostatic, does provide an alkaline environment, and does serve to lubricate the vaginal canal. It does not deter unhealthy sperm from entering the cervix.

2. **Correct Answer:** 3. *Rationale:* A fetus' heart begins to beat during the fourth week after conception.

3. **Correct Answer:** 2, 4, & 5. *Rationale:* A client with dumping syndrome should consume five or six small meals per day, as large meals will promote dumping. Sweets and milk products should be avoided. The diet should contain a moderate to high level of protein. Beverages should be consumed between meals, not with meals. The diet should be low in soluble fiber.

4. **Correct Answer:** 2. *Rationale:* Severe hyperkalemia can lead to dysrhythmia and cardiac arrest. It does not lead to hypokalemia, acute respiratory distress syndrome, or hyperglycemia; although, clients experiencing electrolyte imbalances should have all of their electrolytes monitored closely.

5. **Correct Answer:** 3. *Rationale:* A client experiencing thyroid storm is likely to need a cooling blanket for fever. She will likely receive antithyroid drugs and intravenous sodium iodide. Her fever will be treated with an antipyretic that does not contain salicylate, such as acetaminophen.

6. **Correct Answer:** 2. *Rationale:* All of the symptoms listed are typical manifestations of hypothyroidism except intolerance to heat, increased urine output, and diarrhea. Common sequelae include intolerance to cold, decreased urine output, and constipation.

7. **Correct Answers:** 3, 4, & 5. *Rationale:* Healthy kidney cells are replaced or displaced by cancer cells in renal carcinoma. Male clients may experience nipple darkening or breast enlargement. A nephrectomy may be performed if manifestations and tumor spread cannot be controlled. Renal carcinoma is most common in clients 55 to 60 years of age. Hematuria is commonly a late sign of the disease.

8. **Correct Answer:** 3. *Rationale:* Respiratory insufficiency is a major concern in a burn client who has inhaled toxic fumes, smoke, hot air, or steam. It is a contributor or cause of death in such cases 77 percent of the time.

9. **Correct Answer:** 2,3,5,4,1. *Rationale:* In order, the most common causes of death for African-Americans in 2000 were

   i.   Heart disease
   ii.   Cancer
   iii. Cerebrovascular diseases
   iv.   Unintentional injuries
   v.   Diabetes Mellitus
   vi.   Homicide
   vii. HIV
   viii. Chronic lower respiratory diseases
   ix.   Kidney diseases
   x.   Influenza and pneumonia

Understanding the most common mortality and morbidity statistics can assist the nurse to create appropriate health promotion programs and also alert him to which symptoms to most closely monitor.

10. **Correct Answer:** 4. *Rationale:* The client who wears a pressure garment for burns will still need to perform active range of motion exercises or have passive range of motion exercises performed on his affected body parts. The pressure garment does assist by limiting venous engorgement, helping to prevent contractures, and reducing hypertrophic scarring.

11. **Correct Answers:** 1, 2, 4, & 5. *Rationale:* Fat embolism syndrome can be a serious complication of a bone fracture, sickle cell anemia, pancreatitis, and diabetic coma. It is not a known complication of emphysema.

12. **Correct Answers:** 1, 2, 3, & 4. *Rationale:* Predisposing factors for pregnancy-induced hypertension include multiple fetuses, renal disease, vascular disease, and adolescence. It is more common in a primagravida mother than one with children. Other factors that predispose to pregnancy-induced hypertension include diabetes mellitus, gestational trophoblastic disease, advanced maternal age, and hydramnios.

13. **Correct Answers:** 1 & 3. *Rationale:* The licensed practical nurse is well-qualified to care for the standard post-operative client and the client in need of decubitus ulcer treatments. The client newly diagnosed with diabetes mellitus will require extensive client teaching. The client with severe asthma could have emergency respiratory problems and would benefit from the monitoring of the registered nurse. The client with a high fever of unknown origin would also benefit from close monitoring by the registered nurse.

14. **Correct Answer:** 3. *Rationale:* A normal blood pressure for a newborn is 80 to 60 systolic and 45 to 40 diastolic.

15. **Correct Answers:** 1, 3, 4, & 5. *Rationale:* The neonate should exhibit sucking, rooting, blink, tonic neck, Moro, step, and Babinski reflexes. The neonate should exhibit a Palmar grasp reflex. The pincer grasp reflex does not appear until age 10 to 12 months.

16. **Correct Answers:** 1 & 3. *Rationale:* The umbilical cord should fall off in 7 to 14 days on its own; it should never be pulled or loosened. The area should be cleaned two to three times a day or with every diaper change. The area should be kept dry at all times to prevent infection. There are no nerve endings in the umbilical cord.

17. **Correct Answer:** 3. *Rationale:* It is important to find out exactly what the client is doing. Smoking a poisonous herb is very different from utilizing music therapy. Many clients use complementary therapy as alternative therapy and do not follow their physician's advice. The physician must always know about complementary therapy, as many of them can interfere with prescription drugs or alter lab work values. Complementary therapy can be harmful even if not swallowed. Harmful items can be smoked, inhaled, or rubbed on the skin, among other things. Whether a complementary therapy is part of a religious practice does not make it safe or unsafe.

18. **Correct Answer:** 4. *Rationale:* Most clients do not need a vitamin supplement if they consume a healthy, varied diet. Taking three high-dose vitamin A supplements per day can be harmful and the physician should be aware of this practice. Asking questions in a condescending way will potentially end the conversation and render the client reluctant to divulge other information. Vitamin A is a fat-soluble vitamin, making it more dangerous to over-consume.

19. **Correct Answers:** 2, 3, & 5. *Rationale:* Nicotine does serve as a stimulant that creates a depressant effect when it wears off. It is approximately as addictive as cocaine. Nicotine products combined with counseling

and support are effective smoking cessation tools. Chewing tobacco can lead to several types of cancer and is not a safe alternative to smoking cigarettes. Stress causes humans to produce corticosterone, which reduces the effects of nicotine and causes the addict to need more nicotine for the same effect.

20. **Correct Answers:** Arterial ulcer: 1, 2, & 4. Venous ulcer: 3 & 5. *Rationale:* Intermittent claudication is frequently one of the first symptoms noticed by a client who later develops an arterial ulcer. The foot will usually be cold or cool, and pulses in the foot will be diminished or absent. Venous ulcers typically have brown pigmentation and the formation of granulation tissue.

21. **Correct Answer:** 1. *Rationale:* A hemangioblastoma is characterized by the symptoms described. Schwannomas and neurofibromas are found in the thoracic or cervical area and cause motor weakness and radicular pain. They are treated by surgical resection. Meningiomas are found in the thoracic or cervical area and cause mild sensory loss and back pain in the midline. They are treated with tumor resection and radiation therapy. All of the tumors are extramedullary spinal cord tumors.

22. **Correct Answer:** 1. *Rationale:* Malignant astrocytoma is a serious condition with a high morbidity and mortality rate. The physician must further explain the diagnosis, prognosis, and treatment with the family and client to ensure that they understand. Telling the client's wife that she is in denial is inappropriate at this point, as it may be a misunderstanding. If she is indeed in denial, it can be handled in a therapeutic manner.

23. **Correct Answer:** 3. *Rationale:* The symptoms can be indicative of either a stroke or a transient ischemic attack. The physician should be contacted immediately while another nurse checks the client's vital signs, monitors the symptoms, and provides emotional support. It is imperative to quickly get orders for the client.

24. **Correct Answer:** 3. *Rationale:* The woman should be kept still, and her legs and spine should not be moved at all. It is safe to observe for bleeding after a trauma, as long as the client is not moved. The nurse should next try to keep the woman calm and find out her identifying information if she seems likely to become unconscious.

25. **Correct Answer:** 2. *Rationale:* An absolute neutrophil count of 1,500 or greater is normal. A count of 101 to 500 indicates a high risk of infection, while a count of 100 or less is life-threatening. No count is considered to place the client at "low" risk of infection because many factors are involved in a client becoming infected with any given organism.

26. **Correct Answer:** 1. *Rationale:* The symptoms described are indicative of homonymous hemianopia due to a stroke. It involves blindness in half of the field of vision. This is a more likely cause than the other responses.

27. **Correct Answer:** 2. *Rationale:* Erotic asphyxiation involves starving the brain of oxygen, often by being choked, during sexual play. It is a deadly compulsion of many males beginning in adolescence. It does not involve sniffing fumes. The nurse may not automatically be able to contact the parents due to privacy concerns, but she must emphasize the danger of this practice to the child and get him to contract not to do it again if possible.

28. **Correct Answer:** 2,4,3,1. *Rationale:* Tremors are generally the first sign of Parkinson's disease and are commonly self-reported. Tremors are followed by rigidity and bradykinesia. Akinesia is a late development of bradykinesia.

29. **Correct Answer:** 1,3,4,2. *Rationale:* Children of two to four months of age are at the highest risks of SIDS. The 5-month-old child is at the

next highest risk, followed by the 9-month-old. Children are unlikely to develop SIDS after the age of one year or before the age of one month.

30. **Correct Answer:** 3. *Rationale:* Honey is considered low phenylalanine and may be consumed by children with phenylketonuria. Chicken is high in protein and, therefore, phenylalanine. Diet soda cannot be consumed. Ice cream also contains too much phenylalanine for consumption.

31. **Correct Answer:** 1. *Rationale:* The liver may be painful due to damage from the toxicity. A headache, fever, or coughing would not be anticipated with acetaminophen overdose.

32. **Correct Answer:** 4. *Rationale:* The hip spica cast covers the abdomen, and children commonly complain of tightness after consuming a large meal. The other possible answers are detractors.

33. **Correct Answer:** 1. *Rationale:* One indicator of child abuse is significant underdevelopment. While other factors may cause underdevelopment, child abuse should be the first suspicion. The other possible answers represent less likely scenarios.

34. **Correct Answers:** 1, 2, 4, & 5. *Rationale:* Whipple's operation, also called a pancreaticoduodenectomy, involves the removal of the head of the pancreas, the duodenum, the gallbladder, and a portion of the bile duct. It is a common treatment for pancreatic cancer. Other treatments include blood transfusions, pancrease and combination chemotherapy drugs. Orlistat would not be indicated, as clients with pancreatic cancer usually lose large amounts of weight and should follow a 2,500-calorie diet.

35. **Correct Answer:** 4. *Rationale:* Addiction, misuse, and tolerance are always possible with narcotic medication (and many other medications). However, narcotics do have a role in pain management and should be

utilized when needed, for only as long as needed. Response 3 trivializes the mother's concern and is inappropriate.

36. **Correct Answers:** 1, 3, & 5. *Rationale:* A 20- to 21-gauge needle is generally used for adults. Some practitioners use a needle as large as 16 gauge. Instead of holding his breath, she should ask the client to take slow, deep breaths to promote relaxation and avoid fainting. Pressure should be held for two to three minutes after the procedure. If the client is taking anti-coagulants, the time may need to be extended to five to ten minutes. It is appropriate to improvise and use a blood pressure cuff as a tourniquet in the home health setting. The cuff should be inflated to a level higher than the client's diastolic blood pressure. The needle should be inserted into the vein at a 15- to 30-degree angle.

37. **Correct Answer:** 2. *Rationale:* Active or passive range of motion activities are critical to helping the bedridden client avoid the development of contractures. The other responses may be partly true, but number 2 is the best answer.

38. **Correct Answer:** 1. *Rationale:* Pedal arterial flow can be detected by Doppler when it cannot be palpated.

39. **Correct Answer:** 4. *Rationale:* Testosterone can cause hypercalcemia, not hypocalcemia. Other side effects include nausea, fluid retention, rash, and dizziness.

40. **Correct Answer:** 3. *Rationale:* A client who has been taking caffeine for a considerable period of time can experience moderately severe withdrawal. His visits with outsiders and his behavior around caffeinated products should be monitored, but his potential for withdrawal is more serious. While his use of caffeine makes him more likely than a typical teen to use illegal substances, it is the physician's responsibility whether or not to order testing for illegal drug use.

41. **Correct Answer:** 2. *Rationale:* 105 to 110 degrees is an appropriate temperature for shampooing a client.

42. **Correct Answer:** 4. *Rationale:* The normal length for a newborn is 19 to 21.5 inches. The normal head circumference is 13.2 to 14.8 inches. The normal weight is 6 to 9 pounds.

43. **Correct Answer:** 3. *Rationale:* Verbal or physical abuse of a client must be treated with the utmost seriousness. The superior must know, and the assistant must be kept away from the client so that further abuse cannot occur. The superior can report the abuse to the proper authorities. In some states, you may have an obligation to report based on the circumstances. As a staff nurse, merely speaking with the assistant does not suffice to solve the problem, nor does recommending counseling. Speaking with the client does not solve the problem, although it is acceptable to process what happened with the client. The nurse should not make excuses for the assistant's abuse.

44. **Correct Answers:** 1, 2, & 3. *Rationale:* The nurse should make the physician aware that the client has suggested that she will not be following the prescribed diet at home. A dietician or diabetes educator can teach the client the benefits of following a diabetic diet. The nurse should also reinforce the dietary information and try to ascertain any stumbling blocks that need to be worked out. In this circumstance, she is not violating the client's privacy by discussing this with the physician or other caregiver.

45. **Correct Answer:** 1. *Rationale:* A common side effect of ECT is temporary memory loss. The other answers are incorrect.

46. **Correct Answers:** 1, 4, 5, & 6. *Rationale:* The suction dilatation and curettage, also called a therapeutic abortion, is imperative if a spontaneous abortion does not occur. A diet low in animal fat, protein, and vita-

min A has been correlated with an increased risk of hydatidiform mole. Methotrexate is the prophylactic treatment of choice to avoid the development of choriocarcinoma. The client will need close follow-up for one to two years to monitor HCG levels and choriocarcinoma development. The client should not attempt pregnancy until her HCG levels return to normal, which can take one to two years. HCG levels are highly elevated during the development of a hydatidiform mole. There is a more than 80 percent chance that the hydatidiform mole is benign.

47. **Correct Answer:** 2. *Rationale:* Group therapy is generally not indicated with hypochondriasis. Treatments of choice include serotonin reuptake inhibitors, tricyclic antidepressants, and cognitive behavioral therapy.

48. **Correct Answer:** 2. *Rationale:* Common symptoms of epiglottiditis include stridor, drooling, swallowing difficulties, and restlessness. It can be a medical emergency requiring intubation.

49. **Correct Answer:** 1. *Rationale:* The performance of any procedure without informed consent can be construed as assault and battery.

50. **Correct Answer:** 167 ml per hour. *Rationale:* Four liters equals 4,000 milliliters. 4000 divided by 24 (hours) equals 166.67, which is rounded to 167.

51. **Correct Answers:** 3, 4, & 5. *Rationale:* It is appropriate to compromise with the client for a small reward for performing a challenging task. It may help the client to become familiar with the environment while no one is around. At some behavioral management facilities, natural consequences (such as missing lunch) are used to encourage healthy behavior. This technique, if utilized, should be accompanied by professional monitoring and therapy to ensure its appropriateness for the client. Threatening to increase her medication is inappropriate and does not

promote rapport. Telling her that the other clients are talking about her is counterproductive and may increase her anxiety.

52. **Correct Answer:** 4. *Rationale:* All of the items mentioned are considered to be contributing factors to the development of paraphilias except having a lot of knowledge about sex. In contrast, a lack of sexual knowledge is considered a contributing factor.

53. **Correct Answer:** 5. *Rationale:* The newborn's heart rate should be around 140. Dark red spots in the diaper usually mean the passage of uric acid crystals, a normal finding during a newborn's first two days of life. A black, tarry stool indicates the passage of meconium, which normally occurs in the first 24 hours after birth. Small, white papules on the palate of the mouth are called Epstein's pearls. They are a normal finding in the newborn. A newborn may not void for the first 12 to 24 hours after birth.

54. **Correct Answer:** 2. *Rationale:* Ringworm is a fungus that causes a ring-shaped rash. It is rarely spread from an infected dog or cat.

55. **Correct Answer:** 3. *Rationale:* A typical Munchausen syndrome by proxy case involves a child with difficult-to-diagnose symptoms presented repeatedly to an emergency room or pediatrician's office by a parent, usually the mother. A child not taken for needed medical care may be a victim of neglect. A child with a broken arm could be a victim of abuse or could have suffered a simple accident. Many children are sent to school with a cold; this is not an abnormal finding.

56. **Correct Answer:** 2. *Rationale:* Bacteria such as E. coli or Klebsiella can affect the ulcerated area. It is not common for a virus to do so. The other responses are all descriptive of necrotizing enterocolitis.

57. **Correct Answer:** 1. *Rationale:* The symptoms are indicative of tardive dyskinesia. Dystonic reactions involve contractions of the tongue,

face, and extraocular muscles. They generally occur within the first few weeks of administration of a new medication. Neuromalignant syndrome occurs in the first few weeks of administration of a new medication and is characterized by elevated temperature, heart rate, blood pressure, confusion, and renal failure. It may progress to coma and death. Akathisia is a reaction to medication characterized by motor restlessness and an inability to sit still.

58. **Correct Answer:** 3. *Rationale:* A person with phenylketonuria should avoid eggs, meat, poultry, fish, cheese, breads, nuts, and legumes. They must also avoid sugar substitutes.

59. **Correct Answers:** 2, 3, 4, & 5. *Rationale:* Intolerance to tube feeding can manifest as tachycardia, not bradycardia. The other responses are all indicative of feeding intolerance.

60. **Correct Answer:** 3. *Rationale:* TENS units should not be used on clients with pacemakers. TENS units may be used in a diabetic client, a client with a herniated cervical disc, and a client with cerebral palsy.

61. **Correct Answer:** 2. *Rationale:* Hypervolemia can lead to hypertension, not hypotension. The other responses are all indicative of hypervolemia.

62. **Correct Answer:** 2. *Rationale:* The various types of shock may be treated with all of the listed medications except nonsteroidal anti-inflammatories or Phenergan.

63. **Correct Answer:** 4,3,5,2,1. *Rationale:* The five stages of grief are denial, anger, bargaining, depression, and acceptance. Not everyone experiences all stages or the stages in order.

64. **Correct Answer:** 4. *Rationale:* Vitamin C enhances the absorption of iron. Milk decreases iron absorption.

65. **Correct Answer:** 1. *Rationale:* When weaning the child, it is best to decrease breast feedings one at a time instead of all at once. The other statements are true.

66. **Correct Answer:** 1. *Rationale:* Seizure disorder does not affect intelligence. Special classes are not required.

67. **Correct Answers:** 1, 2, & 4. *Rationale:* The hips are kept abducted to prevent hip dislocation. The infant may require physical therapy to his legs for a period of time. The infant is at risk of hydrocephalus due to having open cranial sutures. This can manifest as increasing head circumference and/or bulging fontanels. The infant does not normally need a feeding tube after myelomeningocele repair.

68. **Correct Answers:** 1 & 4. *Rationale:* Levodopa can darken urine and sweat. Side effects include anorexia, nausea, vomiting, mental changes, and postural hypotension. Levodopa can cause gastrointestinal irritation and should be taken with food. Persons taking Levodopa should avoid taking supplemental vitamin B6 or ingesting foods high in vitamin B6.

69. **Correct Answer:** 1. *Rationale:* A loss of sense of humor, a lack of energy, and a loss of spontaneity are all symptoms of early-stage Alzheimer's disease. Restlessness, impaired judgment, poor impulse control, wandering, repetitive behavior, and voracious appetite are symptoms of middle stages. Indifference to food, urinary incontinence, and inability to communicate are symptoms of late stages. Be aware that the numbering of stages varies by organization, with the Alzheimer's Association (**www.alz.or**) now delineating seven stages.

70. **Correct Answer:** 4. *Rationale:* Malignant hyperthermia is a concern throughout the course of general anesthesia. It also rarely occurs after the anesthesia has been terminated.

71. **Correct Answer:** 1, 2, 3, & 4. *Rationale:* The capacity to develop malignant hyperthermia is an autosomal-dominant trait passed genetically. As well as being under general anesthesia, it can also be triggered by extreme stress or extreme exercise. It is much more common in children and young adults. It is only a risk with general anesthesia, not spinal anesthesia.

72. **Correct Answer:** 4. *Rationale:* The Romberg test is a neurological test. To perform it, have the client stand with her feet together and her arms at her sides. With her eyes open, see if she can stand upright without swaying. If she does, have her close her eyes in the same position. If she fails, it is considered a positive Romberg test and indicative of proprioceptive or vestibular dysfunction.

73. **Correct Answer:** 3. *Rationale:* Overinflation of the tracheostomy cuff can lead to all of the listed conditions except tracheoabdominal fistula, dysphagia, and psychogenic shock.

74. **Correct Answer:** 2. *Rationale:* A Glasgow Coma score of less than 9 usually indicates that the client is in a coma.

75. **Correct Answer:** 1. *Rationale:* Babinski's sign is normal for an infant under two years of age only.

Appendix D

State Boards of Nursing Contact Information

Alabama Board of Nursing
770 Washington Avenue
RSA Plaza, Ste 250
Montgomery, AL 36130-3900
Phone: (334) 242-4060
Fax: (334) 242-4360
Web Site: **www.abn.state.al.us**

Alaska Board of Nursing
PO Box 110806
Juneau, Alaska 99811-0806
Phone: (907) 269-8161
Fax: (907) 269-8196
Web Site: **www.dced.state.ak.us/
occ/pnur.htm**

American Samoa Health Services
Regulatory Board
LBJ Tropical Medical Center
Pago Pago, AS 96799
Phone: (684) 633-1222
Fax: (684) 633-1869
Web Site: **http://americansamoa.
gov/departments/depts/health.
htm**

Arizona State Board of Nursing
4747 North 7th Street, Suite 200
Phoenix, AZ 85014-3653
Phone: (602) 889-5150
Fax: (602) 889-5155
Web Site: **www.azbn.gov**

Arkansas State Board of Nursing
University Tower Building
1123 S. University, Suite 800,
Little Rock, AR 72204-1619
Phone: (501) 686-2700
Fax: (501) 686-2714
Web Site: **www.arsbn.org**

California Board of Registered
Nursing
400 R St., Ste. 4030
Sacramento, CA 95814-6239
Phone: (916) 322-3350
Fax: (916) 327-4402
Web Site: **www.rn.ca.gov**

California Board of Vocational
Nursing and Psychiatric Techni-
cians
2535 Capitol Oaks Drive
Suite 205
Sacramento, CA 95833
Phone: (916) 263-7800
Fax: (916) 263-7855
Web Site: **www.bvnpt.ca.gov**

Colorado Board of Nursing
1560 Broadway, Suite 880
Denver, CO 80202
Phone: (303) 894-2430
Fax: (303) 894-2821

Web Site: **www.dora.state.co.us/
nursing**

Connecticut Board of Examiners
for Nursing
Dept. of Public Health
410 Capitol Avenue, MS# 13PHO
P.O. Box 340308
Hartford, CT 06134-0328
Phone: (860) 509-7624
Fax: (860) 509-7553
Web Site: **www.state.ct.us/dph**

Delaware Board of Nursing
861 Silver Lake Blvd
Cannon Building, Suite 203
Dover, DE 19904
Phone: (302) 739-4500
Fax: (302) 739-2711
Web Site: **http://dpr.delaware.
gov/boards/nursing**

District of Columbia Board of
Nursing
Department of Health
717 14th Street, NW
Suite 600
Washington, DC 20002
Phone: (877) 672-2174
Fax: (202) 727-8471

Web site: **http://hpla.doh.dc.gov/ hpla/cwp/view,A,1195,Q,488526 ,hplaNav,l30661l,.asp**

Florida Board of Nursing
Capital Circle Officer Center
4052 Bald Cypress Way, Rm 120
Tallahassee, FL 32399-3252
Phone: (850) 488-0595
Fax: (850) 245-4172
Web Site: **www.doh.state.fl.us/ mqa**

Georgia Board of Nursing
237 Coliseum Drive
Macon, GA 31217-3858
Phone: (478) 207-2440
Fax: (478) 207-1354
Web Site: **www.sos.state.ga.us/ plb/rn**

Guam Board of Nurse Examiners
#123 Chalan Kareta
Mangilao, GU 96913-6304
Phone: (671) 735-7406
Fax: (671) 735-7413
Web Site: **www.dphss.guam.gov**

Hawaii Board of Nursing
Professional & Vocational Licensing Division

P.O. Box 3469
Honolulu, HI 96801
Phone: (808) 586-3000
Fax: (808) 586-2689
Web Site: **http://hawaii.gov/dcca/ areas/pvl/boards/nursing**

Idaho Board of Nursing
280 N. 8th Street, Suite 210
P.O. Box 83720
Boise, ID 83720
Phone: (208) 334-3110 ext 21
Fax: (208) 334-3262
Web Site: **www2.state.id.us/ibn**

Illinois Department of Professional
Regulation
James R. Thompson Center
100 West Randolph, Suite 9-300
Chicago, IL 60601
Phone: (312) 814-2715
Fax: (312) 814-3145
Also:
320 W. Washington St., 3rd Floor
Springfield, IL 62786
Phone: (217) 785-0800
Fax: (217) 782-7645
Web Site: **www.idfpr.com/dpr/ WHO/nurs.asp**

Indiana State Board of Nursing
Health Professions Bureau
402 W. Washington Street, Room
W072
Indianapolis, IN 46204
Phone: (317) 234-2043
Fax: (317) 233-4236
Web Site: **www.in.gov/pla**

Iowa Board of Nursing
RiverPoint Business Park
400 S.W. 8th Street, Suite B
Des Moines, IA 50309-4685
Phone: (515) 281-3255
Fax: (515) 281-4825
Web Site: **www.iowa.gov/nursing**

Kansas State Board of Nursing
Landon State Office Building
900 S.W. Jackson, Suite 1051
Topeka, KS 66612
Phone: (785) 296-4929
Fax: (785) 296-3929
Web Site: **www.ksbn.org**

Kentucky Board of Nursing
312 Whittington Parkway,
Suite 300
Louisville, KY 40222
Phone: (502) 329-7000
Fax: (502) 329-7011
Web Site: **www.kbn.ky.gov**

Louisiana State Board of Nursing
7373 Perkins Road
Baton Rouge, Louisiana 70810
Phone: (225) 755-7500
Fax: (225) 755-7585
Web Site: **www.lsbn.state.la.us**

Maine State Board of Nursing
158 State House Station
Augusta, ME 04333
Phone: (207) 287-1133
Fax: (207) 287-1149
Web Site: **www.state.me.us/boar-dofnursing**

Maryland Board of Nursing
4140 Patterson Avenue
Baltimore, MD 21215
Phone: (410) 585-1900
Fax: (410) 358-3530
Web Site: **www.mbon.org**

Massachusetts Board of Registration in Nursing
Commonwealth of Massachusetts
239 Causeway Street, Suite 500
Boston, MA 02114
Phone: (800) 414-0168
Fax: (617) 973-0984
Web Site: **www.state.ma.us/reg/boards/rn**

Michigan/DCH/Bureau of Health Professions
Ottawa Towers North
611 W. Ottawa, 1st Floor
Lansing, MI 48933
Phone: (517) 335-0918
Fax: (517) 373-2179
Web Site: **www.michigan.gov/ healthlicense**

Minnesota Board of Nursing
2829 University Avenue SE
Suite 200
Minneapolis, MN 55414
Phone: (612) 617-2270
Fax: (612) 617-2190
Web Site: **www.nursingboard. state.mn.us**

Mississippi Board of Nursing
1935 Lakeland Drive, Suite B
Jackson, MS 39216-5014
Phone: (601) 987-4188
Fax: (601) 364-2352
Web Site: **www.msbn.state.ms.us**

Missouri State Board of Nursing
3605 Missouri Blvd.
P.O. Box 656
Jefferson City, MO 65102-0656
Phone: (573) 751-0681

Fax: (573) 751-0075
Web Site: **http://pr.mo.gov/nursing.asp**

Montana State Board of Nursing
301 South Park
PO Box 200513
Helena, MT 59620-0513
Phone: (406) 841-2345
Fax: (406) 841-2305
Web Site: **www.nurse.mt.gov**

Northern Mariana Islands Commonwealth Board of Nurse Examiners
PO Box 501458
Saipan, MP 96950
Phone: (670) 664-4810
Fax: (670) 664-4813

Nebraska Health and Human Services System
Dept. of Regulation & Licensure, Nursing Section
301 Centennial Mall South
Lincoln, NE 68509-4986
Phone: (402) 471-4376
Fax: (402) 471-1066
Web Site: **www.hhs.state.ne.us/ crl/nursing/nursingindex.htm**

Nevada State Board of Nursing
Administration, Discipline
& Investigations
5011 Meadowood Mall Way,
Suite 300
Reno, NV 89502
Phone: (775) 688-2620
Fax: (775) 688-2628
Web Site: **www.nursingboard.
state.nv.us**

New Hampshire Board of Nursing
21 South Fruit Street, Suite 16
Concord, NH 03301
Phone: (603) 271-2323
Fax: (603) 271-6605
Web Site: **www.state.nh.us/nurs-
ing**

New Jersey Board of Nursing
P.O. Box 45010
124 Halsey Street, 6th Floor
Newark, NJ 07101
Phone: (973) 504-6430
Fax: (973) 648-3481
Web Site: **www.state.nj.us/lps/ca/
medical/nursing.htm**

New Mexico Board of Nursing
6301 Indian School Road, NE,
Suite 710

Albuquerque, NM 87110
Phone: (505) 841-8340
Fax: (505) 841-8347
Web Site: **www.bon.state.nm.us**

New York State Board of Nursing
Education Bldg.
89 Washington Avenue
2nd Floor West Wing
Albany, NY 12234
Phone: (518) 474-3817 Ext. 280
Fax: (518) 474-3706
Web Site: **www.nysed.gov/prof/
nurse.htm**

North Carolina Board of Nursing
3724 National Drive, Suite 201
Raleigh, NC 27602
Phone: (919) 782-3211
Fax: (919) 781-9461
Web Site: **www.ncbon.com**

North Dakota Board of Nursing
919 South 7th Street, Suite 504
Bismarck, ND 58504
Phone: (701) 328-9777
Fax: (701) 328-9785
Web Site: **www.ndbon.org**

Ohio Board of Nursing
17 South High Street, Suite 400

Columbus, OH 43215-3413
Phone: (614) 466-3947
Fax: (614) 466-0388
Web Site: **www.nursing.ohio.gov**

Oklahoma Board of Nursing
2915 N. Classen Boulevard, Suite 524
Oklahoma City, OK 73106
Phone: (405) 962-1800
Fax: (405) 962-1821
Web Site: **www.youroklahoma. com/nursing**

Oregon State Board of Nursing
17938 SW Upper Boones Ferry Rd
Portland, OR 97224
Phone: (971) 673-0685
Fax: (971) 673-0684
Web Site: **www.osbn.state.or.us**

Pennsylvania State Board of Nursing
P.O. 2649
124 Pine Street
Harrisburg, PA 17101
Phone: (717) 783-7142
Fax: (717) 783-0822
Web Site: **www.dos.state. pa.us/bpoa/cwp/view. asp?a=1104&q=432869**

Commonwealth of Puerto Rico
Board of Nurse Examiners
800 Roberto H. Todd Avenue,
Room 202, Stop 18
Santurce, PR 00908
Phone: (787) 725-7506
Fax: (787) 725-7903

Rhode Island Board of Nurse
Registration and Nursing Education
Three Capitol Hill, Room 105
Providence, RI 02908
Phone: (401) 222-5700
Fax: (401) 222-3352
Web Site: **www.health.ri.gov/hsr/ professions/nurses.php**

South Carolina State Board of
Nursing
110 Centerview Drive, Suite 202
Columbia, SC 29210
Phone: (803) 896-4550
Fax: (803) 896-4525
Web Site: **www.llr.state.sc.us/pol/ nursing**

South Dakota Board of Nursing
4305 South Louise Ave., Suite 201
Sioux Falls, SD 57106-3124
Phone: (605) 362-2760

394 101 Ways to Score Higher on Your NCLEX

Fax: (605) 362-2768
Web Site: **http://doh.sd.gov/
boards/nursing**

Tennessee State Board of Nursing
227 French Landing, Suite 300
Heritage Place MetroCenter
Nashville, TN 37243
Phone: (615) 532-5166
Fax: (615) 741-7899
Web Site: **http://health.state.
tn.us/Boards/Nursing/index.htm**

Texas Board of Nurse Examiners
333 Guadalupe, Suite 3-460
Austin, TX 78701
Phone: (512) 305-7400
Fax: (512) 305-7401
Web Site: **www.bon.state.tx.us**

Utah State Board of Nursing
Heber M. Wells Bldg., 4th Floor
160 East 300 South
Salt Lake City, UT 84111
Phone: (801) 530-6628
Fax: (801) 530-6511
Web Site: **www.dopl.utah.gov/
licensing/nursing.html**

Vermont State Board of Nursing
Office of Professional Regulation

National Life Building North F1.2
Montpelier, VT 05620
Phone: (802) 828-2396
Fax: (802) 828-2484
Web Site: **www.vtprofessionals.
org/opr1/nurses**

Virgin Islands Board of Nurse
Licensure
P.O. Box 304247, Veterans Drive
Station
St. Thomas, VI 00803
Phone: (340) 776-7131
Fax: (340) 777-4003
Web Site: **www.vibnl.org**

Virginia Board of Nursing
Perimeter Center
9960 Mayland Drive, Suite 300
Richmond, VA 23230
Phone: (804) 367-4515
Fax: (804) 527-4455
Web Site: **www.dhp.virginia.gov/
nursing**

Washington State Department
of Health
Health Professions
Quality Assurance
HPQA #6, 310 Israel Rd. SE
Tumwater WA 98501-7864

Phone: (360) 236 - 4700
Fax: (360) 236 – 4738
Web Site: **www.doh.wa.gov/hsqa/**
Professions/Nursing/default.htm

West Virginia State Board of Examiners for Registered Professional Nurses
101 Dee Drive
Charleston, WV 25311
Phone: (304) 558-3596
Fax: (304) 558-3666
Web Site: **www.wvrnboard.com**

West Virginia State Board of Examiners for Licensed Practical Nurses
101 Dee Drive
Charleston, WV 25311
Phone: (304)558-3572
Fax: (304)558-4367
Web Site: **www.lpnboard.state.**
wv.us

Wisconsin Department of Regulation and Licensing
P.O. Box 8935
Madison, WI 53708
Phone: (608) 266-2112
Fax: (608) 261-7083
Web Site: **http://drl.wi.gov**

Wyoming State Board of Nursing
1810 Pioneer Avenue
Cheyenne, WY 82002
Phone: (307) 777-7601
Fax: (307) 777-3519
Web Site: **http://nursing.state.**
wy.us

Appendix E

Quick Quiz Answers

1. Correct answers can vary widely. Examples include infection control, privacy, how to encourage clients to improve their nutritional intake, or management of the disoriented client. Included information may range from legal issues to the latest research on the topic.

2. Correct answers include: gloves, mask, gown, surgical cap, protective eyewear, shoe covers, and drapes.

3. Correct answers include: standard or universal, airborne, droplet, contact, and reverse isolation.

4. October 8 and June 7.

5. Answer 4. Preschoolers cannot understand the wording or even the pictures in a pamphlet well enough to process and retain the information. They can understand verbal and visual instruction.

6. Correct answers may include: repositioning with pillows, massage (especially back and neck), warmth, passive range of motion, and distraction.

7. 1. 16 to 20 gauge
    2. Correct answers include chills, fever, itching, rash, difficulty breathing, and flushed skin.
    3. Correct answers include hemorrhage, and surgery.
    4. Correct answers include cancer and chemotherapy.

8. Correct answers include:

    1. Check the order for correctness.
    2. Take the client's baseline vital signs.
    3. Make sure the blood type is correct.
    4. Identify the client. (Most facility's policy requires two staff members to identify the client).
    5. Ensure the client has an appropriate size intravenous access (usually at least a 16 gauge cannula).

9. It is never acceptable to restick the client with the same needle. A needle must be inserted into the skin only once.

10. Answers are:

    1. False. Only a few medications should be administered via the Z-track method.
    2. True.
    3. False. However, it is frequently used for medications that are painful to receive intramuscularly, such as iron.
    4. True.
    5. False. You should draw up .3 ml of air into the syringe.
    6. True.
    7. False. The needle must be inserted at a 90-degree angle.
    8. False. You should aspirate for blood and remove the needle if blood appears.
    9. True.
    10. False. You should not massage after a Z-track injection.

11. The abdomen, on either side of the umbilicus

12. Correct answers include: puncture of the vein wall, a rapid delivery rate, and a dislodged cannula due to client movement or poor securing.

13. Correct answers include: leaving the IV in place too long (greater than 48 to 72 hours), poor care of the dressing site, and failing to properly clean the IV site prior to inserting the cannula.

14. Correct answers include pediatric clients and clients with congestive heart failure.

15. Correct answers include, but are not limited to, mental status, cardiac, respiratory, musculoskeletal, neurological, urinary, and gastrointestinal.

16. 2. Pregnancy does not increase body temperature. It would not be unusual for the other depicted clients to have a mild fever.

17. 3. Marathon runners usually have a low heart rate of 50 to 60. The other depicted clients would be expected to have a heart rate around 100.

18. You must pump it up to 20 points higher than the last time you hear the systolic pressure.

19. Correct answers include hemovac, penrose, and Jackson-Pratt.

20. Correct answers include: transplantation (due to anti-rejection drugs), diabetes, and AIDS. Many other correct answers exist.

Bibliography

"2009 NCLEX® Examination Candidate Bulletin." NCSBN. 3 Sept. 2009. 15 Aug. 2009 <**www.ncsbn.org/2009_NCLEX_Candidate_Bulletin.pdf**>.

Karch, Amy M., 2005 *Lippincott's Nursing Drug Guide*, Lippincott, Williams & Wilkins, Philadelphia, Pennsylvania, 2005.

NCSBN. 3 Sept. 2009. The National Council of State Boards of Nursing. 15 Aug. 2009 <**www.ncsbn.org**>.

Ready.gov – Prepare. Plan. Stay Informed. 3 Sept. 2009. The Ready Campaign of the U.S. Department of Homeland Security and FEMA. 1 Aug. 2009 <**www.ready.gov**>.

Smith-Temple, Jean and Joyce Young Johnson, *Nurses' Guide to Clinical Procedures*, Fourth Edition, Lippincott, Philadelphia, Pennsylvania, 2002.

Author Biography

J. Lucy Boyd, RN, BSN

J. Lucy Boyd, RN, BSN has practiced nursing since 1991. She has taken both the LPN state board examination and the NCLEX-RN. Now a registered nurse and full-time medical writer, she enjoys sharing her nursing knowledge and experience with new generations.

Ms. Boyd was valedictorian of her class at the Livingston School of Practical Nursing and later graduated Summa Cum Laude from the University of the State of New York – Regents College with a Bachelor of Science degree in Nursing. She is a proud native of Chattanooga, Tennessee, where she can be found reading and researching in her spare time.

She is also the author of *The Complete Guide to Healthy Cooking and Nutrition for College Students* (**www.atlantic-pub.com**).

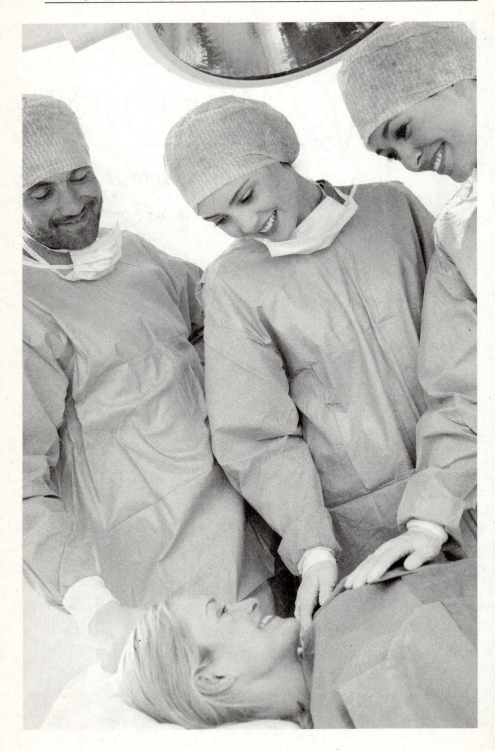

Index

R

S

T

U

V

W

Z